THE ART OF LURE FISHING

The Art *of* Lure Fishing

Charlie Bettell

The Crowood Press

First published in 1994 by
The Crowood Press Ltd
Ramsbury, Marlborough
Wiltshire SN8 2HR

www.crowood.com

Paperback edition 2001
This impression 2002

British Library Cataloguing-in-Publication Data
A catalogue record for this book is available from the British Library.

ISBN 1 86126 411 9

DEDICATION

I dedicate this book to my good friend Steve Gamble.

Sadly, Steve died on Tuesday 14 December 1993, aged 43.

Steve was the man behind the author. He edited my fishing articles and the
draft of this book. He died just weeks after writing the spinnerbait chapter.
Without Steve's guidance and editorial help, I would never have started
writing. Although my name appears on the front cover, this book was very
much a joint effort. Steve and I were a team; we made the perfect lure fishing
writer and editor duo.

Steve's enthusiasm for lure fishing and lure making, inspired me greatly. The
few brief years that I knew Steve were some of the most enjoyable of my life,
Steve was far more that 'just' a friend to me – he was an education.

Steve will be greatly missed by his family and friends.

FOREVER IN OUR THOUGHTS
Steve Gamble
1950–1993

Typeset by Intype, London
Revised text typeset by Phoenix Typesetting, Ilkley, West Yorkshire

Printed and bound in Great Britain by Bookcraft (Bath) Ltd

CONTENTS

ACKNOWLEDGEMENTS

Foremost, I should like to thank Steve Gamble for all his hard work editing the original manuscript. Steve spent many a night at my side as I tapped away at my word processor keys in a very unorthodox fashion! Fortunately, I have come a long way since then and I now write, edit and tap far more competently. Even after so many years, not a week goes by when Steve does not crop up in my thoughts. Without him there would have been no first edition, no second edition, no articles, and probably none of the websites where you can read about my very latest fishing methods and techniques.

Thanks continue to go across the water to Doug Strange, editor-in-chief of *In-Fisherman* magazine, USA, for letting me use various material.

Again, I would like to thank David Smith, John Worzencraft, Steve Gamble and John Bailey for supplying text for the book. Not forgetting those that supplied me with some of the first-class photographs used in the book and to my good friend Paul Groombridge for all his hard work in supplying me with first-class illustrations.

What I would especially like to do is thank those fishing tackle manufactures that have put conservation at the top of their list of priorities. A huge range of unhooking mats and unhooking tools is available nowadays, specifically designed for the predator angler. Those items, I'm glad to say, can be found in many tackle shops throughout the UK, and at very affordable prices! Back in 1994, when this book was first published, most predator anglers had to make do with a pair of flimsy forceps and a piece of camper's bedroll. Times have clearly changed for the better since then. There really is no excuse nowadays not to have the correct equipment with you for laying fish on and unhooking them with. If you can't afford the necessities, then don't fish – it's as simple as that. As for gaining handling and unhooking experience, that can be achieved by fishing alongside a competent angler. Why not treat yourself and have a day out with me?

I'll finish with this, my favourite quote: 'Never keep a fish out of water longer than you would like to be held under it!'

FOREWORD

This book is one of the most amazing I have ever read on angling. Let me explain.

First of all, I truly believe that lure fishing for predator fish must be the way into the future. The days of livebaiting are surely numbered both here and in Europe, and pike fishermen in particular will have to look for new methods as we approach a greener, more conservation-minded age. At first, I have no doubt, there will be great resistance. It is generally thought that the biggest pike of all are caught on livebaits, and so they have been, up to now. The main reason for this is, I believe, that most good, passionate pike anglers have tended to concentrate almost solely on the use of natural baits. Had the same amount of expertise, skill and dedication gone into using artificials, I am sure the picture and record book would be very different. As it is, this remarkable book details dozens of extraordinary fish that have already been caught on artificial lures.

Secondly, I am impressed by Charlie Bettell and his approach to this book. Every single thing in it has been tried and tested again and again. That is obvious, the fact screams out at you. Here there is no hypothesis and no idle theory. Charlie is an absolute stickler for detail, and until he is absolutely happy in his own mind that what he says is true, he will not commit a single word to paper. In short, then, the book rings sound as a bell. It is also important to realize that Charlie is at the centre of a vast network of lure anglers that stretches throughout Europe and to the United States. As a result, he is absolutely up to date with every single development and technique known in the lure-fishing world.

Thirdly, there is the quality of the book itself. Where do I begin? Perhaps with the depth of detail: everything, and I mean everything, is here. Charlie tells you absolutely every last fact on the tackle you will need, on the artificials that exist, how to fish them, how to make them, and when to use them. There is not a stone left unturned as he leads you by the hand through session after session on every water type.

This book is also the most down-to-earth, detailed, instructional book I have ever come across. Absolutely nothing is left to chance or to the imagination. Take, for example, Charlie's instructions on making tackle: they are described totally from A to Z and diagrams illustrate every move. Even a sausage-fingered idiot like me could make lures now!

But, probably, what appeals to me above all is Charlie's obvious understanding of the pike itself. Charlie has thought just as deeply about the fish as about the tackle needed to catch it. His work on pike and light values is extraordinary, and his diagram on pike senses and hunting techniques I find totally stimulating. Charlie's concern stretches beyond this, into an obsession with the well-being of the fish itself. I feel that if you wanted to make an enemy of Charlie then all you would have to do is to maltreat a pike!

Fishing means so much to Charlie: I love the pages from his memory that he inserts here and there to give an imaginative or emotive feel to what is going on. I love his description of piking under the full moon, the pike approaching like a knife of blackness through the silver and then the volcano that is the take. This is enthralling writing from a man who loves what he is doing.

John Bailey 1994

INTRODUCTION

Since the first edition of *The Art of Lure Fishing* was published in 1994, a lot of water has passed under the bridge. One of the biggest changes in my life since writing the first edition has to be my becoming a professional fishing guide. Living in the heart of the Norfolk Broads, I do not have to travel more than ten miles from my house to get to any major river in Norfolk. Since becoming a professional fishing guide I have boated many thousands of pike for clients, the biggest being a cracking 30lb 4oz pike for Guy Chantler in February 2000. It was Guy's first guided pike fishing trip out with me. During that very memorable day Guy boated four pike to a total weight of 76lb 6oz – the second biggest pike weighing in at 19lb 8oz! Was he pleased? You bet he was! For the record, Guy's 30-pounder was lured with a smelly deadbait laid tight on the bottom. The record for the biggest artificial lure-caught pike to come to a client since I became a professional fishing guide stands at 27lb. The captor of that pike, Mr Chris Brookbanks, and his two sons Adam and Jason, have caught so many good pike while out on guided pike fishing trips with me that it would take another book to record all the memorable captures.

It has given me great pleasure over the last few years to teach clients of all ages the techniques and skills required to successfully entice pike using artificial lures or natural fish baits. Fishing is not just about catching fish, though, as I always explain to my clients: it is about having fun too! Many novice anglers, men, woman and children, come out with me solely to learn how to handle and unhook pike. I've seen big beaming smiles, I've seen faces full of fear, and I've seen tears! You never quite know how somebody will react when they come face to face with a fish that has teeth that look as big as a mad dog's, but a damn sight sharper! I have had one or two young clients that have shed the odd tear when the time has come to hold their prize catch, they've been that frightened. With gentle coaxing though, I have usually managed to get them to wipe away the tears and hold their prize catch. Once the initial fear barrier has been broken, it's all systems go from there on! After just a few minutes of returning their prize catch to the water, those once-frightened youngsters can't wait to do battle again with an even bigger fish, to show mum and dad, family and friends, how brave they were when confronted by a monstrous pike. It doesn't matter if you are young or old: under the right supervision you can do what you've always dreamed of doing, but never quite had the nerve or experience to go out and do – i.e. catch a pike. Some people, after only having had one lesson with me, are confident and competent enough to go it alone. Others, who are not so confident, much prefer to have two or three lessons before venturing out alone. Some of my clients like to fish with me regularly, with my knowledge of the Norfolk Broads, my knowing where pike are congregated at the time, and knowing what feeding mood they are in at that time. The feeding behaviour of pike can vary greatly depending on how high their metabolic rate is, the amount of food available to them, the water temperature and clarity, sunlight penetration, air pressure and moon phase! During a four-week period, while updating this book, clients boated ten different 20lb+ pike from a location that was no bigger than a five-a-side football pitch. Those big pike were on a fairly high metabolic rate and were feeding ravenously – a few days later you couldn't catch a big pike from that location for love nor money. To be successful at catching a number of pike in a session, you need to be in the right place, at the right time, doing the right thing. For the newcomer, choice of location, let alone lure/bait presentation, can prove to be a very difficult thing. If only just starting up pike fishing, it's wise to go with a friend a few times who knows how to handle and unhook pike competently, before attempting to go it alone, for the pike's safety as well as your own! Believe me, a hook in the finger is very painful – especially if a pike is still attached to it!

Another change in my life since writing the first edition of *The Art of Lure Fishing*, is the rods, reels and line that I now use. If I had to go back to using some of the items that I was using when I wrote the first edition of this book, I would honestly give up pike fishing – technology has moved on that much! To see what tackle I am currently using, that is, at the time of this book going to print, read Chapter 14. All the rods that I now use were designed by me to fulfil specific requirements. Without doubt, the 7ft 6in Retrieve Technique 5, known as the RT5, has been one of the most raved-about lure rods ever. What many users of the rod will not have known up until now is that I designed it, along with the rest of the RT range. As for main line, I only use braided line nowadays – it really is a must as far as I'm concerned. As for lures, there have been quite a few new and exiting models hit the tackle shop shelves over the last three years, those mainly being jerkbaits and rubber baits. I have seen two or three new top-water lures appear over the last year or so, which are very productive for pike and chub. If you have access to the Internet, check out my web site from time to time to see if any new lures or products have been reviewed or featured by me. The title of my website is *Predator Fishing UK* (www.esox.co.uk). *Predator Fishing UK* has predator articles, a photo gallery, a chat room, a message board, and a host of other features that will help you in your quest to gain more knowledge on the kings and queens of the fresh-water jungle.

I hope that you enjoy the book. If you have any questions that you would like to ask me regarding something featured in this book, or any other questions that you may have, e-mail them to charlie@esox.co.uk. You will find various other useful website addresses in the 'Useful Websites' section at the end of the book.

Good Fishing.

BALANCED TACKLE

Balanced tackle is very important, especially when using small lightweight lures.

Bear in mind that the majority of American plugs that are available to the UK lure angler, especially the small ones, are designed for bass fishing – not piking. Americans, when lure fishing for bass, tie their line directly to the plug, thus eliminating additional weight that could have an adverse affect on a plug's action.

Most British lure anglers, however, tend to use a wire trace, even when lure fishing for species such as chub and perch that do not have teeth like those of the pike. The reason for using a wire trace when lure fishing for chub and perch, is that it acts as a precaution against pike attack. A wire trace will not only allow you to play a pike without risk of your line being cut, but you will also get your lure back,

The longer your wire trace, the less risk there'll be of a bite-off.

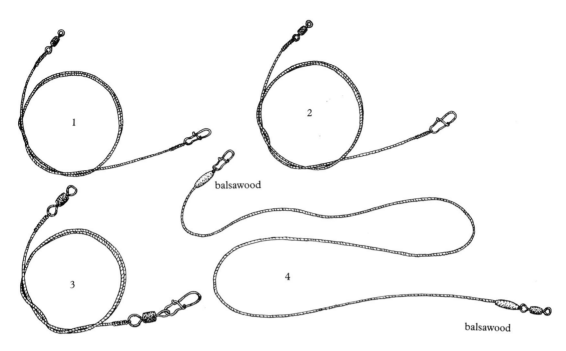

1. small swivel, small snap; 2. small swivel, medium snap; 3. two medium swivels, large snap; 4. small swivel, small snap. Balsawood supports the weight of the wire, swivel and snap.

which in turn may save the life of a pike. I have read articles by anglers who lure fish for chub and perch, but say, in print, that they do *not* use a wire trace. I, personally, think this is very irresponsible of them if pike are present in the waters where they fish. With the modern tackle of today, there is no reason *not* to use a wire trace.

To counter the possible loss of plug action, a balanced, less weighty tackle set-up is a must. Small crankbaits, crawlers and suspending plugs can be affected (for the worse) by over-weight line, wire, swivels and snap-links.

When using small lightweight lures, I would advise you to use the following, or very similar: 8–10lb quality mono line (I highly recommend 15lb Newtech Power Cable braided line); a 50cm (20in) length of 15–20lb fine trace wire; and a quality barrel swivel (size 12) twisted on at one end, with a Fox size 7 'Safe-Lok' clip, or smaller, twisted on at the other end, *not*

crimped. I have even added a small piece of balsa wood at the swivel end of the trace, which really comes into its own when using small crawlers and suspending plugs. I would rather add a piece of balsawood to my wire trace than reduce its length.

Make sure your clutch is set to slip well before your line snaps, especially when using low poundage lines. Clip your lure on to something and apply pressure to the rod while adjusting the clutch. After the initial setting of the clutch, I, personally, do not use the clutch knob for applying extra pressure to a hooked fish. Instead, I use my middle finger as an extra clutch by pushing it against the rim of the spool.

When using big heavy spoons and plugs, I use much stronger items of tackle, for example: 30lb Newtech Power Cable braided line; 20–28lb trace wire; Fox size 7 Specialist Swivels; Fox size 7 'Safe-Lok' snap-link, or one of my own hand-made clips.

ARTIFICIAL LURE CATEGORIES

Before you read the following lure chapters, I feel that it's very important that you know exactly what different categories lures fall into. Some lures are referred to as plugs, which originally just meant that they were made of wood to resemble prey fish. Most modern plugs are now made of plastic, though they are still collectively known as plugs. In my opinion, a wooden plug has a far better action than a plastic one – size for size, shape for shape! Rapala, Ozark Mountain and Bagley's, to name a few, do still make wooden plugs.

Bear in mind when you buy a lure that you don't have to just use it in the way a manufacturer suggests you use it – *experiment*. If I had always followed the manufacturer's instructions, I wouldn't have caught anywhere near as many fish on commercial lures as I have. Remember that most of the lures that are on sale in this country were made for American bass fishing. Therefore, most of the lure descriptions seen in American catalogues are describing how to use the lure for bass fishing – *not* how to use them for catching pike, perch, zander and chub.

Refer to the colour plates for examples of the various lure categories.

TOP-WATER PLUGS

Crawlers

Crawlers can have wings on each side, or a nose plate on the front. Well-known examples are the Crazy Crawler (winged) and the Jitter-bug (nose plate). Crawlers produce gurgling- and plopping-type noises with their vigorous actions. The vibrations they emit are sometimes quite irresistible to 'big' water wolves, especially on a warm summer's day or night.

Chuggers

Chuggers have indented or concave faces and come in several different styles. Water pressure is created inside the concavity when these plugs are retrieved, and they make chugging or popping sounds when jerked. Some also have a nice wiggling action when the face is cranked just below the surface. This type usually have faces which slope backwards from a projecting 'chin', and dive because water pressure on that chin causes it to dig in. Examples are the Heddon Lucky 13 and Bomber's Bomber Popper. A fastish retrieve is needed to make them dive beneath the surface.

Chuggers with faces that slope back from the 'forehead' will not dive, but just chug across the surface until jerked. Chuggers of this type are often referred to as 'poppers', a well-known example being the Gudebrod Trouble Maker.

Stickbaits

A stickbait is a floating plug, and usually resembles a cigar fitted with hooks! It has no diving blade, propellers or action. The action has to be created by the angler. In the USA, this method is called 'walking the dog'. Stickbaits are very easy to make yourself, of wood, cork, or anything else that floats. My favourite is the Heddon Zara Spook, which casts like a bullet, so is great for long-range work.

Propbaits *& propeller blades*

In body looks, propbaits are much the same as stickbaits. The difference is that a propbait has a propeller blade at one end, or one at each end; some even have two props at the rear end. Propbaits are classed as top-water lures, but they can also be very effective when worked just off bottom, or trolled beneath the water's surface behind a weight. Although neither of those methods are suggested by the manufacturers, they are *very* effective. Popular examples of propbait include the Heddon Dying Flutter and Ozark Mountain's Ripper.

SUB-SURFACE PLUGS

These are plugs that run from 30cm (1ft) deep, to Atlantis! The depth they dive to can depend on how hard you crank the plug, the size and angle of the diving blade, or whether the plug is a floater or sinker. Sub-surface lures fall into various categories.

Vibrating Plugs

Most vibrating plugs do not have a diving lip. The trace-attachment eye is located on the flattened head of the lure. The vibrations come from the lure's very tight wobble action on retrieve. Most sink, but in the last couple of years one or two new models have appeared. One is the 'floater' which may have a diving blade. The plug floats on the surface until retrieved, for example Bill Lewis's Floating Rat-L-Trap. The other new type to have appeared of late is the suspending vibrating plug, which doesn't in fact suspend when a wire trace is attached! Vibrating plugs are quite thin in body, just like a bream, and the most common types tend to have very loud sound chambers.

A pike's head appears through the foam. This one was taken on a vibrant wiggle lure.

Trolling Plugs

These plugs were designed mainly for just that – trolling. They usually float at rest and generally have a large flattened forehead which gives them a great wobbling/wiggling action when trolled. I know of none that have metal diving blades. Examples of trolling lures are Swim Whizz, Believer, Kwikfish, Lazy Ike, and Canadian Wiggler.

Jerkbaits

A jerkbait does not usually have a metal diving blade. The front of the lure is shaped in such a way that it will dive when jerked. These plugs were designed for catching *big* pike and muskies. They usually, if weighted correctly, float at rest. When jerked they can be made to dive to about 1.2m (4ft); if jerked many times in quick succession some will dive as deep as 3.5–4.5m (12–15ft), if not more. After a jerkbait has been jerked down, it should start to rise up to the surface – slowly or fast, according to how it's weighted. Most jerkbaits are hand-loaded by the user. By making and loading your own jerk-baits, you will be able to achieve the correct weighting and diving action that suits a particular water. The best known example in this country, at the time of writing, is the Suick Thriller: this has a metal tail which can be bent down to alter the plug's action and diving depth.

DIVING LURES

Crankbaits

Most crankbaits float when not being retrieved. They are called crankbaits because they all have a lip of some sort (plastic or metal) which makes them dive and wiggle/wobble when retrieved. As you wind the reel handle, they dive, cranking the bait down! Well-known examples include the Shakespeare Big S and the jointed Abu Hi-Lo.

Minnow Plugs

These are basically the same as crankbaits. Again most float, but there are quite a few minnow plugs that sink when not being retrieved. Like crankbaits, minnow plugs have diving lips. Some models have a diving lip which is a continuation of the plug's plastic body mould, whereas on other models the diving blade may be glued or screwed in position. The basic difference between minnow plugs and crankbait plugs is that minnow plugs are slim in body and have more of a wobbling action. Some examples are the Rapala Original Floating Minnow and Bomber's Long 'A' series.

SPOONS

A spoon is a piece of sheet metal that is dished in a concave and convex manner to create an action. There are thousands of different types and colours of spoons available.

SPINNERS

A spinner has a weighted or non-weighted wire shaft, around which a blade revolves, usually by means of a clevis. A spinner can be light or heavy and can have one or more spinning blades mounted on it.

SPINNERBAITS, JIGS AND BUZZERS

Spinnerbait

This is a vibratory lure with a V-shaped wire form. The lower arm has a weighted single hook for balance, and it can have one, two or even three spinning blades on the upper arm. Some even have two arms with blades – Colorado or Willowleaf – mounted on. Spinnerbaits can be worked high or low in the water, if the rod tip is held at the correct position, and if the speed of retrieve is just right. They are very effective when used in a sink and draw fashion.

Jigging Lures

These are all types of weird and wonderful things which are used to jig up and down at any given depth of water, including the bottom, for example, Leadheads, Pirks and Tail Spins and thousands of other types. Jigging lures are a great favourite for using through ice holes in cold countries, but they also work over here.

Buzzers

These are similar to spinnerbaits, the difference being that they have a propeller-type blade that allows them to plane the surface water when retrieved. Again, rod-tip position helps these lures. The props can have anything between one and four wings. Some buzzers have counter-rotating twin blades. Buzzers were designed so that their blades would work half in and half out of the water, creating a gurgling noise. Most of them have to be worked too fast to my mind, since they were designed for bass fishing. I found the best one that could be worked slowly enough for pike was Bill Norman's $\frac{1}{4}$oz Triple Wing Buzz Bait. I always carry one with me, especially when fishing!

Another type of buzzer I must mention is the sputterbuzz type. This is a plug without a diving lip, having instead a buzz blade at the front end. These types can work the surface much more slowly than the wire-form types. They are still classed as buzzers however.

FLIES AND BUGS

Flies and Nymphs

Flies imitate aquatic or terrestrial winged insects, while nymphs imitate immature forms of insect.

Streamers

Streamers are like large flies, but, unlike a fly, they imitate bait-fish.

Bugs

Bugs are top-water flies. They are supposed to imitate frogs, insects, mice and so on. Bugs can be made out of just about anything, including hair, cork, rubber, plastic, and lead.

SOFT PLASTICS

These are any types of lure made of soft rubbery plastics such as Worms, Lizards, Crayfish and Grubs.

SKIRTS

These can be made of various materials, such as rubber, feathers, deer hide, marabou, bucktail, and are fixed to hooks to enhance a lure. Although they are mainly intended for use on spinnerbaits and buzzers, I use them on anything.

A selection of lures.

3

TOP-WATER LURES

CRAWLERS

Of all the different types of top-water lure that I've ever used, crawlers have to be my favourite. I get great pleasure from just watching and listening to a crawler wobble and plop across the water's surface. When a big fish hits a crawler, the commotion has to be seen to be believed. Takes can only be described as vicious! The speed at which pike sometimes hit top-water plugs is quite unbelievable: I have seen pike travel some 1.2m (4ft) into the air on the take.

During daylight hours, through the summer months, crawlers worked across shallow, warm, undisturbed water can account for many predators. It is important that no pleasure/speed boats, jet-skiers, swimmers, dogs and so on are around to cause water disturbance. Some of my best catches on crawlers have been at night, when the boats are moored up and the noise-makers are tucked up in bed!

Not only pike take crawlers: perch and chub also like to get in on the act. My good friend David Smith, who is, in my view, a master of the balanced set-up, has caught many chub from the Dorset Stour using small jointed Jitterbugs. I have not had that much success crawling for chub or perch on my local waters, though I have caught a few.

Pike can't resist the erratic action of the author's handmade crawler.

Water pressure against the nose plate or wings on retrieve causes the lure to wobble from side to side. I have had far more success with the nose-plate type of crawler than I have with the winged, but then, I also use it far more!

Action

Crawlers swim with a side-to-side, wobbling action. A crawler's action is created by either a concave nose plate (Jitterbug), or hinged wings that automatically open out from the nose or body of the plug on retrieve (Crazy Crawler).

Preferred Water Conditions

I much prefer to crawl clear water, with a flat calm surface. A slight ripple on the surface is OK, but a good chop on the water will affect the number of takes.

Over the years I have found that pike do not respond to lures as well in murky water conditions as they do in clear water conditions. Why that is, I can only hazard a guess: that the microscopic material that is the basis of murky water tends to slow pike down! Such material will alter the water density, which in turn may affect the breathing and receptors of a pike: that is the lateral line, hearing and especially vision. As we all know, pike take fishermen's baits in very murky water conditions without too much trouble – but then, a pike doesn't really have to chase a tethered bait, does it? Chasing lures takes energy, which a pike may not want to waste if it's suffering from breathing problems! The same holds true for night fishing: I've caught many pike on crawlers at night when the water was flat, calm and clear, but very few when the water was murky.

When crawling clear water during the night or day, I've often seen water disturbance, or a bow-wave, as a pike homes in on my top-water plug from as far away as 9m (30ft) – if not more. These pike most definitely responded to my plug's vibrations via their lateral line or hearing – their vision has played no part in the initial attack response. Often there is thick weed between my plug and the pike; weed so thick that the pike has to push its way through, its back partly out of the water. Taking all that into account, we should get takes all the time – whatever the water colour, or amount of light available; so it makes sense to assume that it is the microscopic particles in murky water that affect the pike. When a water really murks up, even bait fishing is affected.

I have never found perch to be affected by murky water – if anything, I think perch prefer it. Chub, however, like pike, are affected. This is because murky water causes de-oxygenation.

Aerodynamics

Aircraft designers design aeroplanes to be aerodynamic – Concorde is one of the best examples of aerodynamics in flight. To create a violent action in a plug, you have to think 'anti-aerodynamically' (to be strictly accurate it should be anti-hydrodynamically but the

The 'anti-aerodynamics' of a lure have to be just right.

principle is the same). In other words, you encourage vibration by resistance. For a lure to imitate a bait fish in looks, and also to have a similar action, the 'anti-aerodynamics' of the lure have to be just right.

Colour *NOT important*

Having carried out a number of experiments on the appearance of top-water lures from below, I'm convinced that their colour is not that important. Most of the time the fish sees either the silhouette of the lure or the disturbance it creates, the plug's body being lost in the ripples.

Speed of Retrieve *slow*

I like to retrieve a crawler just fast enough to keep it crawling. The plopping noise of a crawler goes hand in hand with its action. In my view, the slower a crawler is retrieved, the better your results. On retrieving, some lure anglers like to stop and start their crawler now and again; I feel this does more harm than good. On various occasions, when retrieving a crawler across gin-clear water, I have stopped my retrieve for some reason only to see a predator appear from nowhere and lie suspended beneath the plug – just staring at it. I have rarely ever got a fish to attack after it has had a really close look at my plug. In those instances, I feel sure that I would have had a take if only I hadn't stopped retrieving.

Very recently, however, I have lure fished a water for the first time where pike will hit a crawler if stopped and twitched above their noses. I think that the reason for it is that the pike in that particular water are very under-nourished. If a pike is hungry enough, it will chase a lure right out of the water!

Some top-water plugs work well when stopped and jerked. This causes a big splash and loud boom to be emitted, which pike then come to investigate. In the crawler's case, on retrieve, it has a constant wobble and plopping noise that cannot be bettered by stopping and jerking. The perfect retrieve speed for any crawler is important because if retrieved too fast, there will be few takes; too slowly and it will not roll from side to side as it's designed to do, and no roll means no plopping noise. It is better to retrieve as slowly as possible while still retaining the wobble action because:

1. The slower the retrieve, the more time a predator has to think about attacking that lovely plopping noise passing overhead.
2. The slower the retrieve, the more time a predator will have to catch the lure.
3. The slower a crawler is moving, the more accurately a predator will be able to home in on it.
4. Hooking statistics are far better on a slow retrieve.
5. At night, or in murky water conditions, a predator will be relying mainly on its hearing and lateral line to locate moving prey. Retrieving a lure too fast in such conditions could greatly reduce your chances of catching by not giving the fish enough time to respond, and then to catch it.

While writing the first edition my son, who was nine at the time, was having some good catches using an 8cm (3in) Jointed Jitterbug. He advised me (his lure fishing tutor!) to jerk my jitterbug now and again just as he did, because he was convinced that an occasional jerk did make a difference to his strike rate.

Time of the Year

Crawlers are at their catching best when slowly retrieved across shallow warm water – during the summer months. For those that do not suffer the close season, May to late October are the best months of the year to go crawling. The rest of us must start a month later, after the end of the close season. To catch pike on a crawler during the cold months is a real challenge! The most productive months are usually in high summer provided it is hot and various other factors are favourable.

Water Temperature

On most of the waters that I've crawled in the past, I have found that a water temperature of 21°C (70°F) or higher is the key to catching pike in numbers. The shallow areas of a water will usually be the first places to reach that temperature. I have found that on big waters that have various shallow bays, all approximately the same depth, pike will start to hit top-water plugs in the largest of those bays first. If there's one bay that is shallower than all the rest, then that bay will usually 'come on' first.

Water Depth and Type

Shallow areas up to about 1.2m (4ft) in depth are ideal areas to explore with a crawler. Water depths as low as 15–23cm (6–9in) should definitely not be overlooked. I have caught many pike in the 5–7lb range from depths of water that would just about cover my ankles.

I have never had crawlers, or any other kind of top-water lure come to that, hit regularly when retrieved over deep water. Sometimes pike will move along with floating weed, so if you spot some over deep water, it's always

Steve Gamble works a crawler along the edge of a reed-bed.

worth sending your crawler over to investigate!

With regard to water type, any type will do, provided it has fish in it! An 'OK water' as opposed to a 'good water', however, can mean the difference between catching one fish and, say, twenty in a day. The ideal type of water for using any top-water lure, is deep water that has shallow areas of some kind – pike love to bask in shallow warm water, or in structures very near to the water's surface.

Features and Structure

I'll go through some of the features and structure that I would look for in a water that I had never lure fished before, and explain how I would work that feature/structure with my top-water lure.

Type: a narrow reeded shelf at the top of a deep drop-off.

Method: if it's a long length of reed-bed, I cast my top-water lure along its length, keeping the lure fairly tight to the reed-bed – within 15cm (6in) to 60cm (2ft). After casting, I retrieve the lure back very slowly. Treat shallow-water reed-beds the same way.

Type: floating weed.
Method: work your plug as near to the weed as you can.

Type: fallen trees.
Method: an old decaying tree is a favourite for a top-water lure: work it over and through the few remaining branches. Strong line is a must for pressuring a hooked fish away from its snaggy sanctuary. If you are unable to work a top-water lure over, or through decaying tree branches, cast as near as you dare to their outer edge. Remember that lures cost money.

Type: floating pontoon and jetties.
Method: work your lure around the edge of a floating pontoon or jetty before walking on it. If possible, hire a boat and work them from a distance. The same method works with moored boats.

Type: submerged weed, gravel bar or submerged island.
Method: slowly retrieve over the top.

Type: weir pool.
Method: work the calm water around the edges of the weir pool.

Trolling

Over the years, I've had great success trolling crawlers. I much prefer to row troll crawlers, rather than use my electric trolling motor (which is too fast). After lifting my boat's anchor to move to a different area, I usually troll a crawler behind the boat to the next anchoring point. Any fish caught while moving to a different area is a bonus. Sometimes, if I'm feeling really fit, I'll troll them all day long.

Effectiveness

Seeing a crawler plopping across the water's surface for the first time can be very exciting, whether or not you hook and land a fish. When I first started crawling, I would be quite content at the end of a lure session if I had only landed two or three fish from ten takes. At first, I missed many takes because of striking too quickly; with time and experience behind me, I don't miss too many now. If everything is working for me, that is, if I have good weather, clear water, not too many bait fish present in the water, plenty of pike about looking for food and so on, I would expect to catch about twelve to twenty pike in a day on crawlers. If I only catch one fish though – that's fishing.

Changing a lure's hooks for sharper, shorter-shanked ones, can greatly increase hooking statistics, especially when top-water lure fishing. I highly recommend Eagle Claw as a replacement treble hook. The nice thing about Eagle Claw hooks is that they are sharper and are made of a finer wire than most factory-fitted lure trebles. Another plus is that Eagle Claw hooks have a much smaller barb, which means that they cause a fish less damage and make unhooking far easier. Some replacement treble hooks will need to be fitted with a small split ring in order to attach them to a lure. As for hook weight, solder can be wound around the shank of the hook if absolutely necessary.

If you have never used a crawler before, you may, after having read this chapter, feel a great urge to get out there and have a go. I wish you all the luck in the world, but remember, if at first you don't succeed – don't give up, keep working at it. When you get everything just right and start landing plenty of fish, I know that you'll agree with me that crawling is the most exciting of all the lure fishing methods.

The time of year, the water temperature, the choice of water and the head of predators present all have to be considered if you are to achieve success. If, during the summer period, you choose a good water to start crawling, you

Undercuts and reed margins are the perfect place for pike to hold up.

shouldn't have long to wait before you too are experiencing the excitement of crawler fishing. Usually my adrenalin starts to flow as my crawler passes over, or close by a feature that has produced fish for me in the past. After six or seven casts to that feature without a take though, I calm down and my body relaxes once again. It's usually then that a bite occurs!

I always concentrate very hard visually, and

listen to my crawler attentively as I retrieve it, far more so than I do for any other top-water lure. This is possibly because crawlers are far more visual and noisy throughout their retrieve; other types of top-water lure usually have to be jerked in order to get enhanced sound effects. Because I concentrate so hard on my crawler, the first take of the day (usually very early in the morning), comes as a sudden shock to my nervous system.

Reflections

To help you to understand what effect crawlers have on me, here is a page out of my memory . . .

It's 1 a.m. and the moon is full. I cast my crawler out some 20m (70ft) and start to slowly retrieve it towards my boat . . . As I wind, I feel that strange eerie feeling coming over me once again. It causes my heart to miss a beat and my nerves to tremble. A splash close by makes me jump . . . I'll . . . that duck!

As my crawler approaches an area of water that I've had many a take from in the past, my adrenalin really starts to flow. The moon's reflection on the flat, calm water is suddenly broken: a sizeable pike is homing in on my crawler – shark style! I watch the bow-wave change direction with every turn of my reel handle. Within a second the water erupts – a good sized pike launches itself into flight and returns to the water with an almighty splash – and I almost part company with my boots! As I jump in fright, I unintentionally strike on my rod. This jerks the crawler out of its captor's toothy jaws and it whizzes through the air towards me. It misses my ear by a whisker and lands in the water some six metres behind me. I couldn't quite make out the tune it was humming as it passed by my ear!

I wind in and recast to the same area. I start to retrieve again, nice and slowly . . . again, there's another bow-wave followed by an explosion of water around my crawler. I manage to keep control of my nerves this time, and strike about two to three seconds after the

An old photo of the author's old friend!

eruption. There is a solid resistance and my rod bends double. I start to play the fish towards the boat. It puts up the fight of its life but is no match for an old hand at night crawling. I slip my landing net under a good twenty-pounder and raise the net arms some 45cm above the water's surface. I turn on my head lamp and quickly unhook it in the confines of the net. After admiring her for a few seconds, I see that she's an old friend. There's no need for a picture, so I lower the net arms deep into the water and let her slip away over the rim. She waves farewell with her tail and vanishes into the night . . .

CHUGGERS

Chuggers are also top-water plugs. They come

in various shapes, sizes and forms, but they all have in common a concave or indented front end, or 'mouth'.

Over the years, I've caught many pike in the 1–7lb range on small chuggers, but few doubles. Big pike have never seemed that interested in them. Chuggers fished on your waters, though, may prove to be a killer for big fish. There must be quite a few waters around stuffed full of pike, perch, zander or chub, where any type of lure would not keep its paint coat for long! Or is that wishful thinking?

Some chuggers just have a concave mouth, while others have a concave and indented one. Some chuggers have a long top lip (Cotton Cordell Near Nuthin'), and some have a longer bottom lip (Heddon Lucky 13). Some chuggers are weighted heavily at the rear end and will sink back-end first after casting (such as the Cotton Cordell Near Nuthin'). Whatever their little differences, they are all collectively known as chuggers. For the DIY lure enthusiast, a chugger is one of the easiest to make of all top-water plugs.

Action

As I've said, chuggers have various mouth designs. Each of the mouth designs can be made to perform differently to the others. In order to get decent catch results from any design of chugger, you have to use imagination and artistic flair! For example, a small chugger can be made to imitate realistically a topping fry. Use your rod like an artist would use his brush when creating a work of art! Lure fishing is an art just like fly fishing. Chuggers (and stickbaits) are not the easiest lure to fish; you might find you are more successful using lures that require a more down-to-earth approach.

I have had far more success using small 6cm (2$\frac{3}{8}$in) chuggers than I have using large 8cm (3$\frac{1}{4}$in) ones. An extra 2cm ($\frac{3}{4}$in) might not sound like much, but it does appear to make a difference to my strike rate.

Below, I'll go through the well-known chugger mouth designs and explain how to work

them to their full fishing potential. First let me explain the difference between a twitch, flick and jerk. A twitch is a gentle 7–15cm (3–6in) twitch of the rod tip. A flick is a sharp 15–60cm (6in–2ft) flick of the rod tip. A jerk is a fairly hard 60–90cm (2–3ft) jerk of the rod tip.

Concave Mouth with Longer Top Lip
The longer top lip stops the plug from diving below the water's surface; in fact, it can cause its head to rise slightly on retrieve. The main difference between this design and the next one is that when jerked, this one makes more of a gurgling noise; while the following design makes a popping noise.

Application: twitched, flicked and jerked on a slow retrieve.

Concave/Indented Mouth with Longer Top Lip
As above, the longer top lip stops the plug from diving below the water's surface, and can cause its head to rise slightly on retrieve. When the plug is jerked forward, a popping sound can be heard and water flies forward in an upward direction! As the water lands back on the surface, a noise similar to that of topping bait fish will be heard.

Application: twitched, flicked and jerked on a slow retrieve.

Concave Mouth with Longer Bottom Lip
Size for size, this mouth design will dive deeper than the following design. When jerked forward, the mouth will throw a small amount of water forward – at the same time emitting a muffled gurgling noise.

Applications: twitched, flicked and jerked on a slow retrieve. Alternatively, when retrieved fairly fast, it will dive beneath the water's surface. Every now and again, stop, letting the plug rise to the surface. When in view, flick and twitch it, then send it diving again – this is a very productive method.

Concave/Indented Mouth with Longer Bottom Lip
Basically, this is the same as the above design,

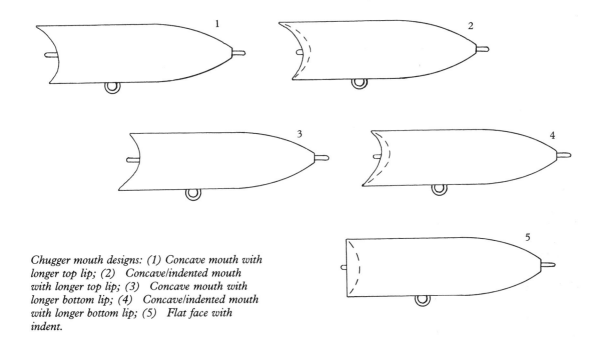

Chugger mouth designs: (1) Concave mouth with longer top lip; (2) Concave/indented mouth with longer top lip; (3) Concave mouth with longer bottom lip; (4) Concave/indented mouth with longer bottom lip; (5) Flat face with indent.

but it will not dive as deep. When jerked forward, the mouth will throw a small amount of water forward, emitting a fairly loud muffled popping noise.

Applications: *see* previous application.

Flat Face with Indent
This shape will not raise its head like the first two designs nor will it dive like long bottom lip mouth designs. This mouth shape makes the plug run straight and true across the water's surface when retrieved slowly. If retrieved faster, you can expect a small 'back-end wiggle' action. If jerked hard, a loud explosion or boom will be heard by one and all!

Application: twitched, flicked and jerked – sometimes fairly hard on a slow retrieve.

The use of the rod tip to make a chugger move in different darting directions can make all the difference to the strike rate. Also, I prefer to retrieve all top-water plugs slowly. Slow retrieving with jerk, twitch and flick, is the key to a chugger's success.

With reference to colour, time of year, water temperature, water depth and type, features and structure and preferred water conditions, everything I said about crawlers applies equally to chuggers.

Leger Retrieving and Trolling Chuggers

Chuggers, hybrid chugger propbaits and propbaits get very good results when 'leger retrieved', or 'leger trolled' just off bottom.

For leger retrieving, use a 1–2oz leger weight on the main line, running leger style, or attached to a 4lb breaking strain weak link, and cast out and wait for the leger weight and plug to sink to the bottom; then slowly retrieve it back, keeping the leger weight in constant contact with the bottom. To date, I've caught more pike by leger retrieving with hybrid chugger propbaits than with any other type of top-water plug. Chugger hybrids have a nice swimming action when worked beneath the surface; pike find it very hard to resist the vibrations and flash emitted by the spinning prop-blade. When working a rough snaggy bottom, it pays to use a 30cm (12in) wire up-trace to eliminate line abrasion.

For leger trolling, use a 2–3oz leger weight on the main line, or attached to a weak link (no stronger than 4lb breaking strain), cast out well behind the boat and wait for the leger weight and plug to sink to the bottom. Then close your bail arm, or engage your multiplier, and place your rod in the rod holder. When all is ready, start trolling – *slowly*. If you get a take, set the hook by accelerating the boat forward, using either arm and oar power, or the electric motor.

The good thing about leger retrieving and leger trolling chuggers and propbaits is that they do not dive below the leger weight when

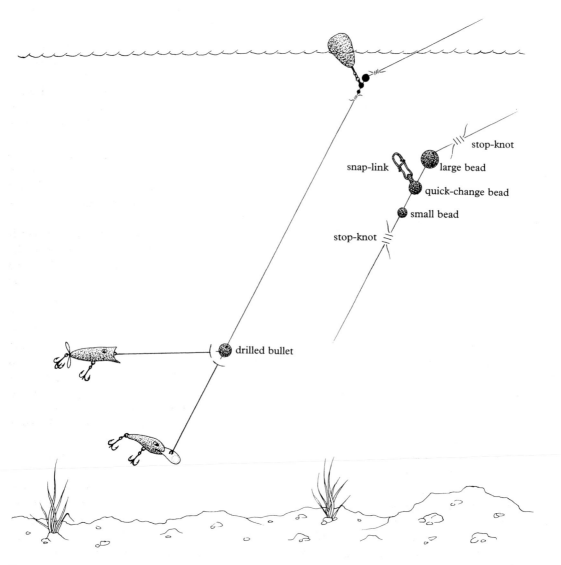

Using a controller float and weight to govern the lure's working depth.

retrieved/trolled slowly: this means, there is less chance of snagging on the bottom. Remember that chuggers with long bottom lips will dive if retrieved fast.

I rarely ever troll chuggers, propbaits, or hybrid chugger propbaits on the surface; in this case, I much prefer to use crawlers.

Float Retrieving and Float Trolling

Float retrieving and float trolling are very effective methods, for which I make my own very buoyant floats – controller floats (*see* Chapter 18).

My large controller float will easily take a 1–2oz drilled bullet. It can also be used to govern the depth you require a plug to work at: you can make a plug that dives to 7m (23ft) work at 3m (10ft), or whatever, by altering the float. If you want to retrieve or troll a top-water chugger, hybrid chugger, propbait, or a shallow diving plug, at depth, all you need do is slide a 1–2oz bullet on the main line before you tie your trace. (*See* diagram on p.24.)

I prefer to use chrome- or glitter-finished plugs when depth trolling for pike. In my opinion, these highly reflective lure finishes do get better results.

Reflections

Although I'm no gambler, I could never resist a little flutter with my friends when out lure fishing together during the colder months of the year. Our usual stake would be £1 for the first fish, £1 for the biggest fish and £1 for the most fish.

On our arrival at a water, my first method would always be to put a hybrid chugger or propbait on a 45cm (18in) trace with a 1oz Arlesey bomb on the main line. My friends would use other lures like crankbaits, spoons, spinners and spinnerbaits; leger retrieving top-water plugs was a method they never could get to grips with. During the many times we fished together, I cannot remember ever having to put my hand in my pocket! More often than not,

that method was responsible for earning me the full £3 stake.

STICKBAITS

A stickbait is a top-water plug, which usually looks like the name suggests: like a crudely shaped stick! The reason I said 'usually', is that I have seen a couple of models of stickbait that differ greatly from the norm: one, for example, had a 90-degree non-diving blade positioned just in front of its belly hook hanger, which, being anti-aerodynamic, causes the plug to wobble as it's retrieved. When jerked, it causes a fair amount of disturbance.

The normal type of stickbait has to be the easiest plug for the DIY enthusiast to make. Once made, it can have a prop added – converting it into a propbait.

A stickbait has no nose blade, wings, concave, indent, prop or any other type of external feature that might help it to catch fish. All it's got going for it, is you, the angler. Some stickbaits have a weight added at their rear end (such as the Heddon Zara Spook), which tends to stop the stickbait from skimming across the surface too much when twitched, flicked and jerked. The added weight actually enhances the plug action created by the angler! In my view, models without a weight added do not perform anywhere near as well as the weighted models. The unweighted models tend to skim over the water's surface too much for my liking. When a weighted stickbait is jerked forward hard, a splash of water will be seen coming from it and a fish-like topping noise heard. Shortly after the jerk, it is not unusual to see a pike swirl close by.

If you have a supply of propbaits with the eye-type hook hanger at the rear end (such as the Heddon Dying Flutter), why not convert one into a stickbait? All you have to do is unscrew the short rear hook hanger and replace it with a longer one – 35mm being the ideal length. Before you screw the replacement hook hanger into the body, slide a drilled brass or nickel metal bead onto it to act as a rear weight. If you cannot get hold of drilled metal beads, just use a length of plumber's solder instead: wrap a length of it around the shank of the rear treble. If you use this method, you do not have to replace the hook hanger, or even remove the prop blades! Old spinner bodies can also be used as a substitute for metal beads. You'll have to enlarge the centre hole of the spinner body to be able to slide it onto the hook hanger. For lure-making equipment, *see* 'Useful Websites' on page 159.

Action

If a stickbait is retrieved at a slow speed, medium, or fast speed, it will just cut straight through the water because of its very aerodynamic shape (apart from the non-diving blade type!). Very little sign of water disturbance will be seen coming from it. 'Boring', I hear the crawler, chugger and propbait users saying, and I would have to be the first to agree with them after using crawlers, propbaits, hybrid chugger propbaits and chuggers (listed in my personal order of preference).

Although stickbaits lack any type of external feature that would create action on retrieve, if the angler jerks, twitches or flicks the rod tip (which is preferably held at 10 o'clock high and pointed in the direction of the stickbait), the plug will zigzag over the water with each alternate jerk, twitch or flick. Americans call the method either 'walking the dog' or 'walk the dog'. If you gently flick your rod tip to the left or right, you can make the plug move in one specific direction.

Stickbaits, of all surface plugs are the most annoying for me! When retrieved, you may often witness, like I've done, a big vortex open up near the plug. These are created by big 'just interested' pike! In my opinion, a top-water plug needs to act, look and sound more than 'just interesting' to cause predators to attack it. Yet on the days when crawlers, propbaits and chuggers do not get any type of response from pike, stickbaits, for some reason, start catching!

Water Conditions

To get any type of a result using stickbaits, gin-clear, flat, calm, warm water is a must. As I've said before, though, there's bound to be a water that will prove me wrong.

My biggest pike to date taken on a Heddon Zara Spook, fished over weedy clear water, is 17lb 4 oz – not a bad fish for a boring-looking plug! I had caught the same pike two days previously on a 8cm (3in) jointed Jitterbug; yet on the day that I caught it on the Zara Spook, I had been using the Jitterbug for some time to no avail. As soon as I put on a boring-looking Zara Spook, the fish took – read into that what you will!

When vibrant crawlers are not producing the goods, stick on a stickbait. Their less vibrant actions could be the answer to their success.

The comments I made regarding colour, time of year, water temperature, water depth and features and structure for crawler fishing, are just as valid here.

Reflections

It was a summer afternoon... I cast my Heddon Zara Puppy up-river and slowly retrieved it back towards me. As the plug passed within inches of a reed-bed, a sizeable pike struck. The pike left the water and tail-walked for some distance with the plug in its mouth; then, to my horror, it shook its head and sent the Puppy flying. On that occasion you could say the pike 'walked the puppy'!

Without such memories of the one that got away, fishing, in my opinion, would be rather dull. My most memorable fish to date is not my personal best 33lb pike – but another monster that grabbed a pike of about 7lb that I was playing. Unfortunately, I never landed either. That big pike is the one that I'm always hoping to hook again, even when I'm fishing a different water!

PROPBAITS

A propbait is a top-water plug that has either one, two or three lightweight propellor blades mounted on it. Blade mounting and blade design can vary enormously. I feel that the size and type of prop-blade used in plug construction can, more often than not, be compared to that of the attacking predator! Meaning – big prop-blades seem to attract big pike, and small prop-blades tend to attract the smaller predator, with the odd exception here and there.

In order to get good results using propbaits, I would suggest that you pay great attention to prop-blade design. Prop-blades like those on the Ozark Ripper and Luhr Jensen's Nip-I-Diddee, are, in my view, far superior to the type on the Heddon Dying Flutter, which usually need extensive tuning. The latter are very good lures, though, when tuned.

The most popular blade combinations have one or two prop-blades at the rear, or one blade at the front and one at the rear. Propbaits with just one blade at the front, or with one blade at the front and two at the back, are far less common. A propbait fitted with a large 'counter-turning' prop-blade at the front end, can often cause trace snagging problems when casting. To get over this, feather the spool while the propbait is in flight. A counter-turning prop-blade fitted at the front end is worth any amount of reduction (by feathering) in casting distance.

Action

Like crawlers and chuggers, propbaits work best when retrieved slowly across the water's surface. Twitching, flicking and jerking the rod tip now and again causes the blades of a propbait to make a buzzing noise as they cut through the water. Some blades throw water into the air when flicked or jerked, creating a noise like a topping fish.

I like to slowly retrieve a propbait about 2.5m (8ft) before giving it a twitch, flick or jerk to

The author feathers the spool with his middle finger. He also uses the finger as a fine-tune clutch.

create added sound effects, which can often cause instant strikes from big pike. The 2.5m (8ft) part of the retrieve without a twitch, flick or jerk gives a predator ample time to hit the propbait while it is slowly moving over the calm surface, its prop-blades flashing an enticing message to the approaching predator's eye: 'come and get me!'

Blade Type

The size and type of prop-blade, in my view, can make a difference to the strike rate – sometimes, a big pike difference. A standard nickel prop-blade tends to cut through the water on retrieve, whereas an aluminium counter-turning blade, or buzz blade, slaps the water's surface. When a propbait with nickel-plated blades is jerked forward the blades make a buzzing noise. When a propbait with aluminium counter-turning blades, or buzz blades is jerked forward, a loud slapping noise is emitted from them. That loud slapping noise brings pike in from much further afield.

Reflections

One day in June, I set off afloat to go and fish top-water lures in a shallow weeded bay that I had never worked before. It was about 10 a.m. when I arrived in the bay. To the touch, the water was not as warm as I would have liked, although the sun was scorching hot and the water temperature was rising with every minute that passed. I had had no luck after an hour, so I upped anchor and set course for another bay some half a mile to the north. I positioned my boat on the outer edge of a big bay and dropped anchor; then cast various top-water plugs into the bay – but, like the previous bay, nothing stirred . . .

I put on a silver spoon and cast it out into the deeper water. Straight away I was into a double. I cast again and again – and I caught again and again.

Soon after midday something happened in the bay that I had never seen the like of before: it had suddenly become alive with big topping pike. The closest thing that I'd ever seen to such a sight before was carp spawning. I quickly put on one of my handmade counter-turning propbaits and cast it out. The plug landed some 9m (30ft) from a tree that lay lifeless and half submerged in the water. I took up the slack line and then jerked the plug hard. As the blades slapped the water's surface there was an almighty eruption from within the branches of the tree as a big old girl went into attack mode. I don't mind admitting, I jumped at the sight. My head went into tingle mode as I saw the fish's bow wave heading straight for my lure . . . as the water erupted, I went into shake mode! Her toothy jaws closed on the plug and I was into my best ever top-water lured pike. She weighed 25lb 4oz and was of solid build. After

photographing, I lowered her carefully to the water; I remember thinking as I watched her slip from my fingers, 'take care my darlin'.' She replied by thrashing water straight in my face. By the time I could see again she was gone.

FISH SIZE

The size of fish I have caught over the years on the various types of top-water plug (worked on the surface), may be of interest.

Crawlers have consistently caught me double figure pike: In one midsummer month, I caught no fewer than seven pike over 17lb using a 8cm (3in) Fred Arbogast Jitterbug – plus a few smaller double- and single-figure pike and chub.

A handmade propbait with an aluminium counter-turning blade mounted front and rear has, to date, accounted for my biggest top-water caught pike – 25lb 4oz. Propbaits with standard nickel-plated blades mounted on them (such as the Heddon Dying Flutter), have caught me a greater number of pike than any other top-water plug, most of them under 10lb in weight.

Small chuggers have accounted for many pike in the 1–7lb range, plus a few doubles.

Large hybrid chugger propbaits have not been too successful worked on the surface, but have accounted for many pike when worked below it! (*See* section on leger retrieving, page 23.) I have also caught many pike on propbaits leger retrieved just off the bottom (*see* diagram opposite).

Stickbaits have not accounted for that many pike to date, mainly because I never used to be all that keen on using them. The pike that I have taken on them, have all, barring a couple, been over 10lb in weight.

The amount of time that I spend using each specific type of top-water plug obviously plays a major part in my catch statistics. If you prefer to use different types of lure to me, your overall catch statistics will differ from mine: for example, if you enjoy using a stickbait and

Large handmade propbaits.

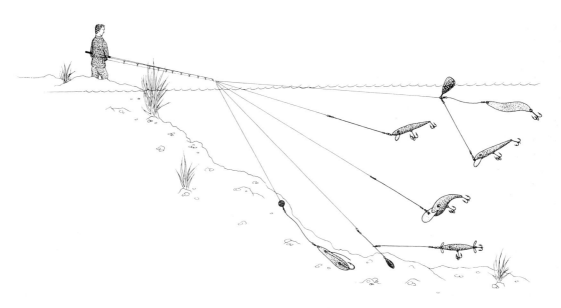

Different ways to retrieve a lure.

spend most of the summer 'walking the dog', you can expect to catch a lot more pike on a stickbait than I have. If you enjoy using a specific type of lure, then use that lure irrespective of how many fish it catches: lure fishing is all about enjoying yourself, not playing the size and numbers game.

My favourite type of lure is a crawler (a 10cm Jitterbug in particular). As I enjoy using that specific lure so much during the summer period, I catch far more fish each time I use it than I do on any one of the other lures lying idle in my lure box!

A lure angler's catch statistics are usually based on the number of fish that a specific lure has caught for him. What most lure anglers tend to overlook is the amount of hours that one specific lure has been used by them in relation to all the other lures they have! Usually, the more fish a lure produces, the more that lure becomes your favourite and so, in turn, the more it's used.

The author carefully returns his 25lb 4oz pike.

4

SUB-SURFACE PLUGS

TROLLING PLUGS

Trolling plugs are sub-surface workers, originally designed for trolling. There are many different models available today but the one thing they all have in common is the design of the 'forehead', which is usually flattish in appearance. Some models also have an indent like that of the indented chugger, which causes enhanced plug action. .

I have seen it written that trolling plugs are difficult to cast from the bank, because they tangle very easily with the trace when cast. All I have to say to that is, those writers obviously lack personal experience using them. Many different models of trolling plug can be cast from the bank with ease: I have only one model that can be difficult to cast. I say 'can be' because, in the right hands, there is no problem. This one model is the jointed Quikfish which, when cast into a head-on wind, will often come to a halt in mid-flight, while the trace attached to it keeps on going, so that it ends up caught around the plug. To overcome this 'boogie' problem, feather the spool while casting; that is control the amount of line coming off the spool with your index or middle finger (*see photograph on page 27*). Some casting distance will be lost by feathering, but the trace and plug boogie problem will be eliminated. When there is a fairly strong head-on wind, it also pays to cast in between gusts.

If the wind is coming from behind you, great casting distances can be achieved with the lightest of lures. So on windy days, it definitely pays to give a little thought to the position you cast from, in relation to the wind direction.

Jan Arends of Holland displays a nice pike, taken on a Believer lure.

Action

The actions of trolling plugs vary greatly. Some have a nice wide, lazy wobble, while others have an aggressive wobble and wiggle action.

Like any lure, the body action of a trolling plug will be defined by the speed at which it is trolled or retrieved. The first time you have a go at trolling lures, it pays to troll the lure just under the water surface for the first couple of minutes! If you can see the lure, you will get a good idea of how fast to row, or what gear/throttle position is best suited to that lure. When the trolling speed is right for the lure, look at the rod tip and mentally take in its action; it usually starts to bounce when the optimum trolling speed of the lure is reached. Rods of $1\frac{3}{4}$–2lb test curve are ideal for indicating whether or not your lure is still working as you want it to. If the rod tip action starts to differ from your mental picture, the lure is either being worked too slowly, it's tangled, or it's dragging bottom. There's just no substitute for experience with this technique.

Depth Trolling

When trolling at depth you really need to know at what depth your plug is working. There are a number of alternatives you could use for determining a plug's working depth, including coloured lines, 'clip on the rod' depth counters and the trusty old stop-knot, which is the easiest method and is described below.

To start with, if you're intending to troll a trolling plug without any form of weight, such as a leger weight or downrigger, it's no good using a model that only dives 1.8m (6ft) below the surface, if you want to explore the 3.6m (12ft) layer of water. When trolling at depth, it's always better to use a plug that will dive deeper than actually required; the length of line let out, or a controller float, will govern the lure's working depth.

The simplest method of controlling a plug's working depth, is to use a stop-knot. Nowadays, most anglers use a 10ft or 11ft rod, so all you have to do is use your rod as a measure for positioning the stop-knot. If you want to troll your deep-diving trolling plug along the 2.7m (9ft) layer of water, set your stop-knot at 3m (10ft) from the plug. If the stop knot remains about 15cm (6in) above the water's surface the plug should be working the 2.7m (9ft) layer. This is because of the effect of forward movement balanced against water pressure that makes the plug dive. This makes an angle of around 60 degrees from a horizontal line through the rod tip to the fishing line, when the plug is working correctly.

Make sure your reel clutch is set so that line can be pulled off the reel under excess pressure. The clutch needs to be adjusted just tight

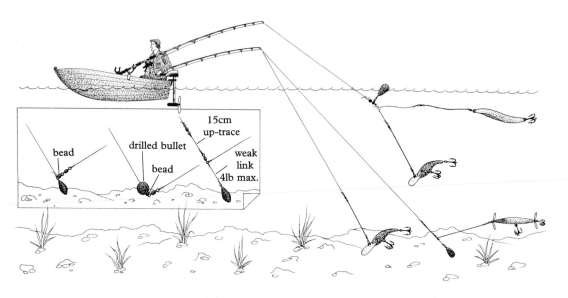

Various ways to troll various types of lure.

enough to be able to set the hooks without any risk of the clutch slipping. If a clutch is set too tight, a good fish could snap the line before you get a chance to alter it. With your rig set up, you will be ready to go in search of big water wolves . . .

Cast the trolling plug over the back end of the boat and wind it back in until the stop-knot is about 60cm (2ft) from the rod tip; then put your rod in its holder and start trolling. Build up speed until your rod tip starts to react in the manner that you require (refer back to your mental picture!). If the stop knot is out of sight below the water's surface, or well above it, either feed out, or retrieve line until the stop knot is just above the surface. All you have to do when everything is to your liking, is keep on the move until you get a take.

When I get a take, I accelerate on the oars or engine to set the hook. It doesn't matter what test curve the rod is (it could be 1¾lb or 3lb), you will drop fish if you do not put instant pressure on the striking fish. When trolling a lure from a downrigger, it is even more important to accelerate because of slack line (*see* Chapter 17)!

Reflections

The first time that I used trolling plugs, was at a southern reservoir. On that first day, between six of us (two to a boat), we caught around 150 pike. We trolled our trolling lures tight to the bottom in water depths that ranged from 6–9m (20–30ft). Further trolling sessions on that particular water produced many more pike, as well as perch to 4lb, and trout to about 3lb.

JERKBAITS

Jerkbaits are sub-surface 'pike' plugs. After casting a commercial jerkbait out, it will lie floating flat on the water's surface until 'jerked' forward. It will then dive a certain depth beneath the surface: that depth is defined by the power put into the initial jerk, the density

of the plug's body, and the nose shape and angle.

Since the first edition was published a great many new jerkbaits have appeared on UK tackle shop shelves – far too many to mention in this revised edition. The Suick Thriller, though, is still one of my favourite jerkbaits.

When the Suick Thriller is jerked forward, it will dive 30–60cm (1–2ft) below the water's surface. The buoyancy of a jerkbait's body is the key factor in determining diving depth: the more buoyant a jerkbait is, the shallower it will dive. The Suick Thriller is a very buoyant plug. After its initial jerk forward, it will rise to the surface very quickly indeed; that is, if no further twitches, flicks or jerks are offered forthwith. To stop a jerkbait from rising to the surface straight after it has been jerked forward, keep jerking, twitching or flicking the rod tip. The jerkbait should then keep moving forward beneath the water's surface. I like to let my jerkbaits bob back to the surface now and again. After each jerk, twitch, or flick of the rod tip, take up the slack line as quickly as possible. If you don't do this, and a pike hits, don't be surprised if you drop the fish.

American muskie hunters work jerkbaits very fast. Fishing from a boat, using a short rod and multiplier reel, the jerkbait is retrieved very quickly. At the same time, the rod tip is continually being jerked downwards, towards the water. Quite often, muskies will be seen following through, but not taking. To overcome that problem, American pro muskie hunters do what's called the 'figure of eight'! As the jerkbait starts to ascend near the boat, they take the rod tip off to the left then out and away from the boat; when the jerkbait is as far from the boat as is humanly possible, it's brought back in a right-hand motion towards the boat, and then out and away to the right – working the rod in a figure-of-eight fashion. The rod tip is actually held beneath the water while doing this; sometimes the rod is even half-submerged to get the jerkbait deep. I've watched a video of Doug Stange and Al Lindner of America's *In-Fisherman* magazine, muskie fishing in this way; believe me, it was breathtaking stuff – muskies followed in and took beneath the boat as Doug did the figure of eight. On the same video, Al Lindner landed a muskie of at least 40lb. To join the *In-Fisherman* magazine, *see* 'Useful Addresses'; as well as the magazine, they do some great videos, which will need converting!

It would appear, after watching the video, that English pike are very lazy compared to American muskies. They may look the same – but they sure as hell don't act the same!

The Friendly Fisherman has now started to bring in the Smitty Muskie jerkbaits and propbaits, all of which can be used for pike.

Is There a Doctor in the House?

American lure fishermen 'doctor' their jerkbaits; they drill holes in the bellies and push in large amounts of lead. The additional weight makes a jerkbait rise to the surface that much slower. Finely tuned, a jerkbait can even be made to suspend at various depths beneath the surface. After jerking a 'negative-buoyancy' jerkbait down, it will lie suspended at a certain depth beneath the water's surface until it's jerked forward again. A negative-buoyancy plug may appear far more appetizing (visually and vibration-wise) to the eye, lateral line and hearing of a pike, than a fast-rising model would. After the first initial jerk to get a negative-buoyancy jerkbait beneath the water's surface, all that has to be done is to give short sharp twitches, flicks and jerks of the rod tip to make the jerkbait move forward, mimicking a small pike. Some jerkbaits tend to zigzag with each alternate jerk, whereas others may have a tendency to go in one specific direction: (that is, left-straight-right).

To make the Suick zigzag better, screw in another trace attachment eye (a 2cm (³⁄₄in) eyed hook hanger) above the existing metal eye. For a wide zigzag, attach to the new top eye, for a medium zigzag, attach to the original bottom eye.

After being jerked forward (beneath the surface), a negative-buoyancy jerkbait will glide forward (left-straight-right) and then come to a halt. It will lie motionless, patiently waiting to be jerked forward again, or to be chomped by the mother of all pike!

A 'walking the dog' retrieve can be very effective when using buoyant and negative-buoyancy jerkbaits.

The Suick Thriller (175mm model) is probably the easiest of all jerkbaits to doctor. The larger the overall body dimensions of a jerkbait, the more doctoring (that is, drilling and loading) that jerkbait will require. Some of my own handmade jerkbaits have required 2oz of lead, if not more, to get them to suspend. American lure fishermen who hunt big pike and muskies seem to love using big heavy jerkbaits. In general, I much prefer to use lighter weighted jerkbaits, which are less prone to rip my arms from their sockets as I try to heave them into flight!

Tail Angle

The Suick jerkbaits have a metal tail that can be bent to any angle down to 180 degrees. The tail can help the plug to dive deeper, or to stay up in the water. In the photo showing you how to doctor a Suick (*see* opposite), you will note that the tail is bent down on the bottom finished plug. The angle that I've set that tail at does three specific things to that plug.

1. On the initial jerk to get the plug to dive, the tail angle makes the surface water boil, which calls pike in to check out the disturbance.

2. It stops the plug from gliding too far forward after each jerk. If that happens there is a risk that its hooks will get caught up on a slack trace.

3. Depending on the power put into a jerk, the tail angle will allow the plug to be cranked down that much deeper than it would otherwise; a hard jerk, keeping the rod tip at about seven o'clock, will make the plug dive, while a medium jerk with the rod held at eight or nine o'clock will keep the plug working at a specific depth.

The height at which the rod tip is positioned plays a big part in depth control, so practise holding it in different positions. Practice makes perfect.

Weighting

All you need to weight a Suick Thriller is a piece of 17swg sheet lead – the type used for roofing is ideal. I cut a piece 45mm long by 13mm wide and then roll it up. It should make a 9mm-diameter cylinder when rolled. Using a 9mm drill bit, I then drill a hole just behind the front belly hook hanger, to a depth of 14mm. Use an elastic band on the drill bit as a guide to show the required drilling depth. Then I apply some glue to the hole and gently hammer in the lead roll.

To fine tune the plug I wrap plumber's solder around the shank of both hooks; this might be any one of three different diameters – 18, 16 or 11swg. The solder used on the hooks of the finished Suick Thriller is 16swg. I found that

Solder comes in very handy for finely tuning a plug.

it was best to wrap the complete shank of each hook and then cut off small pieces from the bottom of the hook until the correct buoyancy is achieved.

I have tuned my Suicks so they suspend off the horizontal plane, and weighted them so the head sits 25mm (1in) higher than the tail. I found that they dived deeper if the plug was weighted 100 per cent horizontally or forward.

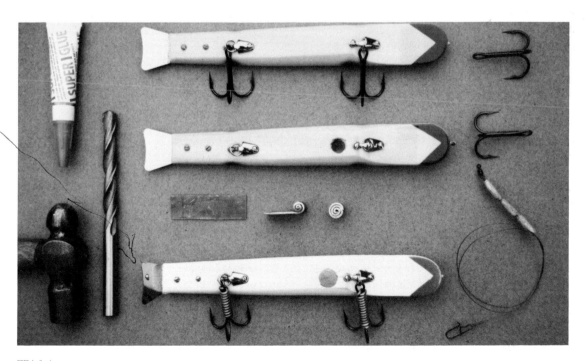

Weighting.

Sinking Jerkbait

Since the first edition was published, many cottage lure-making companies have popped up across the UK. Without doubt, Loz Harrop has to be one of the most successful – his range of jerkbaits is second to none. Check-out Loz's complete range of floating and sinking jerkbaits on www.TackleDirectory.com.

Reflections

When retrieving negative-buoyancy jerkbaits I have seen pike following behind: with each jerk of my jerkbait the pike would move forward . . . interested, but not hungry enough to strike. On occasion, I have a take the instant my jerkbait smashes down on the water's surface after casting. Sometimes, when jerking a buoyant jerkbait, I have seen a *big* vortex appear close by, caused by a *big* pike coming to investigate. So far, I have been unlucky with the really big ones, the biggest pike I've taken to date on the Suick being 17lb. At the time of writing, however, I've only been using the Suick for a matter of weeks!

Another memorable recollection to do with jerkbaits, has to be when Andy Lush opened his mega-sized lure box up at the first PAC-Rapala lure championships held at Ardingly Reservoir. Andy's box was stuff full of giant jerkbaits and propbaits, and anglers swarmed around like flies. If the interest shown on that occasion was anything to go by, big jerkbait fishing is destined to catch on in the UK. In that case, I would advise you to up your life insurance policy, or start wearing a hard hat!

VIBRATING PLUGS

Vibrating plugs are sub-surface lures with a very tight wiggle action, which produces high-frequency vibrations. Over the years, I've taken many fish under 10lb on them, but very few over: it would seem that the vibrations emitted by them appeal to the small predator rather than the large. If I were able to devote more time to using them, I dare say my catch rate would soon alter for the better. Unfortunately though, sinking vibrating plugs are not best suited to the shallow murky waters that I usually lure fish – the Norfolk Broads.

Sinking vibrating plugs between $^3/_8$oz and 2oz, are more at home in slightly clearer deeper waters, say 2.5m (8ft) plus. For slower retrieving work use vibrating plugs of up to /oz in weight. These lighter plugs are really at home in shallow waters up to 2.5m (8ft) deep. For casting such small, lightweight VPs, a light tackle set-up is a must (see 'Countdown Minnows' in Chapter 5).

Up until the 1990s all models of vibrating plug would sink after casting out – there were no models that floated at rest. Standard vibrating plugs sink because of the vast amount of weight and rattles inside their bodies. They usually have to be retrieved at a fair old rate of knots to keep them up in the water, otherwise they drop down and sometimes end up dragging along the bottom. That would not be a bad thing if it were not for the fact that they snag very easily on the bottom.

With the ever-increasing demand for new types of lure, the floating and suspending models evolved . . .

Standard Sinking Vibrating Plugs

These can weigh anything up to 2oz. The small lightweight models are perfect for perch, zander and chub.

I prefer to work a sinking vibrating plug like I would a countdown minnow plug: cast out, count it down, and then start to retrieve. On retrieve they will usually hold their depth quite well, provided your retrieve speed is fast enough. Obviously, with each different weight of plug used, a different countdown and retrieve speed is required to get them to work at the same depth.

Floating Model

These dive when cranked and some are now equipped with a diving blade. I would class this bladed type of plug as a hybrid rather than a straight vibrating plug (that is a vibrating/crankbait plug).

The new generation of floating vibrators do unfortunately sink! Basically, they were designed for tying directly to your line, not for use with a wire trace; I would not advise you, however, to fish them without a wire trace. To overcome the problem, you can make a special trace with one or two small pieces of balsawood threaded on to it (see Chapter 1). The balsawood neutralizes the weight of the trace. If you can get the balance between lure and the trace just right, you could be on to a real winner, since the floating vibrator can be fished in a variety of enticing ways once the weight of the trace has been sorted!

Crank it down and then stop the retrieve; the plug will start to rise slowly to the surface. After a few seconds, twitch, flick or jerk the rod tip, then start to retrieve once again; repeat this process over and over. It really is a good method for imitating small erratic prey fish; small pike definitely approve.

Suspending Model

The suspending vibrating plug suffers from the same problem as the floating model: the additional weight of the trace sinks the lure. Follow the same cure instructions.

A suspending plug, if weighted correctly, will either rise very, very slowly in the water when the retrieve is halted, or hover almost static in mid-water. If you find one that works as intended, guard it with your life – they're as rare as rocking horse droppings!

Jigging

If you are in the right situation, sinking vibrators can be very effective when jigged up and down in the water. The best places to jig are: the corners of a river where the water pressure cuts the bank away; from a boat over deep water; from a bridge provided you can get down to land the fish; from a floating pontoon; from a jetty. These are just a few ideas to point you in the right direction.

Spice them Up

Vibrating plugs can be spiced up by removing the rear treble and adding a Colorado blade; Americans call this type of bait a 'tailspin'. When cast out, the Colorado blade will slow the plug's sinking rate right down! As it sinks, the tail spins – hence 'tailspin'.

Another way that I like to fish vibrators, is to add a jig spinner frame to the trace attachment eye. When equipped with a Colorado or willow blade, this really does increase the strike rate.

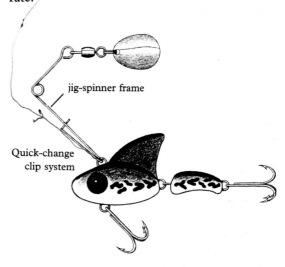

jig-spinner frame

Quick-change
clip system

A jig-spinner frame can be attached to many different types of lure.

Reflections

The one thing that always stands out in my mind about vibrating plugs is that when fishing them from my fibreglass boat, I can hear some models rattling from as far away as 6–9m (20–30ft). My fibreglass boat acts as a receiver and amplifier! The ultra-loud noise (high frequency vibrations) that some models emit doesn't deter the smallest of pike from attacking.

5

DIVING PLUGS

CRANKBAITS

Crankbaits are diving plugs. Ninety per cent of them float at rest; those that do not will be covered further on in the Chapter in the minnow plug section, under the heading 'Countdown Plugs'. The vast majority of today's crankbaits have a diving blade of some sort (except odd exceptions like the Bass Oreno, Predator and Equaliser), which enables the plug to dive beneath the water surface when 'cranked in' by the angler ('cranked in' being an American term for retrieving). As diving lipped plugs have to be cranked to get them to dive, American lure fishermen aptly named their fat-bodied floating diving plugs crankbaits. The word 'bait' is often used by American fishermen instead of 'lure'.

This is where it starts to get a bit complicated. American lure fishermen divide crankbaits into two distinct categories: fat-bodied crankbaits come under the simple listing 'crankbaits', and the thinner slim-bodied ones, under the heading 'minnow plugs'.

A crankbait's diving blade, body shape and size, the density of the wood used in body construction, and the amount of air in a plastic plug's body all contribute in some way to the plug's swimming action. That said, diving plugs come in hundreds of different shapes and colours; for the novice lure angler it can be a real nightmare choosing the right lures. I'll try to cover as many of the different types of crankbait that you're likely to come across. As for lure colour, *see* Chapter 12.

It pays to carry two or three duplicates of your favourite lures. It also pays to carry back-ups of lures that have proven themselves time and time again: losing a lure that has accounted for a good number of fish can only be described as absolutely soul-destroying. A back-up of that particular lure will allow you to carry on as you were before. A back-up lure will also help you to get over the heart-ache that usually occurs when your line cracks free from the wire trace!

If I snag a lure on the bottom of my local water when fishing from the bank, I attach a small cork float to the main line, then I cut the main line above the cork float, leaving it to float free on the water's surface, supporting the line ascending from my snagged lure. Later that evening, I'll return with my boat and free the lure using my lure retriever. Some anglers will go to even greater lengths to get a lure back: Gord Burton, who has never got round to learning to swim, has in the past donned a life jacket in order to get across to the far bank of his local river, to retrieve a plug that I'd made for him.

Diving Blade Construction

A crankbait or minnow plug's diving blade will be made either of a metal or plastic material. When cast out, most crankbaits float on the surface until retrieved. As they have to be cranked to make them dive, they're categorized as crankbaits. The shape, size and angle of a diving blade will determine a plug's diving depth. The action of a plug, though, has to be created by its designer! The narrower a diving blade is, the less action the plug will have, and vice versa. Usually, the longer a diving blade is, the deeper the plug will dive, and vice versa. The greater the angle a diving blade is set at –

Mark Wilson shows a 19lb 8oz pike taken on a Magna Strike Predator lure.

off the horizontal line of a plug's body – the shallower the plug will dive. The more horizontal a diving blade is in relation to the plug's body axis, the deeper it will dive.

To give you some idea of what various shapes and angles of diving blades do when retrieved, refer to the diving blade chart on page 40.

Body Construction and Strength

A plug's body construction, density and strength are important for a number of reasons, listed below.

1. If a plug's body is too dense, the plug will lack action. Action (wiggle and wobble) is created by the amount of air in the body material and the diving blade's width and its angle(s). The less dense a plug's body material is, the more that plug will want to float. A diving blade will have other ideas for the body and will try hard to get it to dive. What results is a battle between the buoyancy of the plug's body and the diving blade. The battle between the two forces will be evident in the plug's action: it will vibrate.

2. A plug's body has to be tough enough to stand up to punishment from needle-sharp teeth, and to withstand the odd bang against a bridge support, rock, boat and other solid objects.

3. If the body of a plastic or wooden plug starts to take in water, the action of that plug will suffer, and it will no longer work at its suggested diving depth. It therefore has to be carefully sealed.

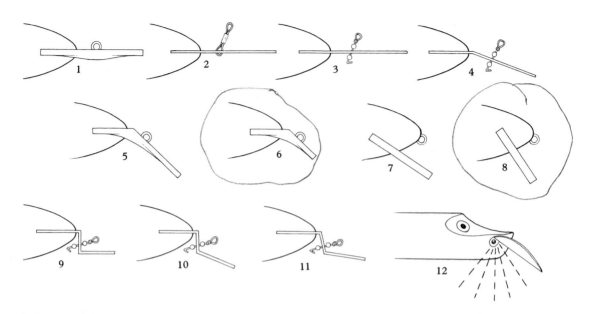

To give you some idea of diving depth . . . 1. Plastic diving blade; deep diver. 2. Metal diving blade; deep diver, with a flip-over lip. 3. Handmade metal diving blade; deep diver, with a flip-over lip. 4. Same as 3, but does not dive as deep. 5. Plastic diving blade; medium diver. 6. Plastic diving blade; shallow diver. 7. Plastic (or handmade metal) diving blade; medium diver. 8. Plastic (or handmade metal) diving blade; very shallow diver. 9. Handmade metal diving blade; shallow diver. 10. Handmade metal diving blade; medium diver. 11. Handmade metal diving blade; medium to deepish diver. 12. Variable depth diving blade.

I much prefer wooden plugs to plastic because they have a far better action. At the time of writing, Bagley's Monster Shad, is, in my opinion, one of the most realistic-looking of all crankbaits. It imitates a ¼oz roach perfectly. The flat sides of the Monster Shad emit plenty of flash, which makes it a far better target to the eye of a pike when the plug is side-on, rather than facing the fish.

Electronics

In years gone by, many kinds of electronic and wind-up gadgets have been installed into fat-bodied plugs. Inventors have tried out all sorts of ideas to eliminate the use of a diving blade. I have seen battery-powered plugs that have a small engine inside the body, which drives a prop shaft with a propeller mounted on the end. It was recommended that the plug be suspended beneath a boat, or large float. As the propeller turned, the plug swam forward.

When writing the first edition, I received from Andy Lush crankbaits and minnow plugs that had red, battery-operated, flashing lights inside their bodies. To switch on, you load their batteries, and remove them to switch off. Andy also sent me a crankbait that emits a musical tune, which automatically switches on when it lands in the water. When taken out of the water, it switches off. Switch-on is caused by water bridging the belly and rear treble hooks.

When bait fishing, I have legered electronic sound devices next to my dead baits. Does electronic sound frighten fish off? Does it hell! The thing that I've not been able to prove over the years is whether or not the loud noises (vibrations) emitted from my sound devices,

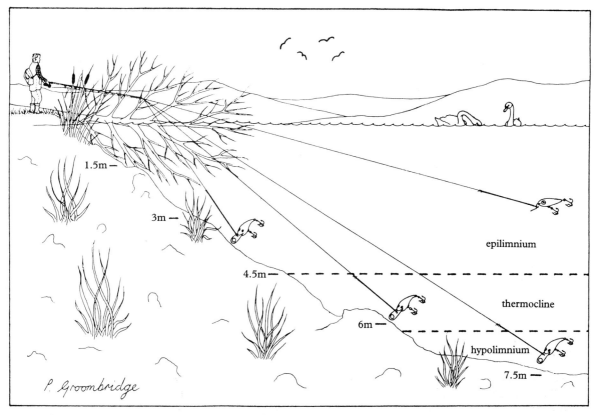

Explore all the depth layers using different types of lure.

have actually enticed pike to my bait. I believe they have. It is a fact that while underwater transmission tests were being carried out by the American Navy in World War II, sending messages to frogmen, it was observed that huge shoals of fish came in to investigate the source of the frequencies. Unfortunately, though, I haven't a clue as to the range of frequencies being transmitted.

Action

Every different named lure that works beneath the water surface, be it a crankbait, minnow plug, trolling plug, vibrating plug, spinner, spoon, or whatever, will have its own personal action. I feel that it is important to carry as many different types of lure as you can. If one type doesn't get a take, try another, and another, and another, until you get results.

Alter the size of your plug regularly. Work different depths. Don't be afraid to work deep divers hard along the bottom. In the past, while out lure fishing, I have advised anglers that I've met, to work one of the deep-diving crankbaits that I've seen in their lure boxes, hard along the bottom where pike lie resting. Usually they don't want to try this for fear of losing their plug; but if you want to catch pike, you have to be prepared to make sacrifices. Deep-diving crankbaits are designed to go deep and search out predators that are resting on, or just off bottom, or patrolling deep. To be successful with lures you have to work them to their full potential – don't be frightened of losing one or two. In my view, it's worth losing the odd lure to catch a twenty-pounder. I won the 1992/3 PAC Ryobi Pikemasters by working spoons tight along the bottom; I lost two spoons in the process, but look at what I won – two handbuilt rods by SRS England worth £280, a season ticket to a trout water worth £90 and two really nice trophies. Say no more!

Long-lipped, fairly buoyant crankbaits are far less prone to snagging than short-lipped ones. As the long lip of a deep diver hits the bottom, or a snag, the plug will tend to flip over, keeping its hooks clear of the obstacle.

Speed of Retrieve

I like to retrieve any type of lure slowly – worked just fast enough to get its action going. Sometimes, I throw in the odd fast crank, twitch, flick or jerk here and there, since breaking the pattern of a lure's action can sometimes work wonders. On occasion, when retrieving a plug that floats at rest, I stop for a few seconds and let it rise up in the water – the number of takes I've had on the rise is amazing.

Pike respond well to low-frequency vibrations. The faster a plug moves through the water, the faster it will vibrate and the faster a plug vibrates, the higher the frequency it emits. The speed at which a lure is retrieved determines the frequency emitted from that lure! The speed at which a lure is retrieved could therefore be the single most important factor in its success. A plug's action emits vibrations, as does hook movement, or rattling balls hitting against the side of a plug's body. Chapter 12, relating to sensory perception, covers vibration in much greater depth.

Hooks and Hook Hangers

Quality hooks and hook hangers are a must in my view. Cheap and cheerful plugs with 'Mickey Mouse' hook hangers are not worth bothering with. Although cheap, they don't last very long, while quality plugs do last. Provided, they don't snag up! If the trace attachment eye of a cheap and cheerful plug were to snap while you were playing a fish, the plug might later cause the pike's death. Buy reputable brand names if possible. If you are going to buy a plug that has the eye-type hook hanger, make sure they are good strong eyes.

Plugs like the 7.5cm (3in) Abu Hi-Lo, which have screwed-on hook hangers, are very reliable indeed. Plastic plugs with moulded-in hook hangers are very reliable nowadays. A few years back such plugs used to suffer from water leaking into the plastic plug body around the hook hangers, but better-quality plug moulds seem to have solved that problem.

I like plugs that have a one-piece wire system running from the trace attachment point to the rear hook hanger. Rapala and Nils Master plugs have the wire system running right through the plug body. If you want to check to see if a plug has such a system buy yourself a cheap battery-operated circuit tester.

As for hooks . . . In 1990 American lure companies started to use short-shank trebles on plugs, which I have found results in far fewer miss-hits. The longer a treble hook shank is, the less chance a hook has of ending up where it's wanted, that is inside the predator's mouth! On many occasions when using a plug equipped with long-shanked trebles, I have hooked a fish outside its mouth, which is possibly because the predator has not had its mouth open wide enough to be able to engulf the plug body and hooks. What usually happens is that the smaller-mouthed predator grabs the plug's body, and the angler feels the take and strikes – setting the long-shanked treble outside the mouth. Short-shanked trebles do seem to help in overcoming that problem; certainly, using them has upped my hooking statistics.

Another hook worth investigating is Heddon's Excalibur, described as a rotating treble hook. The three hooks that go into the making up of an Excalibur treble are off-set. As you strike into a fish, the treble hook's torque-accelerated twist action engages a second hook point into the fish. It is said that the Excalibur can increase your hooking statistics up to 30 per cent over conventional trebles.

Always keep your hook points needle-sharp. I always carry a hook sharpening stone and some spare hooks with me.

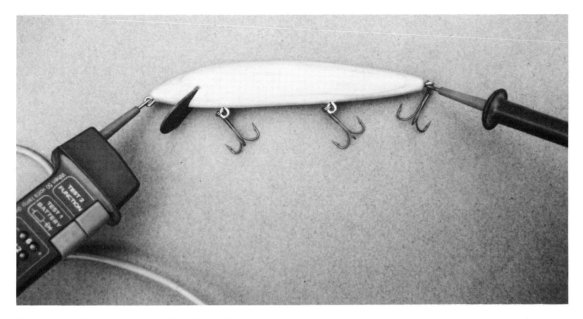

Testing to see if wire runs right through the plug body.

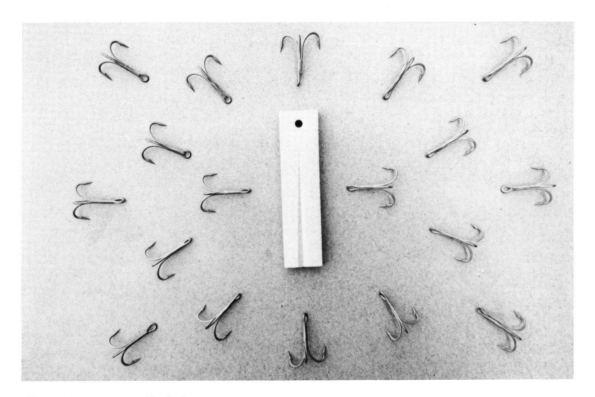

Always carry some type of hook sharpener.

Jointed Crankbaits

Jointed crankbaits and minnow plugs have a far better action than the unjointed variety. I would love to see some jointed plugs made so that the two halves knock together while being retrieved, giving off extra sound effects. Commercial jointed plugs are usually tapered off at their joint(s), eliminating any chance of the two halves knocking against each other (for example, the jointed Abu Hi-Lo).

Snagless/Weedless Crankbaits

Some crankbaits are designed to snag less! Such plugs have a long diving lip and a bar-like trace attachment point (such as the Heddon Hellbender). When the diving blade hits a snag, the plug is automatically flipped over, keeping its hooks clear of the obstacle. In fact, most long-lipped crankbaits and minnow plugs flip over in much the same way, though they are not as effective as plugs that are specially designed to do so.

Some plugs come with a weed- or snag-guard attached to the body, while others have weed-guards attached to the treble hooks. On both types, weed still gets caught on the diving blade, which is why I, personally, hate both types; there's no reason for you to hate them, however.

Searcher Crankbait

This is a special crankbait that I designed for getting down to the bottom quickly – much

Crankbaits. (1) Searcher Crankbait; (2) Magna Strike Equaliser; (3) Bass Oreno; (4) Magna Strike Gladiator (previously named Grandma); (5) Abu Hi-Lo; (6) Magna Strike Predator; (7) Monster Shad.

quicker than any other type of diving plug. To get the plug to dive quickly, it is heavily weighted at the front end with sound chambers that act as ballast. At rest, the plug usually floats with its head just below the surface, although, depending on the density of the wood I'm using, some may sit vertically. Because of varying wood density, you never really know beforehand just how a finished wooden plug will sit, or act, in the water.

The instant my weighted searcher crankbait starts to move forward, it's down there looking for big girls! This plug is very effective for trolling and normal casting work.

Tuning Plugs

If a plug tends to work to the left or right on retrieve, all you have to do to get it to run true, is adjust the trace attachment eye at the front of the plug. If your plug retrieves to the right, bend the trace eye of the plug to the left and vice versa.

In some lure fishing situations, it can be very rewarding having a plug that does work to the left or right, because you can then get it to go under moored boats, floating weed, or work an area of water that you are unable to cast to. Detune accordingly!

Reflections

It was about two o'clock in the afternoon when I dropped anchor. I was roughly in the same position where I had taken 150lb plus of pike (in two hours) the previous day. It would have been well over 200lb if the numerous big pike that I had seen following my searcher crankbait, had struck.

A couple of anglers were trolling close by and we exchanged conversation. 'Hi Charlie, how's it going?' 'All right mate,' I replied, 'I've had a few. I had a really good day yesterday.' 'What on?' 'Using my trace emitters over small trout mostly. I also had a few on this searcher crankbait that I'm using. It's a new type of plug

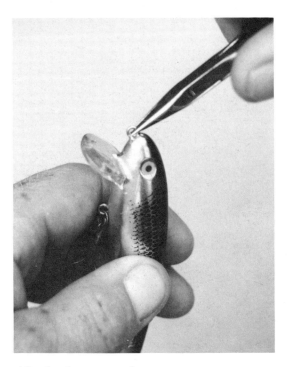

Adjusting the trace attachment eye.

This 22lb 8oz pike took the plug just as the author praised it.

MINNOW PLUGS

Minnow plugs are slim-bodied crankbaits. About 95 per cent of today's minnow plugs float when not being retrieved; the remaining 5 per cent mainly consist of the sinking, count-down type. There are minnow plugs that (should) lie suspended in mid water if the retrieve is halted; others dive shallow, medium, deep, and very deep. They may be jointed or unjointed, short or long, with rattles or with-out. Unlike the fat-bodied crankbaits, there are almost as many wooden-bodied minnow plugs available as there are plastic. Again, the wooden variety, in my view, have a better action.

Action

Most fat-bodied crankbaits tend to have a good back-end wiggle, with a small amount of side-to-side body wobble. The slim-line unjointed minnow plug has the reverse: a good side-to-side wobble, with just a touch of wiggle at the rear end. Jointed minnow plugs, especially large models, tend to have both a good side-to-side wobble and rear-end wiggle.

Size for size, and retrieved at the same speed, the slim-line minnow plug will have a much faster vibration action than that of the fat-bodied crankbait. In murky water conditions, or at night, I much prefer to use fat-bodied crankbaits because of their lower-frequency vibrations. In clear water conditions during daylight hours, minnow plugs, in my opinion, have the edge over fat-bodied crankbaits, especially when used in shallow water. Minnow plugs look far more appealing to the eye. Small pike definitely seem to prefer the action of the minnow plug to that of a fat-bodied crankbait. This could possibly be because the small fry they hunt emit higher frequency vibrations than larger prey fish do.

I have found over the years of using small and large lures, that my small lures get plenty of takes from predators under 10lb in weight (with the odd, exceptional big fish), and my bigger lures regularly catch more sizeable fish,

that I've been testing out. I had a few big fish follow it yes . . . yes!' It was text-book stuff. I had been casting and retrieving as we talked. As I was about to say 'yesterday', I was cut short – my rod had bent into a good fish . . . Within a couple of minutes I had landed a nice pike of 22lb 8oz.

That has to be one of my most cherished memories using a searcher crankbait, simply because it was taken as I praised it.

For those interested, my searcher crankbait had a gold glitter finish. Nowadays, I only ever use gold or silver, or mixed gold and silver glitters on my own handmade plugs. I never bother with fancy paint jobs.

night or dk water use fat bodied crankbaits otherwise use minnow plugs

The author prepares to hand-land a pike that took a minnow plug.

but very few small ones. I feel sure that a predator knows by the vibrations it receives, whether or not it can handle that 'presumed' meal. Vibrations from big lures are probably classed as 'danger' by smaller predators. I have found, however, that it is possible to 'make' small pike attack big plugs – by adding a swivel and a no. 4 Colorado, or no. 4 Willow blade to the rear hook hanger; when fishing in clear water, I have witnessed small pike grabbing the blade. An identical plug, without a blade mounted on the rear hook hanger, would not get a touch. Whether it's the flash that attracts the smaller pike, or the higher frequency vibrations emitted from the spinning blade, or both factors combined, I just don't know. What I do know is that it works – try it for yourself and see.

A small prey fish, due to its body size and erratic actions, will emit higher frequencies than those of larger prey fish. With that in mind, it's easy to understand how the size of a meal can be judged by the vibrations emitted by it.

Exceptions

There are one or two very fat-bodied crankbaits that do seem to break all the rules with regard to fish size! For example, the Magna Strike 15cm (6in) Predator, and the 18cm (7in) Equalizer take small and large pike in numbers. It could possibly be to do with their unique wobbling action, which is very similar to that of a minnow plug!

A water that holds a big head of small predators and not too many large, will also totally go against what I have said about lure size. When a lot of small predators are hunting in the same area, no meal is overlooked.

As always, the speed at which you retrieve can make all the difference to your strike rate

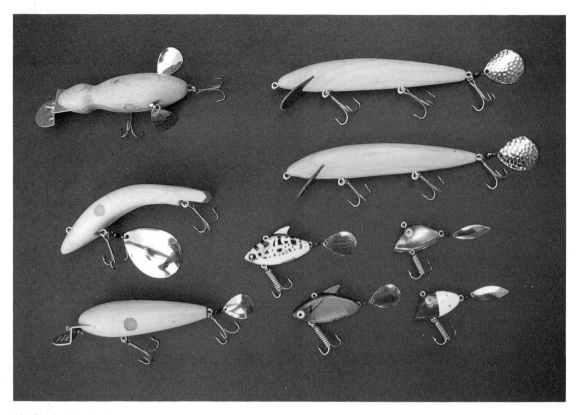

A selection of spiced-up plugs.

– think *slow.* If that doesn't get results, alternate your retrieve speeds between slow, medium and fast.

Shallow and Deep Divers

A selection of shallow and deep-diving minnow plugs is a must for the serious lure fisherman.

Long and short-bodied shallow divers that fall into the 30cm–1.5m (1–5ft) diving range, work very well during the summer months in clear waters of about 2m (7ft) in depth. My friend Mark Wilson has had tremendous success on the unjointed, flat-sided, 15cm (6in) Magna Strike Gladiator minnow plug. In the summer of 1992, Mark caught around 200 pike on one (now retired) Gladiator. The flat sides of the Gladiator minnow produce more flash (because of the chrome finish) than any other

minnow plug that I've used before. Because of its flat sides, I would think that it also emits a totally different vibration wave to other minnow plugs. Whether it's the flash, or the different vibration pattern, or both combined, I'm sure that the Gladiator will become one of the truly great names of the 90s.

The nice thing about shallow-diving minnow plugs is that they are usually true to their suggested diving depth. If, for some reason, the retrieve is speeded up (because of an approaching boat, for example), it is rare to have a minnow plug dive below its suggested diving depth and snag on the bottom.

When using deep-diving minnow plugs, I prefer to work them up and along drop-offs, rather than at depth in deep open water (where I much prefer to use deep-diving fat-bodied crankbaits, spoons or spinnerbaits).

Just because I may have a preference for fishing a lure one or two specific ways, doesn't mean you have to follow suit. Some anglers, for example, like my friend Jan Arends of Holland, have done very well when retrieving shallow-diving minnows (like the Gladiator) over very deep water.

Countdown

Countdown minnows sink when cast out. The speed at which they sink depends on the line, trace wire, swivels and snap-links used. If you use a light set-up – for example, a 10lb main line, a 45cm (18in) Drennan 15lb breaking strain wire trace, a Rosco size 12 swivel and a Cotton Cordell G2 snap-link – a countdown minnow will usually sink about 30cm (1ft) per second. I would advise you to count slightly slower than a clock: one *and* two *and* three *and* four, and so on. Believe it or not, the heavier your set-up, the longer it may take a countdown plug to reach your required depth, because thicker line acts as a drag.

Suspending

Suspending minnow plugs are rather disappointing! When I first heard about minnows that suspend in mid water, I had to have one. I bought one from my local tackle shop and went straight over to the pit to play with it. I attached it to the trace via the snap-link, cast it out a short distance, and was most upset as I watched it sink to the bottom . . .

I later found out (this was during my early days of lure fishing!) that suspending minnows were designed to be used without a trace and snap-link: you are supposed to tie your line directly to the plug. This may be acceptable in some countries, but in the UK a wire trace is called for at all times when fishing for pike, perch and chub. For bass, sea trout and salmon, a trace is not required, provided you are fishing for them in salt water. Sea trout and salmon do travel up some freshwater rivers where you will find pike.

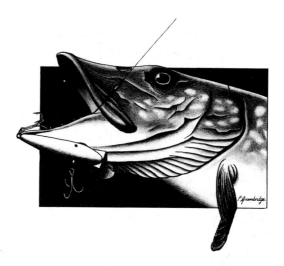

The minimum trace length that I would use is 45cm (18in).

To overcome the problem of suspending minnows sinking, you can mess about with the trace! For instance, you can counteract the weight of the wire, swivel and snap-link, by using small pieces of balsawood (*see* Chapter 1). I, personally, prefer to make my own suspending plugs that can be used with one of my own standard wire traces.

Jerk Minnows

I really do like the jerk-type minnows, although some far more than others. My favourite, at the time of writing, is the Bill Lewis Slap Stick. At rest it sits with its nose out of the water, with its body almost vertical. When jerked, it makes a nice 'topping fry' noise. If retrieved at a constant speed, it will dive to about 90cm (3ft); I prefer to retrieve the Slap Stick slowly, making it dive to about 30–60cm (1–2ft). Small pike can't resist the plug's fast action and amazingly loud rattle.

Specific Lures

You are probably wondering by now, why I

haven't mentioned more lures by name. This I have done for a very good reason: at the time of writing, many of my favourite lures are sadly about to be discontinued. In my view, there would be nothing more annoying for you to be told all about this and that fantastic lure, only to find out that it is no longer available.

I feel that by discussing body shape, diving blade angles, and how to work various types of lure, and showing pictures and diagrams, you will have a good idea, after reading or looking through the book, what type of lures do what, and when and where to use them.

As regards diving blade construction, body construction and shape, speed of retrieve, hooks and hook hangers and tuning plugs, everything I said for crankbaits applies equally to minnow plugs.

Reflections

It was one day in July 1993, when I was fishing a 8cm (3in) Fred Arbogast Jitterbug at a local water . . . The flat, calm water's surface had bubble lines in all directions from where I stood! My crawler had failed to stir a single thing, so I changed to a Bomber Long 'A' 15J, a silver-flash, blue-back, jointed minnow. I cast it to my left, and it landed some distance away with a quiet plop. I started to retrieve it nice and slowly . . . I could see it flashing away beneath the water's surface, but as I watched, it vanished! My rod bent double – I was in to a good one. The pike weighed 19lb 8oz and was almost as long as my Mega Ulti-Mat. I'd caught the pike only a few days previously on my favourite 8cm Jitterbug – the very same Jitterbug that had not stirred a single thing on this occasion! Don't fall into the 'favourite lure trap' – *diversify.*

A large unhooking mat is a must.

6

SPOONS

Spoons are pieces of shaped sheet metal. There are many different types of spoon available to the lure angler, for using in various situations. All spoons can be cast and retrieved from the bank, boat, or trolled. Some types can be far more productive than others though, when fished in specific locations/situations. Weight, colour, flash, action, weed-guards and so on, can be the 'make or break' for success.

ANTI-KINK VANES

It pays to use a good quality swivel at either end of a wire trace when using a spoon/spinner, or anything else that rotates. Some spoons tend to rotate non-stop when they are being retrieved or trolled, which in turn can cause havoc with your line. Even using good-quality swivels doesn't always solve the line twist problem. Standard shop-bought plastic anti-kink vanes do not entirely overcome the problem, as they, too, have a tendency to rotate when the swivels are under pressure during a fast retrieve or troll. Lead anti-kink vanes are OK, but too heavy for my liking; they can overtake the lure when casting, causing even more

havoc. To get over the problem of line twist, I designed a '100 per cent foolproof' plastic anti-kink vane that will not turn one single revolution when under pressure.

What I finally did was cut a 2cm (¾in) length of 2cm (¾in) diameter balsawood dowel, and shape it into a ball using sandpaper. I then cut the ball in half and glued one half on each side of my handmade plastic anti-kink vane. The balsawood, being buoyant, will not allow the anti-kink vane to revolve at all. All the spoon's rotation is taken up by the two trace swivels and the ball-bearing swivel which is fitted to the rear end of the anti-kink vane; of late I fit a standard swivel to the front end. If line twist occurs while casting, the line will untwist via the standard swivel.

My handmade anti-kink vane is made from plastic. Using a set of (sharp) double-pointed calipers, set to 3cm (1¼in), scribe a circle on to a piece of plastic. Keep scribing until you have cut right through it. When complete, sand

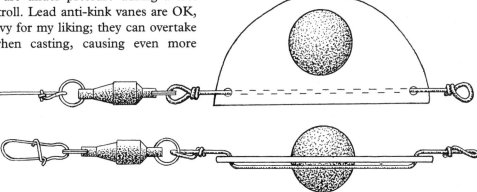

The author's foolproof anti-kink vane. (Standard swivel not shown.)

the circle's edge with a piece of fine sandpaper. You should then be left with a 6cm (2½in) plastic circle. Cut this in half and you will have the makings of two anti-kink vanes. The vane's wire system is totally straightforward.

TYPES OF SPOON

Standard Spoons

Standard and trolling spoons can both be cast from the bank or a boat, or trolled: the main difference between them is that standard spoons are thicker and heavier, size for size, than trolling spoons.

Standard (heavy) spoons are more effective for searching out predators that live in deep water. To make heavy spoons work high in the water, you have to retrieve them much too fast, which is why I invented the top-water spoons (*see* page 55).

When spoon fishing in deep waters, it pays to use a heavyish spoon of about 15cm (6in) or longer, although spoons longer than that tend to be too heavy for my liking, or, if lighter-weight, their casting distance will be reduced because of body size. Casting distance is very important for searching out predators that hold deep, or tight to the bottom. You need the weight, aerodynamics, and hydrodynamics of a spoon to be just right for distance casting and retrieving at depth.

To get good results working standard spoons tight along the bottom, cast the spoon out, and when it lands, leave your bail arm open until line has ceased to leave the spool of your reel. When you're sure the spoon has hit bottom, close the bail arm and slowly retrieve the spoon back. This can be risky, but to catch fish that hold up tight on, or close to, the bottom, you have to be prepared to lose one or two lures. You can fit a snagless (*see below*, page 54) wire hook-guard on to your spoons if you're really worried about losing them. Don't let the cost of a lure put you off fishing snaggy areas of a water, since these are the most productive

places to fish a spoon, so long as it is the right spoon (a snagless one). Submerged tree stumps and branches are prolific holding places for predators like perch and pike.

Trolling Spoons

Trolling spoons are lighter (size for size) than standard spoons. When trolling using a weight of some kind (a 2oz lead on line, or a downrigger weight of 1–12lb), you want a spoon that flutters horizontally behind that weight, *not* below it with very little action! Heavy spoons have less action when retrieved fast, or trolled.

On most of the waters that I troll, water clarity leaves something to be desired! When you're working a spoon at depth in coloured water conditions, you want to use a spoon that vibrates and rotates as much as possible, hence the importance of a reliable anti-kink vane. Movement and rotation provide not only vibration but maximum flash as well.

Lightweight spoons are very effective when trolled just beneath the water's surface, but clear water is a must for this method.

Spoons that emit good vibrations and flash can totally outfish heavier ones at depth! I have had far better results using a lightweight spoon with a ½–2oz weight attached to the main line, than I have using a spoon weighing the same as the weight and light spoon combined!

At depth, lure action, vibration and flash are a winning formula for strikes. Steve Gould, the well-known hairstyle trend-setter, caught four 20lb pike (casting from a boat) in one day from Llandegfedd, Wales. He was using a silver/copper '00' Kuusamo Professor spoon. He also caught a 29lb pike on that same day using a spinnerbait, which is shown on page 75. I rate the lightweight Kuusamo as the best commercial spoon for trolling and retrieving above weed-beds.

My own handmade, lightweight, stainless steel spoons cast better than the average commercial trolling spoon. Up to 1993, the biggest fish taken on one of my lightweight silver

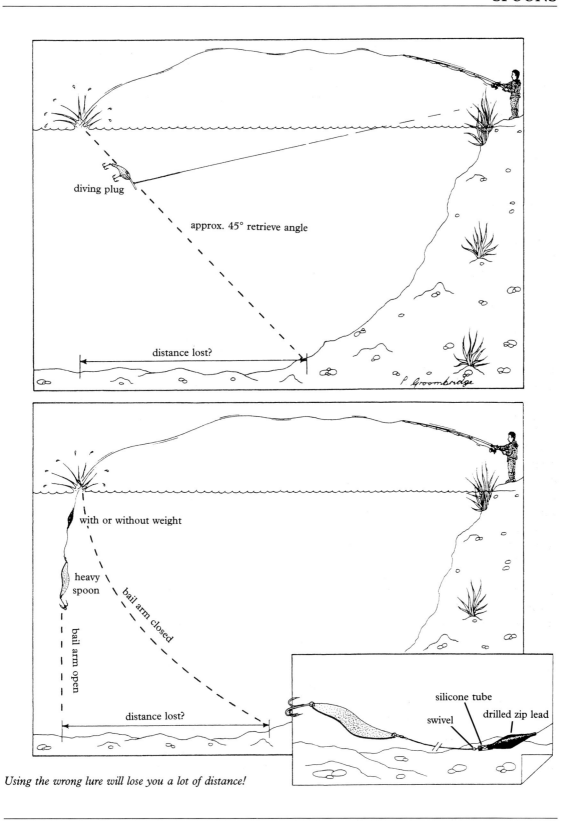

diving plug

approx. 45° retrieve angle

distance lost?

P Groombridge

with or without weight

heavy spoon

bail arm closed

bail arm open

distance lost?

silicone tube

swivel

drilled zip lead

Using the wrong lure will lose you a lot of distance!

Derek MacDonald with a 31lb pike, taken on one of the author's handmade mirror-finish spoons.

spoons, is a 31lb pike. Derek MacDonald, the 1989 TG lure champion, was responsible for the capture.

Weedless Spoons

Weedless spoons usually have a fixed hook, with wire arm hook protectors riveted to the spoon's body. The wire guard on most weedless spoons is strong enough to cope with weed, but not with snags like old tree branches. I hate to think how many weedless spoons I've lost to snags over the years.

They *will* pick up a certain amount of weed, which being soft and stringy, can't help but find the hook points positioned beneath the wire weed-guards. Weed will also attach itself to any other nooks and crannies in your set-up, such as swivels and snap-links. They are best suited to being worked through weed alone. If you want to work a spoon through lily

pads or anything like that I suggest you change the wire guards for a thicker, stronger gauge.

If a weedless spoon helps you to catch just one fish, that's one more than you may have caught if you had not possessed a weedless spoon! I have lure fished waters during the summer period where you could only fish with weedless spoons owing to the dense weed growth. If I hadn't possessed them, I wouldn't have been able to lure fish those waters at all.

Snagless spoons

'Snagless' is a name of my own making! As I've said, I've lost a lot of weedless spoons to snags over the years, so eventually I decided it was time to do something about the weedless wire system. I drilled the rivet out of one of my existing weedless spoons and replaced the hook-guards with a thicker gauge of wire. I also altered the design of the guards so that predators could engulf the spoon with ease. On most weedless spoon models, the wire guards stick up far too high above the hook points, so that as a predator strikes, the wire hook-guards (on some commercial models) can get in the way. If weed-guards come into contact with a predator's mouth before the body of the spoon, the predator will push the spoon forward via the weed-guard and will not be able to grab the spoon body cleanly. Most lure anglers tend to refer to non-productive pulls on the rod tip as miss-hits. My hook-guard design has totally eliminated the miss-hit problem.

Wiggle Spoons

On retrieve, a wiggle spoon acts similarly to a plug – wiggling along beneath, or breaking, the water's surface. Where a plug needs a diving blade to get it to dive, a wiggle spoon uses a planing blade to stop it from dropping to the bottom like a stone. I call the wiggle-spoon blade an 'ascendant' blade. Instead of the spoon diving, the blade angle makes the spoon stay aloft when being retrieved; if you stop the retrieve, the wiggle spoon will plummet.

By altering your speed of retrieve, you can make the wiggle spoon work at various depths. A fastish retrieve will cause the wiggle spoon to break surface, whereas a slow speed will allow it to work deeper.

The only other spoons, that I know of, that act anything like my own Wiggle Spoon, are the Helins Swimmerspoon and the Cahokie spoon (both, unfortunately, are no longer made). The Cahokie spoon can be seen in Barrie Richards and Ken Whitehead's book *Spinning and Plug Fishing*, p. 3. One other early wiggle spoon was the Wicked Wiggler which was almost identical to the Cahokie spoon. The Wicked Wiggler was made from 1927 to about 1945. Wiggle spoons are not that hard to make. If you ever want to have a go at making one, I'll supply you with a paper template.

Top-Water Spoons

I invented the top-water spoon in 1992. Its main function is to work over the top of weed beds, or to be fished 'sink and draw'. It has been a very productive lure over the years – pike love its enticing silver flash!

A skirt added to the treble hook really does enhance the top-water spoon. As the spoon is sunk and drawn, the skirt opens and closes just like a jelly fish!

My top-water spoon is very easy to make – there is no complicated concave and convex shaping along its body. All you have to do is beat one side of your metal shape with a nylon-headed hammer: a Thorex plastic-headed hammer, with a head size of 2.5cm (1in), is the perfect tool for the job.

Wobbling Spoons

The wobbling spoon is another concept of my own invention! If you can get your hands on some really lightweight aluminium or stainless steel sheet, cut spoon bodies of about 12–15cm (5–6in) long by 5cm (2in) wide, and you will have the makings of a truly great ultra-light-weight wobbling spoon. These are not easy to cast, but they are worth the effort!

Being so lightweight, the spoon will automatically rise to the surface on retrieve. I like to make my wobbling spoons hit surface and then sink them by not retrieving, and then repeat the process (sink-and-draw style). Jerks, twitches and flicks all help to convince a predator that this is the real thing! I would say that a 15×5cm (6×2in), ultra-lightweight wobbling spoon is the best imitation, vibrantly and visually, of a 6oz–1lb prey fish.

Spinning Spoons

Some spoons are fitted with shaped fins that cause them to spin, like the good old Colorado bar spoon, which dates back to Victorian times. I've had some very good catches over the years of using Colorado spoons; the only problem with them is, again, line twist (*see* the 'Anti-Kink Vanes' section on page 51).

SKIRTS

Skirts help to enhance any type of lure, be it spinner, spoon or plug. I prefer to use multi-coloured living rubber skirts myself. A skirt acts as a good target for a predator to strike at; since I started using skirts on spoons, my hooking statistics have definitely increased.

In my view, multi-coloured skirts come into their own when fished at depth. If one colour of rubber skirt is not able to receive and reflect its colour wavelength of light (because the water clarity filters out specific wavelengths of light), then hopefully another of the skirt colours will, making that specific colour a good target to the eyes of onlooking predators.

SPOON SIZE

On some of my local waters, I have found that the size of spoon used can make a big difference to my catch rate.

Most of the local waters where I lure fish, are not packed with predators, and what few predators there are could be just about any-where in hundreds of acres of water. When lure fishing from the bank, it pays to have a good deal of knowledge about where the fish are. This can be achieved in a number of devious ways. For example, stopping off and talking to roach anglers about those nasty old roach-snatching pike seems to work wonders! If they are having trouble with pike snatching their roach away, it could be worth while to return later that day, to that exact spot, and with luck have some good sport – thanks to the match-man's groundbait and maggot feed!

It's not always that easy; many's the time I've spent three or four hours casting big spoons and plugs on those same local waters, without the slightest hint of a knock. When I finally get

Jack Goverde of Holland with a 30lb pike, taken on a spoon. Jack's finger was badly cut while unhooking.

my head together and put on a small spoon, or spinner, I may have four or five fish in a matter of minutes.

On other waters, where large concentrated shoals of predators will strike at just about anything that moves, the size of lure doesn't seem to make that much of a difference to my catch rate. On such occasions, I have even hooked perch on big lures.

On waters where it is hard to catch a fish, lure size can make a significant difference. On such hard waters, small lures will be taken by both small and big pike, but big lures tend to be given a wide berth by the smaller predator. It is not uncommon, in Norfolk, to have a small pike (5–7lb in weight) 'hit' while playing it. The biggest victim that I've heard of locally, weighed 17lb. I feel certain that small pike and perch think before they pounce; big lures may spell danger to the smallish predator, while representing a large meal to a giant-sized pike. Remember though – not all waters follow the same pattern.

Reflections

I have many memorable accounts of spoon fishing. My most cherished memory of using spoons has to be my winning of the PAC-Ryobi Pikemaster Championships of 1992/3.

The event that clinched the title for me was held at Ardingly Reservoir. I had won the pike trophy on the last occasion a lure competition had been held there, back in 1986.

On the day of the event, I decided to fish from the same bank that I had fished from in 1986 (the east bank). The water was very deep out in front of me, about 9m (30ft), so I decided to use my own handmade heavy spoons (equipped with mega-sized, multi-coloured skirts) to search out pike that lay resting on, or patrolling near, the bottom. The vast majority of the pike I've caught from trout reservoirs have been hooked very close to the

bottom, or just as my lure leaves it on its ascent to the surface.

I used a handmade, heavy stainless steel spoon to get casting distance. After casting, I waited for the spoon to hit bottom before retrieving it. Every now and again on the retrieve, I would stop and let the spoon return to the bottom and then retrieve again, to ensure that the spoon was where I wanted it – close to, or dragging the bottom.

It was not too long after the competition had started (9 a.m.) that I was into my first fish, a pike of 13lb plus – a nice start. Not long after that fish, I had another of about 7lb, which, like the first, was a very welcome sight. I had over 20lb to the credit of my heavy spoon and the day was not over . . .

Things did slow up after catching those two fish but I stuck at it non-stop, hoping that the next cast would produce the clinching fish for me. Shortly after two o'clock I lost my heavy spoon to a snag – cries of anguish could be heard echoing round the valley! I had loaned the only other identical spoon I had with me to my friend John Probert. John had gone off in search of a productive swim (not that I would have made him give me the spoon back – er-hem!), so I had to come up with another winning method. Fortunately, I had one 2oz zip lead in my lure box, which I put on my line before retying the trace. From then on, I used a lightweight stainless steel spoon. I found that I could cast even further this way.

At about half-past two I landed a 12lb pike. That fish, as I was to find out later, only just clinched the match (and ultimately, the title) for me. My total weight at the end of the event was 34lb 3oz. The second place went to Nigel Botherway with 33lb 1oz and third place went to M. Jeffrey with 20lb 2oz. My 34lb 3oz was not bettered at either of the two events that followed (Kingsmead and Thorpe Park) so I became the overall winner of the three-event competition, taking the title using my own handmade spoons.

SPINNERS

by
John Worzencraft and David Smith

'We very much doubt that there is another more versatile, varied and exciting angling method than lure fishing with spinners; if there is, we have yet to experience and enjoy it.'

Spinners have been used for centuries, but spinning as a fishing art-form in its own right only really made quantum leaps in popularity and success with the availability of more suitable tackle, especially the fixed-spool reels that have reached such an excellent level of technological development.

All things to all anglers, spinners are special. Often regarded as cheap, quick and easy, they bring instant results for enthusiastic fishermen.

John Worzencraft with a spinner-caught pike. Note the small carry bag and large landing net.

More experienced anglers develop their spinning art to higher and broader levels, catching more and bigger predator fish. With spinners, really skilful lure anglers can reach degrees of excellence at least similar to, if not higher than, those of fly fishermen, and catch a much wider, more exciting range of coarse and game fish.

Pike, perch, chub, zander, trout, salmon, sea trout, and the occasional bream will take well-presented spinners; we have heard of tench, carp, barbel and even eels being caught with them! Spinner hybrids such as spinner-plugs are effective for larger predators and fly-spinners will extend a lure angler's potential range of species even further to include dace, bleak, rudd, roach and one of John Bailey's favourites, the grayling.

This may come as a surprise to those anglers who think that spinning is just a casual form of fishing, or a last resort which only produces small fish; nothing could be further from reality! A good friend of ours, a very successful (and extremely modest) dyed-in-the-wool bait fisherman for pike and zander, used to be extremely sceptical about lure fishing, especially spinning. Eventually we persuaded him to try an Ondex spinner and a small selection of other lures, and within a few weeks he was completely convinced about the benefits of this style of fishing, having caught many double-figure pike; the best was over 17lb, not bad for a beginner! At the time of writing he's looking forward to catching his first chub on a spinner. If you need more convincing, try it for yourself.

HOW SPINNERS WORK

Various types of blade turn at different angles to the spinner shaft. The angle of rotation, rate of retrieve and water flow control the blade's rotational speed. Emitted vibrations and flash attract pike and other predators. Silver, gold and copper are the basic metallic finishes used for spinner blades; they may be smooth and highly polished or have hammered, fluted, or painted surfaces.

The designed-in action of a spinner is a major factor in its fishing success and this can be further improved, or made worse, depending on the way it is retrieved. Pike are especially sensitive to vibrations made by prey fish and lures. They home in on a spinner using their highly developed lateral line acoustic sensory detection system until they are close enough to see it (*see* Chapter 12). Only then does a spin-

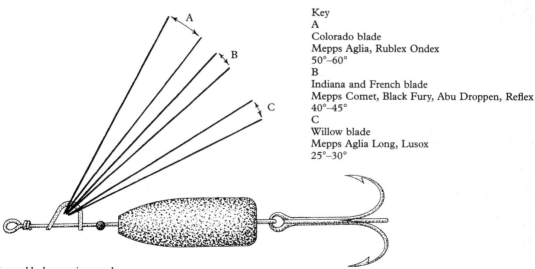

Key
A
Colorado blade
Mepps Aglia, Rublex Ondex
50°–60°
B
Indiana and French blade
Mepps Comet, Black Fury, Abu Droppen, Reflex
40°–45°
C
Willow blade
Mepps Aglia Long, Lusox
25°–30°

Spinner-blade rotation angles.

ner's flashing blade and colours become important visually. Its revolving blade mimics the flash of twisting and turning prey fish, usually triggering the predator's instinctive strike response.

Predators may also perceive certain coloured features of spinners as bull's-eye targets for attack; for example, any areas painted red, which imitate fins, bleeding sores or gill rakers, or contrasting yellow and black eye spots. In contrast to plugs, spinners create a blurred image of light patterns and colours. We have studied this extensively in our own sub-aqua and tank research, agreeing with the earlier experimental work by Barrie Rickards and Ken Whitehead.

Spinners can be made more effective by adding red wool, hair, real or red plastic worms, rubber skirts, teaser tails and even thin strips of mackerel or other fish to the treble hook. Rublex Ondex and all Abu spinners now have hackled hooks.

The underwater world of predators and prey fish is very different from that of the angler on the bank, a fact to be considered when designing and using spinners in deep water. Visible white light from the sun is made up of a spectrum of colours, which we can see when light is split up and refracted by rain water to form a rainbow. As well as refracting light into its component colours, water absorbs some of them more rapidly than others; red, orange and yellow wavelengths are absorbed by surface layers, and only green, blue, and grey colours penetrating the depths. Water also partially polarizes light which penetrates its surface. Of course, if the water contains suspended silt, algal blooms or pollutants, they scatter light and prevent it from penetrating very deeply; then, as they do at night, predators have to rely on their ability to detect prey fish by the vibrations they emit. Very deep, clear water is illuminated mainly by partially polarized green-blue light, and this has a major effect on the appearance of spinner flash and especially colours: reds become blue-black and whites turn to grey. The lower the light intensity, the

shallower the depth at which this effect occurs.

Contrary to some manufacturers' theories, we can see no advantage in putting blue paint on spinner bodies or blades for deep water – red, black and blue all appear grey-black at depth. Colour contrast, spinner silhouette, movement and light reflection are more important than actual colour. Another of John Bailey's favourite fish, the char, and some other species that spend most of their lives in deep water, have extra green-blue photo-sensitive pigments in their eyes which give them better deep-down vision.

The water surface also reflects and partially polarizes sunlight which is seen as glare by the angler; wearing polarizing glasses reduces this glare and gives a better view of what is below the surface.

CHOOSING THE RIGHT SPINNER

Although over the years there have been new ideas for spinner designs, traditional blade shapes such as the rounded Colorado, more oval French and slim Willow-leaf styles are still as popular and successful as ever; this is because these three styles cater for most spinner speeds and actions: slow, medium and fast respectively.

The size of your spinner may need to be in proportion to the area and depth of the water you are fishing. Big heavy spinners on small waters may spook fish; even on large waters, it's worth fishing the margins with lighter lures first.

The ability to cover all depths from the water's surface to the bed of your river or still water with spinners is the key to success in the search for predators. Spinners of different weights, blade types and sizes are needed to achieve this.

Use the table opposite as a basic guide to choosing the most suitable spinners for the depth and flow of water you plan to fish. It's a good idea to get two of each of the most

SELECTING SPINNERS FOR DIFFERENT TYPES OF WATER			
	DEPTH SHALLOW Up to 1.2m (4ft)	**DEPTH MEDIUM** Up to 2.4m (8ft)	**DEPTH DEEP** Over 2.4m deep (8ft)
LAKES PITS RESERVOIRS	Large, light Colorado or French	Medium-weight French or intermediate	Large, heavy Willow or intermediate
RIVERS SLOW FLOW	Light Colorado	Light or medium Colorado or French	Medium Colorado or French
RIVERS MEDIUM FLOW	Light Colorado or French	Light or Medium French	Medium French or intermediate
RIVERS FAST FLOW	Medium Willow, French or intermediate	Medium or heavy Willow, French or intermediate	Heavy Willow or intermediate

SPINNER WEIGHTS		
LIGHT	**MEDIUM**	**HEAVY**
Up to 8gm ($\frac{1}{4}$oz)	8–15gm ($\frac{1}{4}$–$\frac{1}{2}$oz)	Above 15gm ($\frac{1}{2}$oz)

SPINNER BLADE SIZE NUMBERS		
SMALL	**MEDIUM**	**LARGE**
00, 0 & 1	2, 3 & 4	5, 6 & 7

SHAPES AND SPIN ANGLES OF SPINNER BLADES		
SHAPE	**STYLES**	**SPIN ANGLES**
Narrow, fluted or feathered	Willow Mepps Aglia Long, Lusox	25°–30°
Medium	Indian, French Mepps Comet, Black Fury ABU Droppen & Reflex	40°–45°
Intermediate and Broad	Colorado Rublex Ondex Mepps Aglia	50°–60°

Selecting spinners for different types of water.

common spinners with Colorado, French and Willow blade shapes – they are easy and cheap to obtain. This means that you can use one as it is and modify the weight of the other as necessary (*see* Chapter 18). This will give you a good selection of spinners, a light and a medium-heavyweight version of each blade type.

make your own

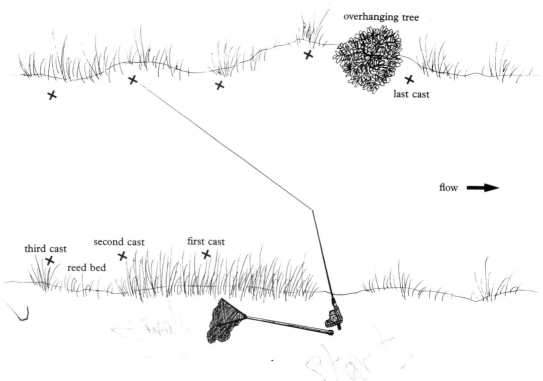

The casting method that David and John both like to use.

SUCCESSFUL SPINNING METHODS

Generally we recommend starting with a spinner which works at the slowest possible speed, which ensures that the lure spends the maximum amount of time in the predator's strike zone. Trout and sometimes perch are exceptions, preferring high-speed spinners! In warm water, spinners rapidly reeled in across the surface can sometimes induce other predators to strike. When the water is very clear, start with small spinners and gradually step up in size if they are unproductive.

Casting, Countdown and Control

Presentation, casting angle and distance play important roles when spinning in flowing water. We have often found that better results are achieved by approaching your intended fishing area from downstream if possible and casting up into it, keeping well out of the predators' field of vision, Chub, trout and, to a lesser extent, pike, seem to prefer spinners travelling downstream into, rather than away from, their strike zone, although this isn't a cast-iron rule. Barrie's findings are similar to ours while Charlie's are the opposite where pike are concerned!

Your first cast should be close to the near-bank margin, up stream and at a distance of about one-third of your maximum casting range. Follow this with a second cast to about two-thirds of your range, again into the margins, and finally a third at maximum range. By doing this you will maximize the number of unsuspecting predators you tempt with your lightweight spinners and minimize the number of those spooked.

Work your series of triple casts along the near bank and across to the other side, which is likely to be very productive if access to the far bank is difficult or if fishing is not permitted. Next, move upstream to the spot where your third cast landed and repeat your casting pattern. Of course, there will always be exceptions and occasions when upstream casting is difficult.

In fast-flowing water, the right choice of spinner will let you fish your lure correctly; it's possible to make a lightweight spinner stay almost stationary in the current without rising to the surface. To get down deeper you may have to allow the spinner to sink after casting while, with your bail arm open, you estimate how far it has sunk by counting down. Sometimes extra up-trace weight, or a paternoster rig is needed to get your spinner down to the depth you want it to work at.

LIGHTWEIGHT SPINNING TACKLE

Lure fishing tackle is described separately but no chapter on spinners would be complete without mentioning the benefits of lightweight spinning. With modern materials, this can be achieved without sacrificing strength or results. High or intermediate modulus carbon and glass fibre blanks enable ultra-light rods to be ultra-strong and sensitive too. Large silicon carbide-lined rings make casting light spinners simple, helped by modern reels and hi-tech lines with low diameter-to-breaking strain ratios.

Small reels are needed for lightweight spinning, and there's one very important point that we would like to emphasize about these, and indeed all reels, with variable drag control mechanisms. Small reels have small drag systems but they still have to cope with the heavy work-load of spinning for big predators.

Prolong the efficiency and life of your reel's drag mechanism by always slackening the drag right off after fishing. Sometimes oil and grease can find their way on to drag washers and disks,

greatly reducing their effectiveness. If that happens, it's best to clean, degrease or replace them, either by yourself, or through your local tackle dealer or the manufacturer's appointed service agent.

Lightweight spinning tackle with links, swivels and trace wire to match, can present small spinners almost perfectly; this is the essence of finesse fishing, amazingly productive for all predators and particularly useful when trout, chub or perch are your quarry. Like Mepps, Abu have UL (ultra-light) versions of most of their spinners, some weighing 2g ($\frac{1}{16}$oz) or less!

Skilled anglers with correctly balanced and sensitive tackle will be able to detect instantly even the slightest takes by predators and strike quickly, avoiding any risk of deep-hooking and greatly increasing their catch rate. We cannot summarize this form of fishing more perfectly than lure maestro Barrie Rickards' single sentence: 'Just a little rod, a reel and two small boxes of tiny lures can provide a staggering day's sport.'

Hooks

Some commercial spinners are badly let down by poor quality or over-sized hooks. We always check standard hooks and replace them if necessary; after all, they're the main connecting link with your fish! Chemically sharpened ones such as those supplied by Partridge, Drennan/Kamasan and Eagle Claw are the best replacements; they are a bit expensive but very worthwhile. Completely barbless hooks are not very effective for spinning – we tend to partially crush normal barbs or use hooks with small barbs.

WHICH SPECIES, WHICH SPINNER?

With superb vibration and visual sensory detection system, pike are fearless predators – we don't know of any spinner that they won't attack if it's presented correctly! When seeking

Jan Arends of Holland was in a spin after boating this beauty.

large pike and fishing from the bank, we still generally recommend that you always start with small, non-spooking spinners before stepping up to larger ones.

On the other hand, some predators such as perch, chub and trout rely more heavily on sight to locate their prey; with characteristic striped camouflage, perch often lurk in shaded haunts while keeping an eagle-eye on more brightly lit water nearby for unsuspecting prey. Spinner flash is all-important for attracting these predators and successful spinning for specimens of these species requires considerable skill. Small blades, particularly hi-spin types, are best when the water is very clear; if the spinner has hackled hooks then so much the better. Try adding a real or plastic imitation worm to the treble hook.

In coloured water, spinners with much larger blades are necessary because they emit more vibrations and flash. Don't be afraid to use size 5 or 6 Colorados, 4 or 5 French or 2 or 3 Willow-bladed spinners; even small predators will take surprisingly large lures.

Zander have ultra-low light vision and are the masters of coloured water and dark conditions. The light-detecting cells in their eyes contain a special pigment which reflects light, greatly increasing their detection sensitivity. This unusual feature, most noticeable in flash photographs of zander, is mainly responsible for the name given to their American cousins, 'wall-eyes'. Prey fish with inferior low-light vision are at a severe disadvantage when zander are on the prowl!

Contrary to some ill-informed opinion, the bigger zander are very clever predators, not easily fooled by lures or baits; we have had most success with lighter and suspending spinners with 'natural' actions. As far as blade colours are concerned, we have found that contrasting ones (for example black and yellow) are very effective.

Salmon, when they return to fresh water to spawn, are unable to digest food because their stomachs have shrunk (atrophied). Consequently they have to be induced to strike by triggering their instinctive response to stimuli using the movement, flash and colour of spinners. Daylight spinning for salmon is one of the most well-established forms of lure fishing. Rapidly changing levels of slightly coloured water are the best conditions; good spinners for salmon are Mepps Aglia Long, Kilty Buck, Devon Minnow and Flying 'C'. John's favourite is a home-made tandem spinner hybrid, a hi-spin blade mounted in front of a Devon Minnow, all on a single wire shaft; it catches pike too!

Sea trout are very difficult to catch in daylight and night fishing with spinners isn't easy, so every fish caught will be well-earned! Choose spinners with medium-sized blades and lightweight bodies; try adding reflecting or luminous materials, paint and hackles to the blade, body and hook.

SNAGGING

Pike are ambushing predators, camouflaged to conceal themselves from view as they lie motionless in weeds, roots and reeds, so those are obviously the best places to fish for them – as the saying goes, 'If you don't lose the occasional spinner, you're not fishing in the right places!' With treble hooks there's always the problem of snagging. This can be partially overcome by using weed-guards.

Spinnerbait hybrids, also known as buzzers, have a large introverted single hook to achieve the same thing (see Chapter 8). There's no doubt that your hooking rate will fall when using weed-guarded hooks, although this may be out-weighed by the extra fish you attract in areas that you would not be able to fish with normal spinners. The old-style Bushwhacker triple hybrid spinner-spoon-fly lure was also good for fishing through weed and lilies. The large blades on Shakespeare's Trilures also help reduce snagging.

If you make your own spinners, you can be much more adventurous about where and how you fish because replacing them is relatively cheap. In very deep water they can be fished in a spoon-like way by dragging them along the bottom; predators tend to strike downwards at the blade and are hooked neatly in the chin; Charlie has used this method very successfully for big perch. Spinners can also be fished using sink-and-draw and trolling methods; for added flash, some anglers combine a spinner with a wobbled deadbait.

Spinning at night can be eventful and is not for the faint-hearted or non-swimmers. A spare torch and extra batteries are essential. If sea trout are your quarry, then you've no choice! As far as spinners for this species are concerned, it's worth experimenting with luminous paint on one or two medium-sized spinners such as No. 4 or 5 Mepps Comet, Aglia or a Flying 'C' for deeper water. Suspending spinners with neutral buoyancy are helpful both during the day and night to avoid snagging. Coloured and luminous lines also help.

WEATHER

It's generally accepted that spinning is more effective in the warmer months. Light intensity and temperature influence the production of hormones and other biochemicals which control predators' metabolic rates; these factors often seem to conspire to make predators feed less frequently as the water temperature drops. When spawning approaches it can be a different matter: then the big females feed more often to gain weight in readiness.

Wet and windy weather can favour the lure angler whose presence on the bank will be much more difficult for the predators to detect. By the time the colder weather arrives, prey fish are more scarce but predators still have to feed, and can give tremendous sport on some freezing days. Pike tend to move to deeper, warmer water and in doing so may gather in substantial numbers. Naturally they stalk shoals of prey fish as they move around, although in some areas large pike very often supplement their diet by eating nutritious rodents, frogs and small water birds. These pike can become very sedentary and may not move far from their summer haunts.

Don't be put off spinning by cold weather – good catches can be your reward for braving the elements. Wear really warm clothes and use the mobility you have as a lightly-laden angler to cover the water in search of gatherings of predators. You only need to carry rod, reel and landing net, as everything else can be put in one of the excellent multi-purpose fishing waistcoats available from Ryobi Masterline, Shakespeare and Barbour. These jackets have plenty of pockets for your licence, spare traces, scissors, forceps, pliers, gloves, plasters, weigh sling, spring balance and camera. Hook bonnets will protect trebles, so you can put spinners safely in your pockets.

John has done a lot of cold-water spinning on East Anglian rivers and has had some super days. Once, when ice on the river only left a 3m (10ft) wide strip of fishable water in the middle, he took eight pike to 13lb in less than half an hour, hardly having to move a foot (though it had taken him two or three hours to find the 'hot spot'). Only when he came to land the first fish did he suddenly realize that the ice along the margins was 1.8m (6ft) wide and his landing net was 15cm (6in) too short. Wading will let you reach the parts that non-waders can't!

SPINNER TYPES

There are dozens of spinner manufacturers throughout the world; some, like Mepps, have decades of experience in spinner development and production. Another French company, Rublex, also has a long tradition of spinner making; their Ondex, Veltic and Voblex spinners have become classics. Spinners are prominent in Garcia's range of lures with all-time favourites such as the Droppen and Reflex versions as well as the weight-forward hi-spin Morrum design. Shakespeare too have a well-established range.

In the table on p.61 we have naturally recommended spinners that are easily obtained, well-

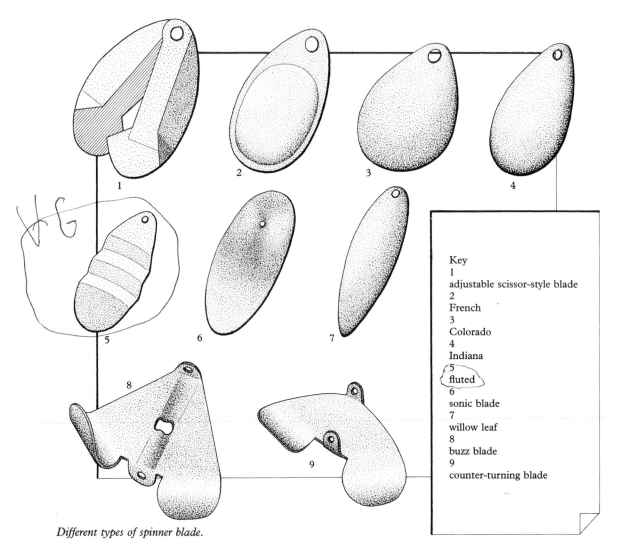

Key
1
adjustable scissor-style blade
2
French
3
Colorado
4
Indiana
5
fluted
6
sonic blade
7
willow leaf
8
buzz blade
9
counter-turning blade

Different types of spinner blade.

tried and tested over the years. For interest and completeness, we have described below most types of spinner design, even though some are now quite difficult to obtain or no longer available; for these, DIY may be the only answer.

Colorado Blade Types

We have emphasized that, unless fishing for trout and occasionally perch, slow, controlled spinning is the way to get the best results. When it comes to choice of spinners to help you do just that, the Rublex Ondex tops the list. We know of no other spinner design with similar weight-to-blade size ratio available in the UK; its treble hook has red wool hackles to improve effectiveness. With several near twenty-pound pike and many large chub up to 6lbs 9oz in weight from Dorset rivers to his credit, David regards the Ondex as one of the best spinners around, very effective for all predators.

Spinners with Colorado blades shouldn't be confused with traditional Colorado bar-spoon spinners which are very different; they and their companion kidney spoons are described on p. 69.

French Blade Types

These are probably the most widely used and versatile spinners. They are available in a wide range of blade sizes, and DIY versions are easy to make. Commercial French-bladed spinners include Mepps Comet, Comet Decoree and Black Fury which, with gold blade, black background and yellow spots, John rates very highly for zander and perch; he always adds a red teaser tail plastic worm to the treble hook. Many other tackle manufacturers produce their own equivalent designs; Shakespeare have their range of Pearl spinners.

Willow-Blade Types

One of the top three, in the spinner popularity stakes, Willow-bladed versions are generally used for deep and faster flowing waters. The

Mepps Aglia Long is a classic example, and is good for salmon and pike; even larger versions called Giant Killers are available by mail order from the USA.

Intermediate Blade-Shape Spinners

Several commercially available spinners have blade shapes which are intermediates between the main designs we have already described. Some of these intermediate types can be very effective; the Mepps Aglia is one of the best. There is also a heavier version of the largest blade size called the Musky Killer which has a well-hackled treble hook. Abu's Droppen is an all-time favourite and Shakespeare's Kilko spinners, designed for distance casting, are good for pike and salmon.

Indiana blades are really intermediate between the Colorado and French styles. A few manufacturers make versions of them, but they are more common in the USA than in Europe.

In-Line Blade Types

The majority of spinners have blades that are attached to the wire shaft by a U-shaped piece of metal called a clevis; this lets the blade revolve freely round the wire shaft. Some spinners have no clevis, however: instead the wire shaft passes directly through a hole in the blade.

Obviously the vibrations and flash emitted by these in-line blades differ from clevis-mounted types. Several commercial versions are available – we like the Ultra from Abu. Mepps have a version, the Elix Fluo, in their range although it's not available in the UK yet; its small blade revolves freely at slow rates of retrieve. John has made several experimental DIY in-line spinners including blade-forward Devon Minnow spinner-plug hybrids, and reckons they're worthwhile.

Hi-Spin Blade Types

Some predators prefer spinners with small blades that revolve at relatively high speeds, called hi-spin types. There are only a few commercial ones available – Rublex's Voblex, Abu's Morrum Spin and Flyer spinners are three good examples. If you have problems getting hold of hi-spin types, they're very easy to make yourself. While perch will often take surprisingly large spinners, they are also attracted to smaller hi-spin blades, as are trout.

Rubber-Skirted Spinners

Popular for salmon for many years, rubber-skirted spinners have spun off into coarse fishing with great success. They tend to be rather heavy, needing a rapid retrieve, and are therefore most suitable for fast, deep water. These so-called Flying 'C' spinner types, such as those from Kilty Lures, Mepps and other manufacturers, do get good results with pike. Slide-on rubber skirts are now also available for DIY enthusiasts – for their spinners of course!

Multi-Blade Types

Few commercial spinners other than spinner-bait hybrids have more than one blade. Multi-blade types do emit a wider range of vibrations and more flash, but we have not found that this has any statistically beneficial effect on the strike rate.

Multi-Faceted Blade Types

Mepps make a spinner, the Lusox, designed specifically for pike; its blade has three facets resulting in greater 'slip' through the water. As the blade is also quite light, it revolves close to the shaft with a fluttering, butterfly action. We believe it is a development of the old Mepps Ardour weight-forward spinner.

The Lusox also has an ultra-lightweight body; its wire shaft is covered with red plastic tubing and just a single brass deflector bead is used with the blade and clevis. The treble hook has red wool hackles. The main weight is mounted in front of the blade on a detachable shaft.

Abu's Morrum Spin, which we also highly recommend, is of similar design. Both brands are suitable for other predators as well as pike, the smaller 'mouche' fly versions of the Lusox being very effective for perch and trout. At the other end of the scale there is the Giant Lusox Fly weighing in at 45g (1½oz)! Not yet available in UK, it can be obtained from the USA by mail order.

Ribbed and Fluted 'Clam'-Blade Types

Abu's Reflex and Shakespeare's Marble spinners are very effective ribbed-blade types.

Fluted 'clam-blade' spinners are becoming increasingly popular; most enthusiasts make their own because there are only a few commercial examples. They get their name from the fluted blade, which looks like a clam shell. John made some for his experiments in 1992 and caught more fish, bream included, on this type of spinner than all his other lures put together; possibly this is due to the extra vibrations emitted by the flutes and the brilliant flash from the highly polished blade.

Perforated Blade Types

Extra vibrations can be created by using perforated spinner blades; again, Abu have an example in their range, called the Sonette.

Prop, Buzz and Counter-Turning Blade Types

Some spinners have propeller-type blades instead of, or as well as, a clevis-mounted blade. Flat-bladed propeller types are designed to buzz or counter-turn, usually in pairs. Commercial ones are rare so DIY is the best answer.

Weight-Forward Spinners

In theory, weight-forward spinners are easier to cast, are less likely to suffer line twist, and spin as they sink, inducing predators to strike on the drop. The three most common examples are the Mepps Lusox, Rublex Voblex and Abu's Morrum Spin. In practice, as the forward weight is mounted on a separate shaft, coupled to the main one, this type of spinner is more prone to tangling, especially in windy conditions. If you make your own, this problem is easily overcome by using a single wire shaft.

Adjustable Scissor-Blade Types

These variable blade-configuration spinners are good in theory but as they are fairly rare, with only one or two types being available in Europe and the USA, we have limited practical experience with them.

Mackerel Spinners

As its name implies, the classic mackerel spinner was originally designed for salt-water spinning. This small spinner has an in-line flat-bladed propeller which is very lightweight and produces little feel when retrieved; many spinning enthusiasts don't like this aspect but John thinks they are missing out! They are good for trout, perch and pike.

With a bit of DIY, extra weight and hook hackles can be added easily to give more feel. If that's not enough, some jumbo mackerel-bladed spinners are available from Kilty (Buck lures) and Shakespeare (Trilures) developed with the help of the thinking lure anglers' guru, Barrie Rickards, who, in our opinion, is one of the greatest positive influences on the sport.

Clattering Spinners

The blades of most spinners are designed to revolve freely, well clear of the body. Clattering spinners have been developed which either have blade-to-body contact or a body and beaded shaft like a miniature bell, which produces extra vibrations. Mepps have one in their very extensive range called the Comet Booster, though these are not readily available in the UK. Blue Fox Vibrax spinners, available through Normark, are an alternative.

Colorado and Kidney Bar-Spoon Spinners

These two classic original lures are derived from spoons and although sometimes still called bar spoons, they are in fact spinners. In the case of the Colorado, it has a central, weighted, wire shaft which passes through the spoon in two places; propeller-type vanes on the outer edge of the spoon make it spin. This is a big heavy spinner which has fallen from favour in recent years, though we're not sure why. Perhaps it's a bit too heavy, tending to spook the fish, or else the red-painted internal concave face of the blade has less flash. Nevertheless, it's still worth having one in your box; they're available from Leeda.

The kidney spoon is really a spinner with a kidney-shaped blade which revolves slowly and erratically. Reckoned by Barrie Rickards to be a much underrated lure, it's also a collectors' item.

Suspending, Neutral-Buoyancy Spinners

To our knowledge none is available commercially – John explains how to make them in Chapter 18. They're great for reducing snagging and catching predators that prefer spinners with slow-revolving blades, which don't sink like a stone if you pause while reeling in; they have good potential for zander.

Off-Set Trace Link and Keel-Weighted Types

These spinner types were designed to overcome the problems of line twist, although we'd rather use a ball-bearing swivel. In fact, we recommend the ball-bearing swivel for all traces used with spinners; anti-kink vanes and the like are really things of the past in our view.

Hollow-Bodied Spinners

This type of spinner allows the lure enthusiast

to add extra weight, if needed, to a custom-designed, sealable cavity in the spinner body. This cavity can also be used to hold absorbent material soaked in attractant oils. Hollow-bodied spinners are available from Malthouse Productions.

Customized, Tandem and Hybrid DIY Spinners

Spinners can be fished singly, joined together in tandem or combined with plugs, spoons, flies and baits to make hybrid lures. Spinner-plug and fly-spinner hybrids combine the pred-ator-attracting benefits of both types of lure and will often get results when other individual lures fail. Hybrid spinners can be devastatingly effective for all predators. John is particularly keen on the development of DIY hybrid spin-ners, having taken his first lure-caught twenty-pounder on one; he describes how to make these and other spinners to your own design in Chapter 18.

Spinning-Minnow Mimics

More like a plug in the way they closely resemble prey fish, these minnows don't have a revolving blade and so rarely spring to mind when discussing spinners; nevertheless they do spin and so should be classified as spinners.

Devon Minnows and their variants are the traditional lures for salmon and are very pro-ductive. Commercial ones are usually made of metal, wood, plastic, or quill; it's easy to make your own floating versions using shaped, tightly rolled glossy paper. John has had good sport using Devons for pike as well, and they are ideal as the basis for spinner-Minnow hybrids too.

In this chapter we have given a brief and com-prehensive insight into the full potential of spinners, how they are designed and when, where and why they work; DIY spinner- and hybrid-making is described in greater detail in a separate chapter. The rest of the road to

David Smith with a nice lure-caught chub.

success is up to you: try some of the ideas and suggestions, experiment and perfect some of the techniques, learn how to apply them in all conditions and venues in your hunt for coarse and game predator fish, and have fun!

There are other bonuses to be had too – John has been lucky enough to catch several bream including his personal best of nearly 7lb on a spinner intended for zander – such is the lure of spinners. Even carp and tench have been caught on lures. Of one thing we are certain – by following our advice and experimenting for yourself, you will see this form of lure fishing in a totally new light. Have a lot of fun and spin to greater success.

This bream took John's spinner while he was spinning for pike, perch and zander.

REFLECTIONS: ZANDER (AND BREAM!) ON SPINNERS

by

John Worzencraft

'Izzat a zander you got there, mate?' The question surprised me as I hadn't seen or heard the other angler approach. 'Yes' I replied. 'Wotchoo catch it on then, mate?' he continued. 'On this spinner,' I said, showing him my home-made fluted nickel Colorado-bladed spinner. 'You're kiddin' me ain'tchoo', he said in disbelief, 'I've gotta see this.'

I said that I couldn't guarantee to catch a zander on every cast but he insisted on watching. 'Mind the hooks please' I warned him as he stood in the way right behind me; 'Sorry mate, didn't think' came the reply.

Thinking that he would soon get bored and move on, I continued to cast and let my spinner sink deep, counting down the seconds as it went, before starting a slow retrieve. Five or six minutes later my spinner came to a sudden halt during the retrieve and for a micro-second or two I thought it had hit some weed; a gentle and firm strike, and the weed started to move – the fish was on! What an odd take, and what a strange feel it gave to my ultra-sensitive lure rod!

'This'll get my rubber-necking friend going' I thought, and sure enough the Harry Enfield look-alike was there in a flash. 'You don't wanna do it like that, mate' he advised. In fact, he was nearly right – the fish was fighting extremely hard and I wasn't able to control it in the way I had hoped. It wasn't a pike and there were no tugs on the line so it wasn't a perch either – 'Must be a nice zander', I guessed. 'That there fish is leadin' you a merry dance ain't it, mate?' Harry Enfield scoffed.

Soon the fish came into sight and seeing its deep body, I felt sure that it was a good fish, though it looked a bit odd. Suddenly, it topped and instantly gave up the fight, and as I drew it over the net, Harry Enfield and I both realized that far from being a zander, it was a nice bream, which was over 6lb when weighed. 'That's a rum do' said Harry; 'A bream onna spinna – I'd nevva b'lieved it if I 'adn't seen it wiv me own eyes!' I nodded in agreement as I took a quick photo – spinners really are winners aren't they!

— **8** —

SPINNERBAITS, BUZZERS AND JIGS

by
Steve Gamble

SPINNERBAITS

Of all the lures in this book, spinnerbaits are probably the oddest-looking. However, when you look at the thought behind the design it all begins to make sense. Predatory fish respond to flash, visual movement, vibration and colour, and these contraptions give them the lot. They were first dreamed up in the USA in the 1960s for catching black bass. Because they provide all the main stimuli except smell, they have proved to be effective for many other species, although certain design features need to be modified in some circumstances. It is their essential versatility that makes them so useful, although a specialized variation called a buzzer, or buzzbait, exists which is used solely as a surface lure.

Appearance and Construction

The V-shaped wire frame serves two purposes. Firstly it separates the blades from the 'creature' made from the weighted hook. It may be that the effect created is similar to a tight shoal of small prey fish. Smaller pike and perch frequently specifically attack the skirted hook perhaps believing that they are picking off the tail-ender of the shoal. Bigger pike just engulf the whole lot. The second function of the wire

frame is to provide the single hook with a fair degree of weed and snag protection. The longer the top arm, the higher the protection factor, but the less efficient the lure is at hooking fish. In general, a top arm which doesn't extend

Steve Gamble with a big Broadland twenty.

quite as far back as the hook point is the best compromise.

The weighted hook can be dressed with rubber strands, plastic, bucktail hair, feathers or tinsel. The effect of the billowing skirt is to suggest the movement of a live creature, rubber strands being the best at this. This appeals to a predator's instincts, even if the dressing looks like no normal living creature. The weight acts as a keel, helping the lure to ride upright through the water, and the upturned hook point means that the body can be bounced and bumped along the bottom with minimal risk of snagging.

The top arm is home to one or more metal spinning blades, A single-blade model has the blade attached to a loop at the end of the top arm, by a swivel and split ring. A snap-link instead of a split ring makes changing this blade even easier. Additional blades are mounted on the top arm with a clevis, just like a conventional spinner blade. Either both blades are the same size, or the swivel-mounted top blade is the larger. Charlie and I have experimented with versions with one clevis-mounted blade only, which dramatically increases the vibration over the standard single blade. The best-quality models have a ball-bearing swivel to get the maximum amount of spin and flutter from the slowest speed of movement. In practice, a good-quality rolling swivel, like the Drennan diamond-eye, is almost as effective.

Because most spinnerbaits available in the UK are made in America for bass fishing, there are one or two things to watch out for when buying them. The first is that most will have an open R-shaped bend at the point of the wire frame. This is because American anglers tie their line directly to the frame without a wire trace. If you clip a wire trace to this type of attachment, the snap-link will usually slide out along the wire arm and the cast will be wasted. You need a closed attachment loop to use a wire trace and snap-link effectively, and I personally prefer the rolled 'coil'-type of loop, as this has a smoother profile to push through weed more easily. If you already have some R-bend models,

Steve Gamble with a pike taken on one of his own handmade spinnerbaits.

you can cure the problem by lashing some fuse wire round the narrow waist to close the eye.

Some American models have overly coarse, heavy hooks with huge barbs – look instead for neat, sensibly-sized, quality hooks. Finally look out for any sharp angles in the wire frame, usually just in front of the body. I have seen one model with almost a right-angle bend in front of the lead head, as sold. This kind of bend weakens the wire considerably and a double-figure pike could always be the last straw, straightening and snapping it.

The shape of the blade dictates the lure's vibration pattern. The rounded Colorado style has a very wide swing with a characteristic throb, which can be felt right up the rod on a steady retrieve. The narrower Willow-leaf style has a tighter, more fluttering spin. The greater resistance of a Colorado blade means more lift in the water than a Willow-leaf blade on the same-sized lure. The more lift the lure has, the more slowly it can be worked at a given depth, particularly in still water. Increasing the size of the blade will increase the lift if the body weight remains the same. In flowing water, when retrieving against the flow, you may have problems keeping the lure deep because of the lift created by steady water pressure. The answer may be a Willow-leaf blade rather than a Colorado, a smaller blade of either type, or a heavier body.

If you have a range of body weights from about ¼oz up to 1oz, with both types of blade, you can ring the changes and come up with a spinnerbait to deal with most circumstances. This is where a snap-link attachment for the top blade is handy – you can always modify your lures this way. Bear in mind that a twin-blade spinnerbait will have much more lift than a single-blade version of the same size and weight. Another trick is to gently bend the wire frame into a wider or narrower V shape. A wider V gives more resistance and lift, while a narrower one gives less.

Size and Weight

So far, spinnerbaits have seen use mainly as pike lures in the UK. They are also very effective on other species, but it isn't always easy to find smaller sizes in tackle shops, not that it's easy to find larger sizes either! The most commonly available sizes in the UK are ⅜oz and ½oz because these are the most popular bass-fishing sizes in the USA. These sizes are good all-rounders, for casting up to about 25m (27yd) and fishing water up to about 3m (10ft) deep. However, to be versatile you need to be able to adjust the size and weight. Sometimes only a certain size or weight will do the job properly and catch you fish.

Smaller ⅛oz and ¼oz models are made, but are very hard to get over here. If you can get hold of them, they are great for perch and chub.

For longer range, deeper water and flowing water, you really need to get heavier lures: ¾oz and 1oz models are essential for all-round pike fishing, and anyone who gets regular access to the big reservoirs or the Scottish and Irish lochs (and loughs) should get some even heavier ones, up to 2oz. Another advantage of heavier spinnerbaits is that they can batter their way through the middle of weed-beds that would deflect lighter lures. Good fish lurk in the weedy jungles and sometimes a 1oz or heavier spinnerbait is needed to get to them. Also, big pike often want a big meal, and a big flashing spinnerbait just shouts out 'dinner!'

Action

If a spinnerbait is moving then it's working. As long as the blade is rotating and the skirt pulsing it is sending out the right signals. A steady, slow retrieve is a very effective way of attracting predators. Start by choosing a swim which allows a steady retrieve close to good cover; for example, along the outside edge of a big weed-bed, or along a reed line. Keep the lure deep and let it bump bottom every now and then; the Americans call this technique 'slow-rolling'. If you get no response hard to the bottom, try again at various depths right up to the surface, keeping the retrieve slow. A single Colorado-bladed model is good for bottom bumping, with its steady throbbing vibration. Remember, to repeat the slow, steady retrieve higher in the water, you may need a lighter spinnerbait, or a twin-bladed model – don't be afraid to play around with them.

If you have a boat, the ultimate steady retrieve technique has to be trolling. By choosing the right weight and blade combination for the depth of water, you can cruise slowly along productive bottom contours and around structural features. You can make a bit of variation in the lure's action by slightly altering the speed of the boat, causing the spinnerbaits to lift or drop slightly as they go.

You can vary the steady retrieve by giving it a nervous twitch. Basically, cast out and begin

Steve Gould with a Llandegfedd 29lb pike, taken on a spinnerbait.

the retrieve as normal, but instead of a smooth, steady pull, add little jerks and flicks, and even stop winding for a second now and again. When you get it right, the lure is still coming steadily back to you, but in a nervous, erratic, jerky way – flopping from one side to the other, sinking and fluttering a little.

Take this a stage further and try a sink-and-draw style. The top blade will helicopter round as the lure sinks. It generally pays to let the lure drop on a reasonably tight line, so you are always in touch with it in case a fish strikes on the drop. Also, slack line has a habit of tangling round the wire arms on the drop – and on the cast if you aren't careful. There are three main answers to tangling on the cast. One is to use a heavier bait, so you aren't forcing the cast to get the right distance. Another solution is to feather the spool to minimize slack line, just as

you need to do when letting these lures sink, especially in deeper water. The third trick is to push a sleeve of silicone tubing on to the trace wire. When you've snapped on the spinnerbait, push this sleeve over the snap swivel and hard up against, or even over, the attachment loop in the wire. It seems to hold the trace away from the top arm just enough to minimize tangles – both on the cast and when sinking.

Another variation is to retrieve the spinnerbait steadily until it reaches a likely holding place for a fish, then let it drop and flutter downwards for a few seconds before resuming the retrieve. The main thing is to experiment and make the most of the lure's qualities.

In clear water, some people like to add a 'stinger' hook to the big single hook, to improve the ratio of hooked fish to strikes. A treble or another single can be added to the bend of the fixed hook, either by wiring on with a bit of trace wire or, as the Americans do, by pushing a short length of tough surgical rubber tubing over the eyes of the trailer hook so it's stretched tight like a drum head. You just punch the point of the fixed hook through the trailer hook's eye, rubber and all, and slide it into place on the bend. The rubber prevents the stinger or trailer from working loose.

A final trick, hardly ever seen over here, is to add deadbait to the fixed hook. A sprat, sand-eel or small/medium freshwater deadbait (such as small eel tail of about 15cm/6in), is pierced through the head and shoulders. A stinger treble, on a short wire extension, can be fixed further down the deadbait to take care of fish that strike a bit short. You can leave the skirt on or remove it, according to taste. Plastic grubs, worms, fish imitations and so on are also effective added to a spinnerbait in this way.

So now you have no excuse; get yourself a basic selection and give them a try. These days I make all my own, in sizes from $\frac{1}{8}$oz to 2oz so wherever I am fishing, I have a spinnerbait that will hopefully 'do the business'. I also know they are made properly and have all the features I want.

BUZZERS

These lures are a specialized variant of the original spinnerbait. They have an upper arm bent backwards at an angle and fitted with a single propeller-style blade. This propellor gives lift, and the basic technique is to cast, start the retrieve immediately and draw the lure back across the water's surface as slowly as possible without the lure actually sinking. The propeller churns and froths the surface and attracts predators to the disturbance, rather like a small creature frantically thrashing as it swims.

The basic type has a blade made of aluminium with two opposed 'wings', rather like a large mackerel spinner. This type needs to be retrieved fairly fast to keep it on the surface, which can be a bit off-putting for all but smaller

pike. The bigger the propeller in relation to the body weight, the easier it is to keep the lure on the surface and the more slowly it can be worked. There are now models available with quite large plastic propellers with three, or even four, wings (known as Tri or Quad blades) and these can be worked slowly enough to attract the better fish. Body weights of around $\frac{1}{4}$oz to $\frac{3}{8}$oz are most effective.

Buzzers are much less versatile than the normal spinnerbaits, and to some extent fill the same role as propbait plugs. They were devised originally for black bass, which respond well to a fast moving lure. Where they are most useful is in weedy water, where the trebles on surface plugs keep getting caught up. With its big single hook and protecting wire frame, a buzzer can be worked without so many problems, especially round stalky and large-leaved weeds, such as lilies. It can also be allowed to sink slightly and then be pumped back on top in the clearer patches. Try casting across the weeds and skidding these lures back across the top of the thick stuff. When you reach a clearer patch, let the propeller do the work. Use a good strong line for this, at least 15lb breaking strain. Then, if you do get snagged up, a good hard wrench will usually free the hook. If the lure hasn't picked up any weed as a result, continue the retrieve. If it has, bring it back and start again.

A lot of good fish hide away deep within 'jungle' swims, and these lures give you one way of getting to them. The fish can sense something coming and when the lure reaches a clear pocket it often gets hit with no questions asked! An ambush specialist like a pike, staking out a small clearing in the weed, often doesn't have time to take a good hard look when a possible victim appears. It usually just reacts, and you can take advantage of this with a number of weedless or snagless lures. When you connect, that strong line will give you a good chance of getting the fish out!

A straight, steady retrieve along the edge of the weed- and reed-beds and around any structural features, like gravel banks or fallen trees, is always worth a try as an alternative to top-water plugs. Another trick is to vary the steady retrieve by occasionally 'ripping' the lure, that is, giving sudden, fierce jerks, making the lure literally buzz across the surface.

The vibrations from the propeller are still quite effective below the surface, so don't be afraid to use it like a conventional spinner from time to time. Sometimes it will produce the goods like this, probably just by being a bit different – just like all lures. If the buzzer isn't proving successful on the surface, let it sink for a few seconds, then perhaps work it back to the top, let it sink again, and so on.

As with standard spinnerbaits, use a fairly crisp, powerful rod action with a reasonably flexible tip, to help set the big single hook, and also to wrestle fish out of weed quickly.

JIGS

In one form or another, the jig is probably the oldest kind of lure known to man, some historic examples being thousands of years old. In its simplest form it is just a self-weighted hook, action and attraction being imparted by the angler and the various dressings and trailers he adds to it. Although the basic idea is simple, by playing around with size, weight and design features there are a whole range of quite sophisticated possibilities. In the UK these lures are almost unknown outside sea fishing, but in the USA they are one of the key lures for many species including perch, pike and wall-eye (zander). Believe me, if they didn't work they wouldn't still be around after all this time. There are four main modern types of jig lure.

Ice Jigs

This is a Scandinavian speciality, and versions are made by the well-known firms Rapala and Nilsmaster. These lures look like modified minnow plugs. The line is attached at the middle of the back and a single treble hook hangs directly from the belly. At the head and/

or tail ends are two downward-projecting fins and a fixed, single hook. These are sinking lures, designed for fishing in fierce northern winters. They are dropped through a hole in the ice, allowed to sink to the required depth and then gently jigged up and down about 15cm (6in). The fins make the lure swim round and round in a swooping, circular path as it is lifted and dropped.

Although in the UK winter ice isn't often safe enough to stroll around on, these are obviously viable lures for boat anglers and for anyone who wants to search around bridge pilings, jetties, pontoons, steeply dropping banks and close-in, clear pockets in weed-beds. They are also good for working undercuts in river banks caused by water pressure – often found where the river bends.

If you can get your rod tip over, or close to the target area, any vertically worked lure offers you an amazingly controlled way of presenting a target and thoroughly searching out small, confined swims. Anyone who has stalked chub and caught them by dropping a slug or lob-worm straight down to them from the rod tip, will immediately see the possibilities here.

Blades

The second type of jigging lure is known in the USA as a 'blade'. These consist of a flat, metal body plate, with a lead head moulded in low at the front (head) end. There are usually two treble or double hooks attached underneath, plug style, and a row of attachment holes drilled along the back for the trace. A blade lure is basically a metal version of a vibrating plug. By changing the attachment hole you can vary the vibration pattern you get on the retrieve.

The rear hole gives a looser, wider vibration, which gets tighter and fiercer as you move down the holes towards the front. The tighter vibration pattern from the front attachment hole allows them to work deeper for a given speed of retrieve.

Although you can jig them up and down vertically, they are normally used like vibrating plugs. Being metal they are more compact, and sink more quickly. They are normally cast and retrieved sink-and-draw style, or buzzed hard over sunken weed-beds. Some new models even have built in rattles for extra vibration, not that they need it!

Jigging Spoons

You may come across another type of lure called a jigging spoon. These are slim, heavy, metal lures, often in the shape of a tapered, flattened bar. They are basically a smaller, freshwater version of the heavy 'pirks' used by deep-water sea fishermen. They are very popular in the USA for vertical jigging around structure located in deep water. Deep structure is located by using a fishfinder echo sounder. They are nowhere near as versatile as the last of the four main jig types: the lead-head.

Lead-Head Jigs

The basic lead-head is just a bent single hook with a lead head moulded on to it below the eye, but there is a lot more to it than that.

The basic types of retrieve are the up/down vertical movements already discussed, or variations on cast and retrieve. The position of the hook eye is important for the effectiveness of the technique used. A jig for vertical jigging will have the eye centrally placed on top of the head, whereas jigs for swimming retrieves should have the eye placed towards the front of the head.

You may find various head shapes on the market, which are all suited to particular techniques. The commonest is the ball head. The eye is on top of the ball-shaped head but its compactness makes it a reasonable all-round pattern. Other head types are the bullet, the banana (a good snag-resistant casting jig) and the shad head, which is shaped like a fish head and designed to be used with a real, or soft plastic, fish on the hook. There are also versions with little wings moulded into them; these swim round in small circles, just like the

Scandinavian ice jigs, when jigged up and down.

Lead-heads can be either dressed with rubber skirts, bucktail, feathers and so on, or left plain. Dressed jigs can be worked as they come, but plain jigs need a little extra to make them attractive. Soft plastic grubs, worms or creatures can be threaded on to the hook to add colour and movement. Alternatively, you can add real worms, or deadbaits like sprats, sand-eels and eel tails, to provide smell and taste as well. Of course, you can also add these extras to dressed jigs for maximum effect.

To use with natural deadbaits, just push the jig hook through the head end of the bait, so that the point projects. Predators, particularly pike, will often attack the head end, apparently to 'kill' the lure and have it in position for swallowing head first. This way they come into contact with the hook immediately. If you find this isn't working, and you are aware of hits from fish you can't hook, try attaching a stinger treble hook, on a short length of trace wire, to the eye of the jig hook. Fix one barb of the stinger treble about two-thirds of the way down the deadbait's body, just as if you were setting up a conventional deadbait rig. Any predator striking at the middle or rear of the lure should now be nobbled by the stinger treble. Obviously you can do this with soft plastic baits as well.

The single hook on a lead-head can be fairly weedless. Some versions come with weed-guards made of plastic, or a bundle of nylon fibres, like one tuft from a king-size toothbrush. You will find that there are two different types of hook used on commercial lead-heads. The first and most common is a fairly fine-wire, unforged, round-bend Aberdeen pattern. These hooks are relatively soft and may straighten out under pressure, which is worth bearing in mind if there are big pike where you fish. The other common pattern is a forged, heavier-duty type, with a more angular O'Shaughnessy bend – a much better bet for big fish.

Lead-head jigs come in a huge range of weights, from $\frac{1}{32}$oz up to several ounces.

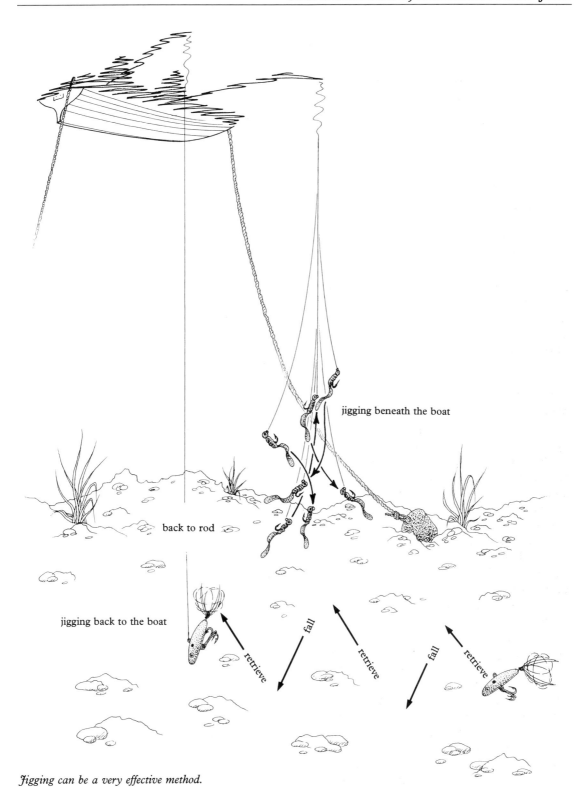

jigging beneath the boat

back to rod

jigging back to the boat

fall

retrieve

retrieve

fall

retrieve

Jigging can be a very effective method.

Choosing the right weight for your technique and venue is important. Light, dressed jigs of around $\frac{1}{4}$oz can be swum off the bottom quite easily, in water depths of 90–120cm (3–4ft), whereas a $\frac{1}{2}$oz jig would hit bottom unless worked at ridiculous speed. In 6–9m (20–30ft) of water, however, you may need a jig of 1oz or more before you can get down near the bottom and still feel what's going on through the rod. In flowing water, you will need to use a heavier jig than you would to work the same depth in still water.

A big bushy skirt and bulky plastic trailers or deadbaits, will all add buoyancy and slow the sinking rate of any given size jig. If you want a big bulky bait to fish on the bottom in deep water, you need to go for weight – say 1–2oz. If you want to swim a lively plastic grub across the top of submerged weed, then $\frac{1}{4}$oz is probably enough. If you want to bully a jig *through* the upper layers of that weed, then go up to $\frac{1}{2}$–1oz. Experiment to discover what's needed each time.

I've already mentioned the basic up-down retrieve. By choosing the right weight for your water you can also try swimming jigs off the bottom at various depths, or over sunken weed or features. Another effective technique is to hop a jig across the bottom, actually thumping the bottom with each hop. Weedless versions can be swung out on a tight line and dropped into gaps in weed, or tight to structures. Jigs can be swum over and around features and also worked through weed or fallen trees. Either a subdued 'feel your way' approach, or an aggressive, busy 'bulldozing' retrieve can be used. Both methods will have their successful days. Start with a subdued approach and if there is no response get faster and more positive.

You can add clip-on jig spinner arms to all lead-heads, turning them into a kind of hybrid spinnerbait. Sometimes the extra flash and vibration is needed. One type, the horse-head jig, comes with a small spinner blade attached with a swivel. You could even try a clip-on buzzer blade, as Charlie has done with some success. Tailspins are teardrop-shaped jigs with

Jason Davies with a Llandegfedd 25lb 12oz pike, taken on a Gamble spinnerbait.

a short wire tail, on which a clevis-mounted spinning blade rotates. Unusually, they are fitted with a treble hook.

A recent innovation is a jig called a 'flying lure'. This is designed so that once cast, it does not sink straight down, but with a swooping curve, down and away from the angler. The advantage of this is that it can be made to go under jetties, boats or overhanging trees where it could never be cast directly.

Rods for jig fishing need to be sensitive, so you can feel what the lure is doing, and also crisp and positive to set the big single hooks. Go for a carbon with a medium-fast action and enough flex to handle biggish fish in confined situations.

FLIES AND BUGS

FLIES, STREAMERS AND BUGS

Since writing the first edition of this book, I have caught countless pike, chub and wild brown on flies. The best fly-caught catch of pike, to date, is eighteen in one day – thirteen of which were doubles – the biggest weighing in at 20lb 2oz!

I thought it would be a good idea to include flies and bugs in the book, along with some of my own ideas on how they can be used to catch pike, perch, chub, or even zander. Fly fishing my way doesn't require fancy fly rods and reels – just a 'whippy' match rod, or similar.

To date, I've been using small flies for catching perch and chub, and large streamer flies and bugs for catching pike. In my opinion, the best time of the year for taking pike on streamer flies and bugs, is during the warm summer months. My favourite method is to twitch and flick the fly/bug as I slowly retrieve it.

Chub, perch and trout respond to flies during the summer or winter periods. Perch and chub are usually to be found in parts of the river that are not regularly fished; I've found some really good perch and chub areas on my local rivers by pushing my way through thick, dense undergrowth. Due to the lack of features or bottom structure, perch and chub are rarely present in the regular swims along my local rivers. During the summer period, perch and chub can often be seen hitting small flies as they dap over the water's surface.

Casting with a fly rod, from deep within thick, dense undergrowth, would be out of the question. I found that I could get takes by using a long match rod to dap flies and bugs on the water's surface, or swing them to holding features. Keeping a low profile is a must when doing this, especially when the water is ultra-clear. Floating dry flies and bugs along on the flow, to features and structure that perch or chub hold up in or around, such as overhanging or fallen trees, can also be very productive.

Bugs are far heavier than dry and wet flies. They can be cast overarm or underarm with just about any type of rod, provided you use a low diameter line. I use 6lb line and a negative-buoyancy wire trace when dapping and floating dry flies and bugs. I grease the end 1.5m (5ft) of line so that it floats. When using wet flies, streamer flies and bugs, I prefer to use a shorter rod. The 7ft 6in RT6 is perfect for this type of fishing. A short rod enables me to cast and flick from within the dense undergrowth that usually surrounds me. Again, I use 6lb line. It is important to de-grease the line when using wet and streamer flies.

If extra casting weight is required when using sinking flies, nip shot on to the line or trace. When using very small flies for chub and perch, a wire trace is not a must. If you are unlucky and a pike or zander should grab your small fly while fishing for perch or chub, no serious damage will be done if it is bitten off. This is the *only* exception to using a wire trace. I consider small single-hook flies to be no more of a risk to pike and zander than a baited match angler's size 16 hook!

When retrieving any type of fly or bug, retrieve slowly, giving little twitches, flicks and jerks now and again. Watch how insect life moves on and below the water's surface and try to imitate it as best you can. It's handy to know a bit about insect life before you begin.

Types of Fly

Dry flies

Dry flies imitate insects landing on the water's surface, and are very effective when swarms of flies are hovering over the water; the dragon-fly imitation is my favourite. When the swarms are no more and there is little sign of predators hitting insects lying resting or dead on the water's surface, a wet fly may be called for!

Wet flies

Wet flies imitate dead sinking insects and aquatic life forms. They can be effective in clear or murky water conditions.

Streamers

Streamer flies are large wet flies that are supposed to imitate fish fry, although I haven't actually seen any fish fry (in my local waters anyway) that look anything like my streamer flies! They do get results, however: perch, chub and small pike are easily fooled by them.

A streamer fly can be made up on hooks as big as a size 4/0, or as small as a size 12. Large streamer flies can be fitted with eyes and a diving blade to make them dive and vibrate. They are probably the easiest to make of the fly family – just about anything goes!

Nymphs

Nymphs imitate young, aquatic insect offspring, such as the dragon- and caddis-fly larvae; they can imitate larval or immature insect forms.

After a major hatch, there will be far more (smaller) offspring than there will be (larger) adult insects. With that in mind, a predator will probably be more attuned to a small fly than it will a large.

Bugs

Bugs come in all shapes and forms. Like streamers, just about anything goes in their making; I especially like the mouse and frog imitations. Pike, perch, chub or trout will attack these amazing works of fly-tying art.

Trolling

When trolling on large water reservoirs (such as trout fisheries), I have rarely caught perch or trout on big lures; probably because they are wary of them. Although I haven't yet tried it, I think trolled streamer flies could be the cure to the wariness problem.

Many trout reservoirs hold large perch. Working a weedless fly tight along the bottom could be a winning method for big perch.

Reflections

The first time that I had a go at fly fishing was back in about 1986. My next-door neighbour at that time (Derek) was a fly fishing noddy! On the day in question, he had gone to try his hand at a trout stock pond in Stambridge, Essex, while I had gone to fish a carp lake in nearby Canewdon with a friend (Barry). On our way back from Canewdon, we stopped off to see how Derek was getting on . . . he was not a happy man, as he hadn't had a touch all afternoon! He asked if I would like to have a go with his fly rod; and as I'd always been fascinated by the way a fly is cast, I accepted. Within ten or fifteen casts, I had landed two trout, the biggest about $2\frac{1}{2}$lb – a good stock-pond fish.

I put my success down to retrieve speed and finger movement – plus Barry's coaching! He was an old hand at fly fishing and gave me some verbal coaching from the side lines: 'Not like that, you pratt!' Derek was right annoyed seeing me land two trout. I offered him his rod back, but he insisted that I carry on! He said something like, 'I'm having more fun watching you, Charlie.' I'm not sure to this day whether or not he meant that as a compliment. Barry had a go with the rod next, and gave Derek and me a lesson in casting the fly, landing two trout in the process.

As Derek had paid £6 to fish the stock pond, Barry and I thought it only fair that he should have the trout. He couldn't bring himself to eat the $2\frac{1}{2}$lb one, however, and returned it to its rightful owner later that evening!

10

RUBBERIZED LURES

Rubberized lures come in all sorts of shapes and sizes: eels up to 60cm (2ft) long, worms from 5cm (2in) to 25cm (10in), lizards, craw-fish, grubs, curl-tails, twin-tails, tripple ripples, tender tubes, toads, talking frogs(!), swamp rats, skirts – the list is endless.

Rubberized baits are mainly used by Ameri-can bass fishermen. As to why they have never caught on in the UK, I can only hazard a guess: import duties and profit margins perhaps. In my opinion, rubber baits do have a market place in this country for perch, chub, trout, pike and zander fishing, but, at the time of writing, very few of these baits are available in the UK. I shall include them anyway.

WORMS AND GRUBS

Soft rubber worms and grubs (grubs being smaller than worms) are very versatile! They can be used on spinners, spinnerbaits, spoons, lead-heads, plugs, or simply on their own, mounted on a single hook. The lighter a worm or grub and mount is, the lighter the tackle set-up required, in order to be able to cast them a good distance.

Worms and grubs can be mounted on a variety of different hooks:

Ian Taylor with a perch taken on a 'spin and grub' combination.

1. A crab hook.
2. A standard single hook.
3. A standard single hook with a 45lb mono weed-guard (*see* diagram on page 143). With this method it pays to have a load of grubs pre-rigged. Then, when a tail gets chomped, all you have to do is pop on a reserve.

4. A treble hook. Remove the treble hook from your lure, push the eye and shank of the treble hook up (from the tail end) through the grub body and then replace the hook. If a treble hook cannot be removed from a lure, *see* No. 9.
5. A weedless worm hook. This is a single hook with a wire weed-guard whipped or

crimped on to it. Hook types Eagle Claw 95XBL or 249W are ideal.

6. A weedless, or standard hook, with shot squeezed on to the wire trace for additional weight.

7. A lead-head's single hook.

8. The weed-guard of a spoon. Thread the wire weed-guard of the spoon through the body of the grub. Push a grub right up the weed-guard and then pull it back slightly; apply a drop of strong glue to the exposed weed-guard and then push the grub back up it, twisting the grub as you push. Within seconds it will be held fast to the weed-guard. Set the grub (by pushing or pulling) to act as a very reliable weed-guard. This method is extremely effective for fishing through snag-riddled areas. When you feel a take, you need to strike hard in order to depress the worm weed-guard, in turn setting the hook/hooks.

9. A spinner equipped with a single, or treble hook. If the treble hook of your spinner cannot be removed, cut it off! Replace it with a new single or treble hook by means of a split ring.

10. A spinnerbait's single hook.

11. A buzzbait's single/treble hook.

12. A single fine wire hook (size 2/0–3/0 or 4/0), Texas-style! Take a size 3/0 single hook and a pair of pointed nose pliers, and make a bend in the hook approximately 1cm (3/8in) from the eye of the hook. Slide 1cm (3/8in) of your grub/worm's body on to the hook point and then slide it up to the hook eye. Now bury the point of the hook in the worm's body, so that the point can just be felt on the other side of the body. For long worms, couple two hooks together with a piece of wire. When you feel a positive pull on the rod tip, you need to strike hard in order to set the hook. Remember that the hook point needs to be forced through the grub/worm's body to successfully hook its attacker!

I have made special 'snap spinner-jigs' to take hooks mounted with prerigged grubs and worms (see photo on p. 85). Perch, especially, like the spin and grub combination. Use the 'snap spinner-jig' on any type of lure to up its strike rate. As with minnow plugs, adding a swivel and Colorado or Willow blade to the rear hook hanger (or flap-tail blade) really does up a lure's hooking statistics. A flap-tail is a lure that has a blade mounted on its rear hook hanger *without* a swivel. Because there's no swivel, the blade flaps instead of spins, hence its name. The only commercially available flap-tail that I know of is Heddon's Big Bud.

Eels

Rubber eels are relatively new to me, but I know through my own experience, that pike absolutely adore real eels. In the future I'm going to give rubber eels a really good go; if I can get hold of some eel scent, I plan to lace my rubber eels with it and try fishing them static! I see no reason why it shouldn't work.

Frogs and Lizards

Rubber frogs, lizards and crawfish look very realistic. In my view, it pays to use these lures when the creatures they set out to imitate are in season (although they will catch outside a creature's seasonal period as well).

Skirts

Rubber skirts can be fitted to just about any type of lure, even wobbled deadbaits. You can either buy them ready-made, or you can make your own; I prefer to make my own. I like to mix various colours of 'living rubber' together, forming mega-sized skirts.

The bigger and thicker you make a rubber skirt, the bigger the hook needs to be. For really big, thick skirts, use a Partridge size 1/0 fine-wire treble.

I like to carry with me a supply of ready-tied skirted trebles. All I have to do if I want a skirt

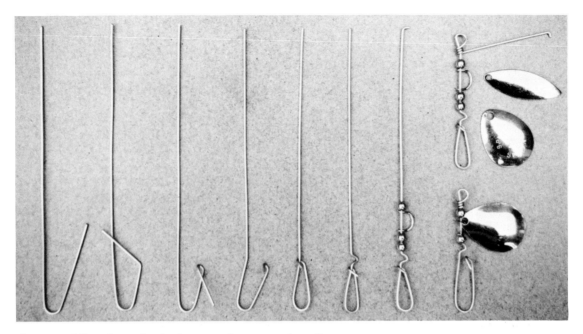

An easy-to-follow picture showing how to make a snap spinner jig.

added to a non-skirted lure, is slide off the existing treble from the split ring and replace it with a skirted one.

Talking Frogs

Rubbery 'talking frogs' or rather 'croaking frogs' made by Burke, have been about for a couple of years now. I'm convinced that the electronic croaks (vibrations) they emit, entice predators to them, usually pike. The talking frog will get takes even when stationary – have a good think about that!

The Advantages of Using Soft Plastic

Like American Express, soft rubbery plastic baits can be used just about anywhere in the world, and attract many hundreds of different fish species. The main advantage of using soft plastic baits in the UK is that they have great lifelike actions which imitate all sorts of freshwater creatures. They are not bulky, which means they make minimal noise as they enter the water – essential when lure fishing for chub and perch. If rigged properly, soft plastic baits will go just about anywhere you desire them to! Predators absolutely adore them.

Reflections

I've caught so many pike and perch over the years by mounting rubber grubs and skirts on my lures that I cannot think of one specific occasion that really stands out from the rest. If pushed, I would say that my best memories of using soft plastics, come from my early days of lure fishing with a small jig-frame, equipped with a small lead-head and rubber grub. Small pike and perch really do love them.

There are one or two waters that I lure fish, where I can only get takes using this type of lure. These hard waters do not have that many pike and perch in, and what fish there are, are fairly small. There are also plenty of prey fish, so your lure has to be very convincing. The small jig-frame, with the small lead-head and grub, I have found to be ultra-convincing.

11

CHOOSING THE RIGHT LURE

PIKE

Winter Period

Pike of all sizes will take lures of all sizes, when food is in short supply. When food is plentiful, the size and choice of lure can, in my experience, make a difference to the strike rate.

Come winter, when prey fish start to shoal up, pike are on the look-out for any size of meal that may happen by looking for its shoaling mates! When all the stragglers have congregated together so that the odd one is no longer to be had, pike will leave their late-summer holding areas and go in search of shoaled-up prey.

I have found that the best time to get any size of pike to take any size of lure, irrespective of colour, shape or features, is in autumn during the first cold snap when the majority of the prey fish have already shoaled up elsewhere. Pike may hold in an area for two or three weeks after the prey fish have migrated to their winter holding areas, and during that time, pike will have a go at just about anything that comes their way. I can go to one area of a local river around November time, when the prey fish are in short supply, and catch ten to twelve pike every session. After a couple of weeks of fantastic action, they're gone, not to be found in numbers in the same area, until approximately the same time the following year. The pike moving off in search of prey fish doesn't bother me very much, as I know exactly where the prey shoal! When pike start turning up in numbers in the prey fish holding areas, they will gorge themselves to bursting point. It's then that lure size becomes important once again,

small silver, flashing plugs, spinners and spoons being highly favoured.

If you can locate a shoal of feeding pike on their way to the prey fish holding areas, any size of lure may get a response. If you are unable to locate the prey fish shoals, you will find that winter lure fishing, using any size of lure, will be a very hit-and-miss affair.

Summer Period

During the summer period, it can pay to choose your lure according to the prey available, that is fish, fowl, rodents and amphibians.

If you're only interested in catching big pike stick to using big lures. If you want to catch plenty of small to medium-sized pike, with the odd big one here and there, stick to using smaller lures. In my opinion, you will catch far fewer predators using big lures all the time, than you would using small and medium-sized lures. For example, using small to medium-sized lures during the summer period, I may catch ten to twelve pike under 12lb in a session, and if I'm lucky, one or two well over 12lb. Using big lures (over 15cm (6in) in length), I may catch the odd one or two small pike, and again, if I'm lucky, one or two well over 12lb. Lure size does make a difference to my overall catch rate, although your catch statistics with regard to lure size, may differ greatly to mine.

If I still lived in sunny 'Southend-on-Sea', where the pike were much smaller than where I now live, the only thing that would differ from what I've said above is the size of the pike. The size of lure for the size of fish rule would still apply – possibly even more so!

Jan Arends of Holland with a huge plug-caught perch.

PERCH

If it were 1986, I would be advising you to use small, medium and large lures for perch! Unfortunately, due to disease, millions of quality perch died back in the 1980s. As quality perch are still thin on the ground, I would advise the perch enthusiast to persist with small-sized lures, especially spinners, spoons, plugs, worms, grubs, bugs and flies. When fishing deep waters with small lures, you may find that they need to be weighted to get them to work or stay deep. Letting the small lure reach bottom before slowly retrieving it is vital for success.

I have spent many hundreds of hours at trout reservoirs, lure fishing for pike with medium-

and large-sized lures, yet I've hardly ever hooked a perch or trout. If I specialize, that is, use only small but heavy spinners, I can, more often than not, catch a perch within minutes. That fact alone tells me that small lures are more realistic and less frightening to perch, in both summer and winter.

Back in 1986, I knew of one or two waters where I could, within minutes of launching my boat, locate huge shoals of big perch by using my fishfinder, but I never wanted to catch them then, being interested only in pike. Now that I want to catch quality perch, I can't locate any! I have no problem catching small and medium-sized perch though. Small, heavy, silver-bladed spinners, dragged along the bottom – *not* spun – really do the business, attracting one reasonable-sized perch after the other.

Location

Perch, when not hunting for food high in the water, or along the shallow edges, can be found in numbers, holed up in shadows created by a fallen or overhanging tree, a moored boat, pylons, or bridge supports, or they will be holding at depth where the light is not so bright.

If you can locate inlets supplying food to the water, such as a sewage outfall, you could be in for some good sport. Perch love to hold near sewage outlets or any other form of inlet that brings food with it.

Perch, like pike, will track down shoals of prey fish (fry): find the fry and you should be close to the perch. Winter, in my view, is the best time for locating and catching big perch as they plunder the fry shoals.

Handfuls of worm-filled compost work really well for getting perch and bream on the feed. Some local anglers have named me 'the compost man'.

CHUB

When lure fishing for chub in flowing water, it pays to think small! During the summer

The author with a nice chub, taken on a Big S plug.

months, chub will take small top-water plugs like Fred Arbogast's 7cm (3in) jointed Jitterbug and Gordon Griffiths' 4cm (1½in) Popper Plug. With regard to sub-surface plugs, chub do have a preference for small lures. I've caught a few chub on big sub-surface lures, but on the whole chub are very wary of them.

As John Worzencraft and Dave Smith have said in their spinner chapter, casting upstream and working a lure with, or across, the flow is the best method for catching chub on lures (this also goes for floating baits, such as Chum Mixers!). Chub are highly tuned to taking food that drifts along with the flow. Lures retrieved up the flow will usually put chub off.

Chub will soon wise up to a lure, so it pays to change lures regularly and keep on the move. Chub are fooled far more easily by lifelike imitations; on 'shy' chub rivers, fly fishing will

probably be the best method of luring them.

During the winter period, chub tend to move into deeper water. The best types of lure then, are small weighted lures, such as flies, rubber worms, spinners and spoons, or small, deep-diving plugs. To weight a small lure just nip shot on to the line or trace.

ZANDER

I have no experience whatsoever of lure fishing for zander; in fact, I've never even caught one. I can only offer you second-hand advice on the size of lure to use for this fearsome-looking creature.

I have talked to many lure enthusiasts that have visited the fens equipped just with lures. Some have told me that zander prefer medium-

Jan shows the potential of continental zander fishing.

sized lures and others have told me they prefer small lures! Who's right? It would appear (from photographic evidence) that small and medium-sized lures both work.

John Worzencraft lives on the Fens' doorstep! I know that John has done fairly well using spinners for zander. If the fens are anything like the Norfolk broads – that is, wind-swept – a small flashy spinner blade, revolving around a well-weighted shaft, would probably be my first choice. If the wind were hitting against my back, I would probably do as I've been advised and use small to medium-sized plugs.

Steve Gamble used to lure fish the Great Ouse Relief Channel back in the late 1960s and regularly took 'schoolie' zander on a plain, but very effective 7cm (3in) silver spoon bumped along the bottom.

It pays to listen to others. Where I may lack knowledge in one area of lure fishing, somebody else may excel – and I'm always ready to listen and pinch a good idea!

TROUT

Unlike perch, small lures (of the non-fly type) rarely ever appeal to trout, any more than medium-sized or big ones. Fly anglers use small, realistic flies to catch trout. While fly fishing for trout, they often take numbers of quality perch. Taking everything into account, the obvious answer, is to use small realistic lures for trout and perch. My good friend Ian Taylor, the manager of Weirwood trout fishery, East Sussex, told me that big trout will take big lures, but you have to put in many hours to catch one.

Ian Taylor with a big 7lb trout, taken on a big Kilty spoon.

SALMON

by
John Bailey

Salmon are not really supposed to take food in during their stay in fresh water, so it is hard to see what size, shape, action or colour of lure could possibly be successful. However, defying the natural rules, lures do work, even if they are not as successful overall as flies.

There are several basic guide-lines that apply when choosing the right lure for the right situation on a salmon river. Obviously, if the water is high and dirty, it makes sense to choose a lure that can get down to where the salmon are, and one that will be seen. Equally, if the water is running crystal low, such a heavy, large lure is likely to be viewed with considerable alarm.

The condition of the salmon also plays some part. For example, if salmon are silver and fresh in from the sea, they are more likely to be

John Bailey with a West Country grilse.

tempted by a spinner of sizable proportions. If, on the other hand, the fish are red and stale, try something a little more conservative.

Action is something to be considered when salmon fishing but again it is hard to see the rules that apply. For example, there are many occasions when a jinking Toby is irresistible, and yet, the favourite salmon lure of all time is the Devon Minnow, whose flight is not in any way erratic. Then, there are some occasions when only a Mepps will be looked at. Probably it is best to take a selection of Tobys, Devon Minnows and Mepps of all weights, sizes and colours and fish those best suited to the conditions prevailing. Once success has been achieved then it often pays to keep on with the same lure rather than chopping and changing.

It is vital to emphasize that these are not strict rules, only guide-lines. There is no branch of predator fishing where the prey is more fickle; the mood of the fish can change totally over the course of a single day.

12

SENSORY PERCEPTION

A big pike is the king, or rather the *queen*, of the freshwater jungle (pike over 10lb in weight usually being females).

Freshwater predators can survive just about anywhere, irrespective of a water's size and depth. The only types of water that a predator will not survive in, are salty or badly polluted waters. Predators will eat live or dead fish of any species, including their own; pike will also eat frogs, ducks, rats and snakes. Perch and chub will also hit small creatures moving across the surface. I have witnessed fowl and rodents being taken by pike: in Norfolk, the home of big-headed pike, it's not uncommon to hear of a fully grown duck being snatched from the surface, never to be seen or heard from again.

Pike and other predators will use their senses in various combinations (depending on conditions) to hunt food. The senses we know of are feeling (via the lateral line), hearing, vision, smell and taste (some species also use touch). So, on the face of it, it seems that a predator has four senses it can use to hunt with, in any one of fifty-two combinations! I said 'it seems', as a predator could have senses as yet unbeknown to man.

LATERAL LINE FEELING

The lateral line is made up of a series of pores running along each flank of a fish. Each pore

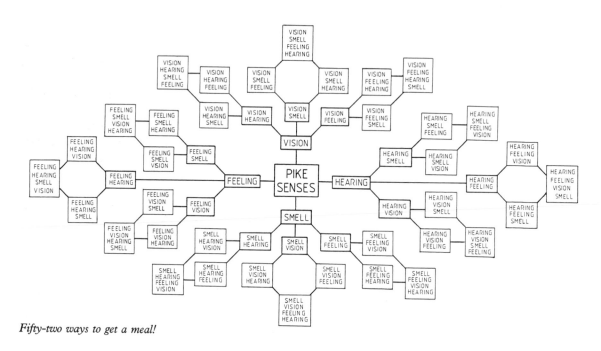

Fifty-two ways to get a meal!

The author's handmade vibrant wiggle lures get the once-over by Gord.

contains sensory cells, which have hair-like processes called neuromast organs. The hair-like cells respond to low-frequency vibrations emitted by other fish, or any moving objects.

A predator can 'localize' vibrations received by means of its sensory cells. Some sensory cells are oriented in one direction and others are oriented in another; the way they're oriented helps a predator to localize its prey. As pike have a very long lateral line, they can probably detect vibrations over a greater distance than any other freshwater predator. Vibrations received by the sensory cells are relayed to the part of the brain that is associated with hearing. The ideal lure action for appealing to a pike's lateral line, is a nice slow wiggle-wobble movement. To produce low-frequency vibrations from a lure, a slow retrieve is a must. The faster a lure is retrieved, the higher the vibration fre-

quencies emitted. Because water is denser, vibrations travel through it five times faster than through air.

I would like to finish this section by quoting Dr Bruce Carlson. Dr Carlson is a professor of physiology at the University of Michigan Medical School, and is an authority on fish senses. 'Fish use their sensitive lateral line to orient in a body of water, stay in a school, find prey, and escape predators.' Using the lateral line, 'They can feel where they are and what's around them.' 'The lateral line detects vibrations from less than one cycle per second to about 200.'

HEARING

Believe it or not, a predatory fish does have ears. Fish have what are called 'inner ears'.

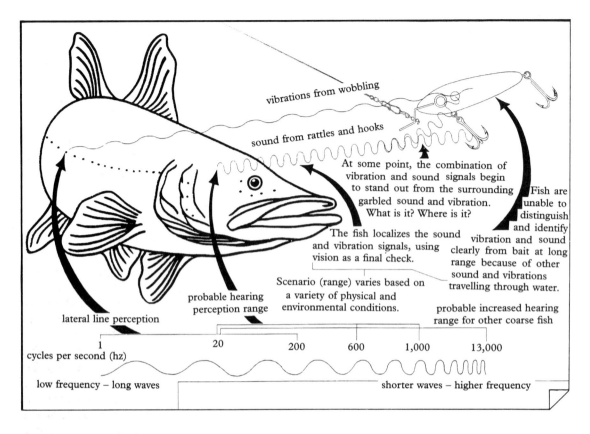

How fish pick up vibrations.

Like the lateral lines, the inner ears also detect vibrations, but higher frequency ones. A fish's ear is very much like our own. It has three semi-circular canals that are used for balance, and three fluid-filled sac-like structures that are used for actual hearing. The sacs are called the utriculus, sacculus and lagena, and are covered with hair-like projections called ampullae. The inner ear also contains calcium carbonate ear bones, called otoliths. As a predator's body is acoustically transparent, vibrations pass straight through its ear protection as if it were not there, just like strong radio waves pass through your house walls. Vibrations passing through the outer-ear protection will hit against the first dense objects they come to, these being the otoliths. The otoliths vibrate at a different rate to the fluid and tissue that surrounds them. The hair-like projections on the cells under the otoliths bend when vibrations hit them, and as they bend, a message is sent to the brain. Like the lateral line, the cells in the inner ear are also capable of localizing vibrations.

Again, I will finish by quoting Dr Carlson:

Hearing is a long-distance as well as short-range sense. Its range depends on the amount of background noise.

'I don't know of studies on wall-eye [zander] hearing, but like bass and pike, it likely encompasses a range from about 20 to 600 cycles per second.

'Given that fish take advantage of every possible environmental cue to feed, or avoid being eaten, they detect and respond differently to slight variations in vibrations. I'm speculating here because few fish have been evaluated for frequency discrimination . . . there's no reason to believe ability to separate slight differences in colour shouldn't be matched by auditory or lateral line capability to separate small differences in vibration.'

I, personally, am 100 per cent convinced that a predator can define the size of another fish (a potential meal!) in murky water conditions, or at night, from the vibrations emitted by it.

VISION

In a pike, the lobes of the brain which control optical activity are very large in comparison to those controlling the other senses. However, we know from countless examples that blind pike are quite capable of feeding and surviving without the benefit of sight. In a pike the nasal organs and the related brain centres are apparently less developed than the hearing and lateral line systems. It seems then, that though pike can use any combination of sight, hearing, lateral line and smell to deal with particular conditions, under optimum conditions of light and water clarity, the relative order of importance of its senses seems to be: firstly sight, then hearing and lateral line, and finally smell. Depending on water colour and light availability (that is, visual range), the pike's visual sense may take a back seat. I feel that the lateral line and hearing frequently play a much bigger role than vision, even though the lobes of the brain which cover optical activity are larger.

The eyes of a fish vary in several ways from our own. Light rays are not bent or focused until they reach the lens, because the tissues of the cornea have the same refractive index as the surrounding water. However, to compensate, the lens has the highest refractive index of all vertebrate lenses. In addition, the lens is both spherically and optically perfect, which means it can transmit a perfect, undistorted image on to the retina. To alter the focus, the whole lens is moved by muscular means, unlike the human lens, which actually changes shape. This means the fish has a more limited focal range than we do, but because of the effects of water on visibility, it doesn't need our flexibility anyway. Most fish have an eye on each side of their heads, which, together with the bulging spherical lens, means that most fish have almost total all-round vision, very useful if you want to keep an eye out for a hungry predator. The disadvantage is that such a system only gives perspective where the fields of vision from the two eyes overlap. In other words, such fish are lousy judges of distance.

If we look at a pike, we can see that both eyes are set higher and more forward-facing, giving binocular vision similar to our own. There are even two 'sighting grooves' running down to the snout. This means slightly less all-round vision, but good perspective. Obviously accurate judgement of distance is particularly important to a predator like the pike.

Research on vision in fish has confirmed that fish tend to be long-sighted. In addition, they have their longest range in their lateral field of vision; in other words, they can see further out to the side than they can see straight ahead. When looking forward, however, the light is directed on to the back of the retina, where the visual cells are densest, which means that the fish will see its clearest, crispest images when looking forwards. In the lateral field of vision the light is directed on to parts of the retina where the visual cells are less dense, causing an image to be less sharp.

Colour Vision

The visual cells in the eye are of two types: rods and cones. The rods are more sensitive, and are capable of detecting very dim light and very vague, shadowy images in low-light conditions. The cones are responsive to bright light, and are responsible for colour vision. A nocturnal fish will therefore have far more rods than cones in its retina, since sensitivity is more important to it than colour. A fish that feeds during daylight will have more cones for dealing with the brighter light.

In the pike's eye, there are roughly four rods to each cone. As the cones are very large, the total mass of each type is about the same. This means that the pike has well-balanced vision, capable of handling a wide range of light conditions, and has excellent colour vision. There is no evidence at present, though, as to how a fish interprets colour. It can hunt effectively from the half-light of dawn, through a blazing summer day, and back into twilight. After darkness falls, a pike will use its sense of smell and vibrational senses more than vision, in its hunt for a late-night snack.

In clear water, a pike can most probably see vague movement up to fifty feet from it; for example, flashing from a spoon or fish, a brightly coloured lure against a dark background, or a dark lure against a bright background. A background colour could be created from a reed-bed, lily stems, a concrete wall, a sunken boat or a fallen tree, to name just a few.

Well out – 25m (80ft) – from the bank in open water there may not be a solid, background colour behind the lure, only the dimness of distance. In bright sunlight any chop or surface movement of the water will break up and deflect the light beneath the surface causing dappling and sunbeam effects. If fishing out in clear open water on a sunny day, the amount of light entering the water in front of, and behind, a lure will define how well a predator will see that lure. We must also take into account that bright sunlight affects a predator's vision; its eyes will take time to adapt to sudden light changes. The light entering the water in front of, and behind, a lure has most effect when a predator is side-on to the lure, rather than looking up at it from below.

In this case, using a brightly coloured lure could, in fact, make it hard for a predator to see. Dark lures probably show up much better against a bright background. On a day where there is no sun, a predator will most probably see a veil of darkness in the distance; this can be used to your advantage by using brightly coloured lures.

During sunny, clear water conditions, imagine a predator is looking up at your nice brightly coloured lure from below; as the lure passes between its eye and the light source (the sun) it will appear very dark, if not black, whatever the actual colour of the lure. Any lure will be a good target as it passes between the sun and the fish's eyes, so in such conditions a plain black lure may prove to be the best catcher.

On a day when the sun doesn't shine, it will be a different ball game altogether. When there is no sun, any colour lure used should show up to a predator's vision as a colour, apart from a top-water lure, which will still appear very dark, if it can be seen at all! A top-water crawler-type action can cause so much surface disturbance, the plug will become effectively invisible to the eye of an attacking/onlooking predator. A predator will home in on vibration and visible water disturbance created by the top-water lure rather than be attracted to its appearance.

Lure fishing clear water, on non-sunny days, is a case of trying all colours and types of lure until you get a take. If predators are not feeding, one specific colour (or plug action) may have a better triggering effect than another, although there is no concrete evidence that predators are triggered more by one colour than another. If pike are feeding during the day, they will often take just about anything you cast their way.

To give you a better idea of how lures appear to pike in sunny conditions, you could try a couple of tests. Hold a lure at arms length in front of a light bulb (switched on preferably). It will give you a basic idea of what a predator would see on a bright sunny day when looking up from the depths. Move the lure about in front of the light bulb and you will see what a predator can, or cannot see under those circumstances. Alternatively, fill a bath with water at night. Switch the bathroom light on, and, using a piece of mono line, work a top-water crawler from one end of the bath to the other. Do not look at the crawler, but at the shape or silhouette of the lure on the bottom of the bath. As you start to pull the lure along – concentrat-

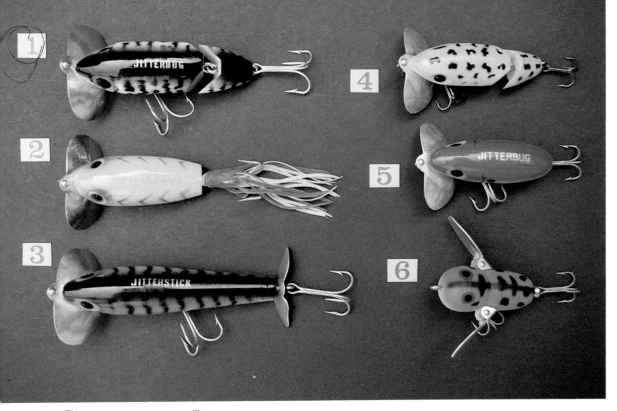

Crawlers. (1) 8cm Jointed Jitterbug; (2) Weedless Jitterbug; (3) Jitterstick; (4) 6.5cm Jointed Jitterbug; (5) 6.5cm Jitterbug; (6) Tiny Crazy Crawler.

Chuggers. (1) Bomber Popper; (2) Hula Popper; (3) Chug Eye; (4) Baby Lucky 13; (5) Trouble Maker; (6) Near Nuthin'.

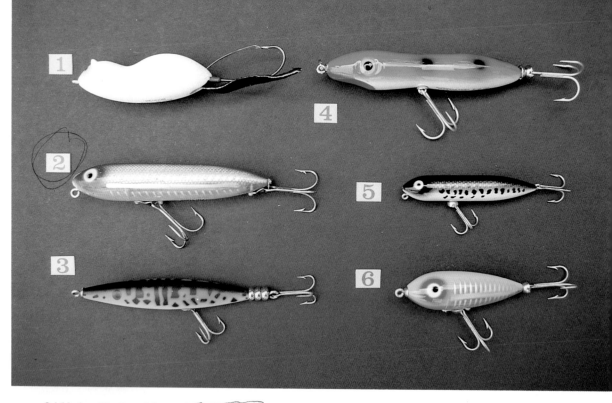

*Stickbaits. (1) Zara Mouse; (2) Zara Spook; (3) converted Dying Flutter; (4) Woodwalker;
(5) Zara Puppy; (6) Baby Zara Spook.*

*Propbaits. (1) Woodchopper; (2) Ripper; (3) Sputterbug; (4) Dalton Special; (5) Buzz'n
Frog; (6) Dying Flutter; (7) Nip-I-Diddee; (8) Baby Torpedo; (9) Bomber Popper (hybrid);
(10) Rat-L-Top; (11) Sinner Spinner; (12) Oval Sprat.*

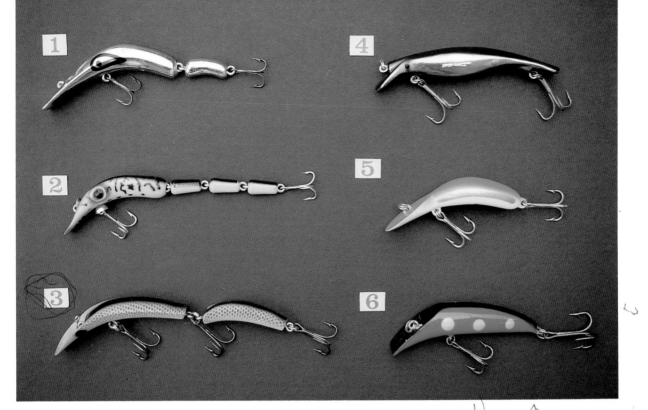

Trolling plugs. (1) Lazy Ike; (2) Beno; (3) Kwikfish; (4) Swim Wizz; (5) Tadpolly; (6) Canadian Wiggler.

deep ↑

Jerkbaits. (1) Cherry Bomb; (2) Zara Gossa; (3) Smitty Jerk; (4) Smitty Diver; (5) Wood Tick; (6) Suick Thriller; (7) Smitty Surface; (8) Big Tuffy.

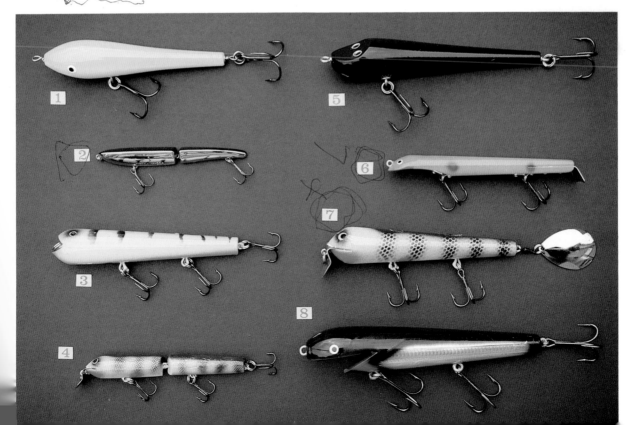

Vibrating plugs. (1) Floating Rat-L-Trap; (2) Suspending Spot; (3) Longbill Spot; (4) Ratt'L Spot; (5) Bayou Boogie; (6) Tiny Trap; (7) Tiny N-Ticer.

Crankbaits. (1) Hot'N Tot; (2) Wiggle Wart; (3) Shallow Reflect 'N'; (4) Little Jack; (5) Abu Hi-Lo; (6) Creek Chub Pikie; (7) Killer Shad; (8) Fat 'A'.

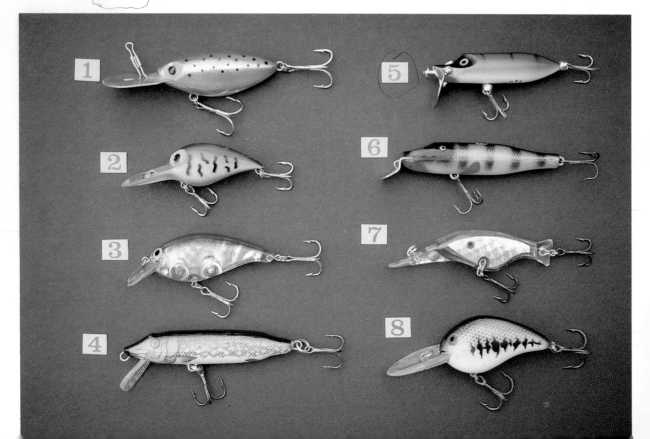

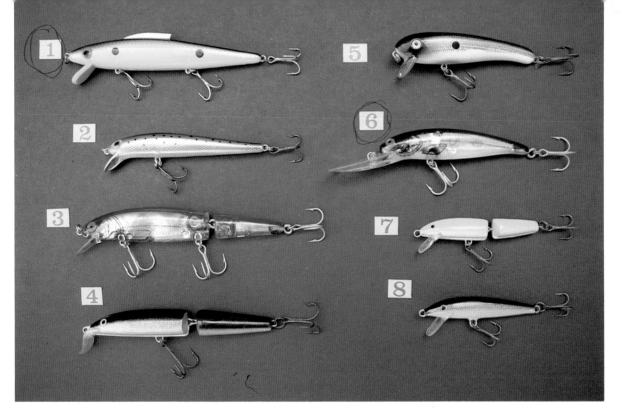

Minnow plugs. (1) Slap-Stick; (2) Thunderstick; (3) Jointed Long A; (4) Jointed Floating Rapala; (5) Baby Stretch 1; (6) Bomber Long A; (7) Jointed J7 Floating Rapala; (8) Original Floating Rapala.

Spoons. (1) Silver Minnow; (2) Rasanen Weedless; (3) Landa Pikko–35gm; (4) Handmade 'Snag-Less' Spoon; (5) Rasanen; (6) Jamtland–16g; (7) Landa Pikko–17g; (8) The author's foolproof anti-kink vane.

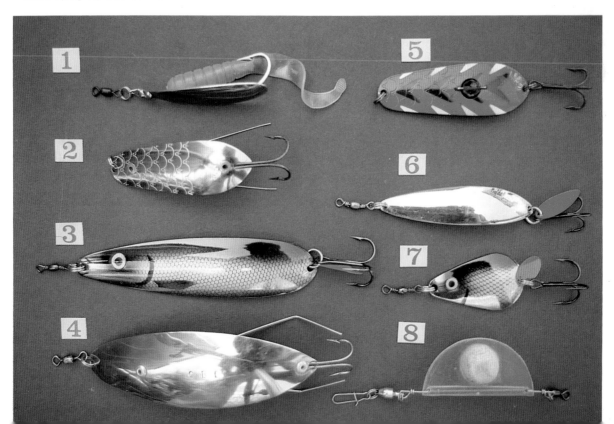

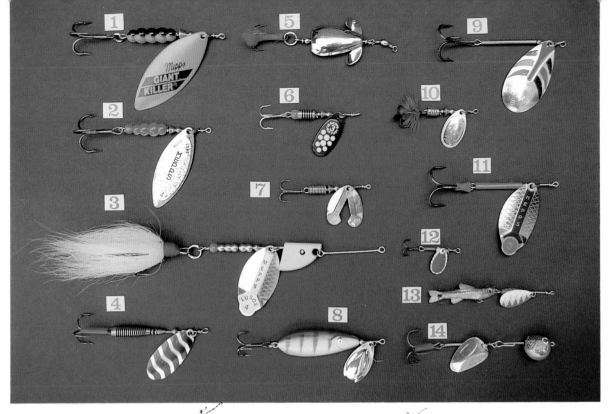

Spinners. *(1) Giant Killer; (2) Aglia Long; (3) Lusox 4; (4) Veltic 5; (5) Colorado Spinner; (6) Black Fury; (7) Scissor Blade; (8) Lotto; (9) Ondex 6; (10) Aglia 2; (11) Lusox 3; (12) Special Celta; (13) Calicocat; (14) Voblex 12.*

Spinnerbaits, buzzers and jigs. *(1) G-Tri-Hatchet; (2) G-Double Willow; (3) G-Double Colorado; (4) Jiggin' Spoon; (5) G-Single Colorado; (6) G-Buzzer; (7) Rattling Sonar Flash; (8) Tailspin; (9) assortment of jigs.*

Flies, bugs and streamers. (1) Divin' Streamer Fly; (2) Weedless Mouse; (3) Surface Popper; (4) Streamer Fly; (5) Dragon Fly; (6) Crawfish; (7) selection of bugs; (8) selection of small flies.

Rubberized lures. (1) Texas Rigged Worm; (2) Crab Hook; (3) Rubber Grub; (4) Texas Rigged Eel; (5) Sparkie Jig Head; (6) weedless Worm hook; (7) round jig head; (8) extension hook; (9) Texas Rigged Grub; (10) Rubber Lizard; (11) Swimmin' Jig Head.

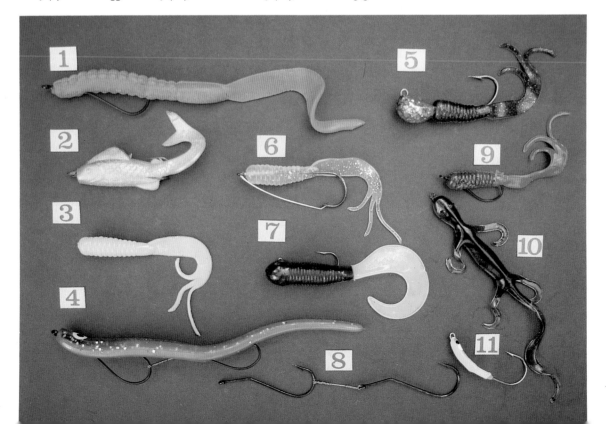

The author with a nice pike taken on a Jointed Jitterbug.

A nice double-figure pike, taken on a Suick Thriller lure.

Charlie Junior with a nice pike, taken on a Jointed Jitterbug.

Michael Bettell plays a hard-fighting, tail-walking, double-figure pike.

ing on the silhouette – you will 'see' the lure as a predator would see it. When looking from below in other words you won't see it at all!

If you should use, say, a green lure along a dam wall that is covered in green algae, (as they usually are during the summer), your green lure will be somewhat lost against the background green to an onlooking predator. Using a red lure against the green algae background, could greatly increase your chances of catching that predator, because it will show up much better.

In my view, the lure colour you choose in clear water conditions should be one that stands out against a given background. Does a specific colour lure have a great deal of influence on a predator? I see no reason why a specific colour shouldn't trigger a predator into striking. Years ago, I used to be convinced that red-headed, white-bodied lures caught me more pike. Veteran pike anglers were always telling me that lures with a bit of red on caught more. Back then, I was not following my own instincts, I was following theirs, and indeed I caught plenty of pike on lures that had a dash of red on, or following close behind, such as a red-skirted hook. Why did the lures with a dash of red really catch? It was because I was only using lures that had a splash of red on! When I started lure fishing there were very few lures sold in this country that didn't have a splash of red somewhere on them. If, back then, I had had some of the knowledge I now have about background and lure colour, I'm sure I would have caught far more pike than I did.

The question is, does a predator associate a specific colour with prey, or does it just see one colour better than another, making that colour a better target? I would say the answer is that one colour shows up better than another in certain light and water-clarity conditions. I would not dismiss the possibility of a colour-trigger factor though; if a predator can see something move because of its colour and flash, it will associate the movement with food, and have a go at eating it, regardless of what shape or form the thing is.

Let's face it, how many red-headed, white-bodied, or, as I look at my lures in front of me, yellow polka-dotted roach, rudd, bream or perch do you come across when fishing? I'm sure that a predator will not associate a yellow polka-dotted lure, doing the weirdest dance through the water you ever did see, as anything down there in its everyday life. No, it hears, feels or sees it as a potential meal. Pike have lasted many millions of years now because they are not too fussy as to what they eat. If something moves, a pike will try to eat it. In order to do that, it must be able to see, hear, feel or smell its prey.

Appealing to a Pike's Vision

To appeal to a pike's vision in clear water, I use shiny spoons, spinners and plugs. Some of my lures can reflect light over a great distance under water. My spoons, being fairly big in size, also emit very good vibrations. I use glitter on my wooden plugs to achieve the same reflective qualities as from my spoons. With regard to spinners, I make my own using mirror-finish, stainless steel blades. In my view, silver flash imitates the flanks of moving bait fish far better than any colour. Some people like to paint perch patterns and such on wooden lures that I've given them, which is fine, but they will not reflect as much flash from their paint finish. Here we have a case of swings and roundabouts. A perch-patterned lure will not be seen from as great a distance as a flashing lure, so it will get fewer follows. However, it will be heard and felt just the same, and if a pike does decide to home in on the vibrations emitted from a perch-patterned lure, and does come into visual contact with it, the pattern will possibly appear more lifelike than a glittered lure. Basically, a painted patterned lure could possibly get more takes, but from far fewer follows!

I also like to use glitter plugs in murky water for visual reasons; when predators are not on a feeding spell (as is often the case when I'm around!), I have found they usually hold up in the reeds, fallen trees or on the bottom, and have to be coaxed into attacking. I have found that a shiny, highly vibratory lure can be very effective if worked very slowly and close to those holding areas. Specialist lures are in order for this type of slow work, as most commercial plugs have very little action when worked at ultra-slow speeds. Also, commercial plugs that have sound chambers do not rattle very much when retrieved slowly. With a specialist lure, you can have action and sound when retrieving slowly. The slow speed of retrieve that can be achieved while maintaining action and sound output, gives a predator more time to think, hear, feel and see your lure. Spoons and spinners dragged along the bottom are a very effective method for catching perch and pike.

If lure action is maintained, a predator will hear or feel the lure coming slowly closer and closer. On many occasions in murky water, a lure will probably pass very close to a pike but out of its vision, the lure's vibrations getting louder, then fading into the distance. A slow retrieve allows a pike to go and casually investigate the vibrations. It can home in on its prey at a nice easy speed, not having to waste valuable energy chasing. As a predator approaches the source of the vibrations, it will hopefully come into visual contact with the lure. Glitter, or mirror-finish stainless steel, maximizes the range of visibility of a lure, unlike a dull-finished lure, which a predator might not see until it is right on top of it, if it spots it at all.

Understanding Colour

Daylight is made up of wavelengths of different coloured light. These wavelengths form the basis of colour; a red object is red because it is able to reflect the red wavelengths of light, blue is blue because it can reflect the blue wavelengths of light, and so on. Coloured water acts as a filter: depending on the water colour, specific wavelengths of light will be blocked and unable to penetrate deeply. If a lure cannot reflect its own colour wavelength of light, it will appear black. Even very clear water can absorb

wavelengths of light if deep enough. Red wavelengths of light, the first to be filtered out by water depth, will penetrate fairly deeply in perfect water conditions. As it starts to get dark, wavelengths of light will only penetrate a matter of feet into the water, if that. When darkness falls, all the underwater-world colours will darken, possibly turning black.

British waters are usually well coloured due to vegetational matter, or bottom-churning caused by high winds, so British anglers need something to tell them what colour can, or cannot, be seen at a specific depth! If you want to be a step ahead of the rest in colour, you could buy yourself a Color-C-Lector from America. This item has a mother unit and probe; the probe is lowered down in the water to the depth you intend to lure fish, and will then tell you, via a dial on the mother unit, what coloured lures to use. You can even buy colour-coded lures for use with the Color-C-Lector.

SMELL

Although fresh water predatory fish like pike, perch, zander and chub have a fair sense of smell, it is poor compared to that of an eel's.

Tank tests carried out in America have proved that bass hold on to a scented worm or grub (without hooks attached) far longer before ejecting it, than they do a non-scented lure. When bait fishing, I rate scent very highly. When fishing for big pike, I always inject my herrings with pilchard oil. The biggest pike I have taken to date, using herrings injected with pilchard oil, is 33lb. I will always remember Mark Wilson, who was with me at the time of capture, saying, 'Those baits of yours stink Charlie – you're not going to use them are you?' I explained to Mark how I inject and dip my herrings in oil before I freeze them. A few hours after the smell of my herrings had cleared from Mark's nostrils, the proof that smelly baits do catch fish could be seen clearly through his camera's viewfinder!

The author's personal-best pike of 33lb, taken on a smelly deadbait.

LURE FISHING AT NIGHT

I first started to come to grips with vibration back in 1987, after witnessing pike bow-waving over weed-beds to get at my highly vibratory lures. The many night assaults that I've undertaken using only lures, has helped no end to confirm my thoughts on the subject. I set about proving my theories, by comparing lures with and without sound chambers. The outcome of my night experiments was about nine to one in favour of lures with sound chambers. When lure fishing at night, I found that a lure with a good action and sound chamber caught many more pike than a lure that didn't have either, or only one of those qualities.

Any lure that is moving, however slightly, will emit vibrations. The better the sound chamber or the swimming, wobbling, wiggling action a lure has, the further its vibrations will carry through the water – hopefully causing responses from predators further afield.

13

CARE OF FISH

STRESS

The following headings all cover the well-being of fish. Some readers may not agree with what I have to say in the following text. I can only say this to them: of all the predators that I've landed and boated since 1986 (well over ten thousand), I've only knowingly had one pike die on me – and that was because it swallowed a deadbait without giving me any indication.

Over the years, I've found my methods to be very effective, but I'm always looking to improve them. I have fished many deep and shallow waters and I have found that predators in both types of water need to be played and handled with care, to keep their stress level to a minimum.

Stress is the name given to over-exertion of the body systems. When a body needs more energy than usual, extra oxygen and glucose are mixed together in the blood. This high-octane mixture is what allows humans and fish to move much faster and exert more power. As a predator chases another fish or lure, it will automatically go into stress mode because it will be using extra energy. What anglers need to consider, to help preserve fish stocks, is how to keep fish stress to a minimum while playing and handling.

A body can only handle so much exertion before it breaks down. Stress, with regard to fish, can be caused by a number of things going on outside its body. The main factors are lack of oxygen in the water, salt tides, pollution, and bad handling. Any one of those factors could cause a fish serious stress, which in turn could trigger off a whole string of unhealthy changes within its body. If we can help in some

way with these external stress-related problems, the fish's internal problems should, to some extent, take care of themselves.

I would class pregnancy as an internal stress factor. The heavier a female becomes, laden with spawn, the more that female is likely to suffer stress. If a female is hooked while suffering from ante- or post-natal stress, the excess stress could prove fatal to her. A pregnant female needs to be played and handled with the utmost care.

Oxygen Supply

As fishermen, we have no control over general oxygen levels in water. What we do have control over, is the amount of time we keep a fish out of water and away from its oxygen supply! A speedy return to the water after unhooking is of the uttermost importance. You may take years to fulfil your dream of catching a 20–30lb fish, so when you do finally catch one, the last thing that you want is to be the cause of its death. It pays to think well in advance of catching a big fish. Ask yourself, 'What will I need? What should I do? How will I react? Should I tell others, or do I keep it to myself? What shouldn't I do?' and so on. You *must* be in total control of the situation. Go over your unhooking and photography routine time after time until it's fixed firmly in your mind.

When a fish is returned to the water, it needs to be free to swim away and recover in oxygenated water, *not* cooped up in a keepnet, sack or tube, just so that you can show it off to others throughout the day. If a fish is retained where there is a lack of oxygen (e.g. in shallow water) the fish cannot even begin to recover. It has to

The pressure's on. Note the rod's nice through action.

use a lot more energy extracting oxygen from poorly oxygenated water, which will cause it even more stress. Even if a fish is in the water, retained in a sack, tube, or keepnet, it may still be suffering. Retained in such a way, your catch may die before your mates or the *Angling Times* reporter arrives.

Salt Tides and Pollution

Since I've lived in Norfolk (four years at the time of writing), I have on two occasions witnessed thousands of dead fish killed by salt water being pushed right up the tidal rivers. The only way anglers can help the fish in such a situation is to promptly notify the NRA, who will implement a rescue plan. The same also applies for pollution.

With regard to the Norfolk Broads, plans have been made to erect a barrier at the mouth of the River Yare in 1996. The barrier, which should protect the Yare, Bure and Thurne – as well as the many broads and systems leading off those rivers – will, if it works, improve the fishing no end for future generations of anglers.

While keeping an eye open for stressed fish, I would also advise you to keep both eyes open for shady characters! Fish stealing is on the increase.

Understanding Stress

I think it's a good idea to understand just what a fish must feel like when suffering . . .

With regard to humans, mild stress can be caused by many things, such as swimming, a game of squash, a bit of football with the kids, running for a bus, or even a game of chess! Each and every one of us has suffered stress at some time in our lives. If your body is not used to being pushed beyond its normal everyday working routine, stress will occur when it is so pushed. It doesn't matter how fit a person is, he can still suffer stress. Think back to the times when you have suffered stress. Think what it must be like for a fish being kept out of the water for about ten minutes, and being unable to take in oxygen. Think what it must feel like to be returned to a sack, or pike tube, at the edge of the water, where oxygen levels may be far too low to aid recovery.

I used to suffer stress two or three times a week when I was one of thirty to forty karate students training in a small hall (*dojo*), all 'fighting' for oxygen, puffing, panting, gasping and groaning. The *sensi* (teacher), 5th Dan Ken Bailey, showed us no mercy! The higher our grade, the harder we were pushed. Achieving black belt made life in the *dojo* very hard work. Similarly, the 'higher' a fish's weight, the more it can often be made to suffer, because of excessive playing, handling and retaining. As with me, a fish's advanced age will not help the situation – I'm forty-six now!

The more students there were present in

A big, long-dead Norfolk pike found floating on the surface. Dean (seen holding the fish) was almost sick as the author slit the stomach in order to sink it. The author does this out of respect for the pike. It is a smelly, disgusting task which he doesn't enjoy.

This time Dean took the pictures – I wonder why?

the *dojo*, the greater the competition for the available oxygen. Quite often I had to bow out and go in search of oxygen outside. There was nothing better than the drive home after karate: the van window wide open, my lungs taking in as much oxygen as I could breathe. By the time I arrived back home (six miles away), I had fully recovered – apart from one or two aching limbs!

Because I exert myself regularly, I know what it's like to suffer serious stress; do you have an idea what stress feels like? If not, get out of that armchair and go for a quick run. You will

experience first hand what a fish feels when kept out of water for any period of time. Within seven minutes of finishing your run, you should have fully recovered. Unlike humans, however, fish can take hours or even days to fully recover from a really stressful ordeal. Some, unfortunately, never recover.

Reddening of the flanks is the first visual sign of stress, but fish will be suffering in a keepnet, sack or tube well before this reddening of the flanks occurs. I cannot see the point of retaining any type of coarse fish for long periods of time.

Photographing Fish

Trout fisheries hold many big species of fish in

them. In my view, they need to protect their specimens by means of rules and fines. If you break their rules, you get fined – no ifs or buts.

If trout fisheries are prepared to open their doors to us, we should respect their rules. They are making good money out of us, but don't forget that they opened at our own request! They are running a business, and businesses are entitled to make money.

Why is it that every time you seem to open up a weekly angling newspaper between autumn and spring, you see an angler photographed with a pike well away from the water's edge. When you read the headline, it usually says something like, 'Tony Takes A Twenty Trolling', or 'Boy Boats Big Beauty'. There they are, pictured with their catch – on a grass bank! How on earth did they get the fish ashore? Trout managers really need to put a stop to this practice. In my view, anglers that tow their catch ashore, for whatever reason, need to be penalized. An experienced boat angler will probably be able to tow a large pike ashore without harming it too much; it's the inexperienced boat anglers that concern me more. They may tow a pike ashore too fast, or hit the fish with an oar as they row, or even with the prop of an electric trolling motor. The only way to prevent the inexperienced boat angler towing their catch ashore is to put a complete stop to it.

Why cause a fish even more stress towing it ashore, when you can photograph it in the boat in private? I think that anglers who tow their catch ashore, are just out to seek attention for themselves. In the heat of the moment, they pay little or no thought at all to their catch. In all the years that I've fished trout reservoirs, I've never taken one fish ashore to be photographed. I go boat fishing because I enjoy it; when I catch a good fish, I want my memory and picture of the fish to be where I caught it! That is, in the boat, above the spot where the fish took.

A potential record is the only exception to taking a pike ashore, because a pike weighed aboard a boat will not be considered for record status. Ken Crow, fisheries manager at Bough Beech, has a policy that no angler must take pike ashore, full stop. If a pike looks big enough to beat the record, Ken will allow the fish to be weighed ashore, but it must be taken there in Ken's boat, which is equipped with a large water-filled tank.

We all make mistakes from time to time – we're only human. If we can eliminate mistakes before they happen by thinking ahead, then we're on the right track.

PLAYING FISH

The Summer Period

It has been said that we shouldn't fish for pike during the summer, but the people that come out with this never seem to put forward solid evidence as to why we shouldn't! I've caught many hundreds of pike on lures during the warm summer months and as far as I know, not a single fish has died. Gord Burton, the 'piking, plugging pirate of Pool Street', who has caught many thousands of pike during the summer months on lures, has also never experienced problems with summer-caught pike.

The anti-summer pikers have stated that pike suffer when caught during the summer period. I would agree that they suffer to some extent, but not much more than a big spawn-heavy winter female! Any fish when hooked will suffer a certain amount of stress. What both the summer and winter angler needs to be made aware of, is how to minimize the amount of stress caused to a fish. With regard to playing, this can be done by slowly and gently playing a fish to the net, or getting it there fast. Do not think 'This one's a goer, I'll play it for a few more minutes.'

If conditions allow, I prefer to play a fish slowly and gently to the net. Some pike that I've caught during the winter, I'm pretty sure, don't even know they're caught until they're safely netted, and even then they will often lie very still in the confines of my landing net.

The legendary 'piking plugging pirate of Pool Street' in action.

confirm, my personal-best pike of 33lb probably never knew it was hooked until it caught sight of my boat. Furthermore, when a fish is played gently, there is less risk of damaging its mouth, especially in the case of perch.

When conditions do not allow for slow gentle playing of a fish – for example, when fishing near structure, weed, anchor ropes and so on – extra pulling pressure *must* be applied to the rod.

Most of the pike that I have caught on lures during the summer period, go bananas as they realize something's not quite right! A jumping, tail-walking pike will suffer more stress than a non-jumping, non-tail-walking pike. In my view, a pike that jumps and tail-walks is a fish that is a cut above the rest! Whatever a fish does while playing it, though, I have never had a problem getting a summer-caught pike to swim off after capture. In fact, they usually leave my hands as aggressively as they attack my top-water lures – leaving me drenched!

Below are listed four ways of playing a fish; the first two should not cause the fish any suffering, but serious stress problems may result from the third and fourth.

1. **Slow and gentle**. Play the fish slowly and gently, letting it have as much line as it wants. When netted, the fish should be unhooked and returned to the water *quickly*. Better still, unhook the fish in the water, within the confines of the landing net.

2. **Apply pressure**. Apply extra rod pressure when playing a fish near structure, thick weed, or anchor ropes. Get the fish to the landing net as fast as you can, without letting it take too much line at any one time. When netted, the fish should be unhooked and returned quickly. When fishing near structure or from a boat, make sure you use a strong poundage line that is fairly abrasion-resistant; when excess pressure is applied to a fish, you can expect it to fight even harder, causing excess stress.

3. **Over-playing**. Over-playing basically

When boat fishing, the netting is suspended into the water from the spreader arms, the net handle being tied firmly to the gunnels of my boat, or in the rowlocks.

I prefer to play a fish slowly and gently because I feel that if it doesn't know it's caught, it will not go into stress mode until it does know, which could be as late as when it catches sight of my landing net, or realizes that it's in it! So playing a fish slowly could reduce prolonged stress by two or three minutes. As I'm sure my good friend Mark Wilson would means playing a fish too hard for too long. It is caused by not having the reel clutch set correctly for netting the fish. When eventually netted, unhooking and return is far too slow.

4. **Weak line.** Having to worry about the strength of your line while playing a fish spells disaster, because you start thinking that you need to play the fish for longer to wear it out before trying to land it. When eventually the fish is netted, unhooking and return is far too slow.

Have your clutch preset as tight as possible for the poundage of line used; for example, if you're using 15lb breaking strain line, preset your clutch to slip just under that. Use line that is strong enough for the playing method. If you're using small lures for seeking out perch and chub using a low poundage line, play the fish gently. The more pressure you apply to a fish, the more it will fight and the harder it will be to net. Do *not* use a poundage line that is too strong for the rod. If you do, make sure your clutch is set to slip before your rod snaps!

The Winter Period

During the winter, a fish's body metabolism slows right down (more so in still waters than in fast-flowing ones). Fish hooked in still or slow-moving water during the winter often come in far more easily than they would if caught during the summer. Because a fish puts up less of a fight, you may be led to think that it is not suffering stress – wrong! As I've said, any fish will suffer a stress response when it realizes something's not quite right, whatever the time of year.

Male pike caught during the winter period will probably suffer far less stress than a spawn-heavy female. Over the years of summer and winter fishing on the Norfolk Broads, I have seen many dead females; only one of them had died during the summer period. That fish, which probably went 30lb, I found on 16 June 1990; it had been dead for some time so I

didn't put its death down to angling – but you never know. The other dead females that I've seen have all died during the winter period; their deaths were probably brought about by being hooked, played for too long, handled badly, caught again too soon after a previous capture, or being kept too long on the bank or in a sack.

I spend far more time at the water's edge (or over the side of the boat) nursing winter-caught pike – waiting for them to swim off – than I do with summer-caught pike. The latter usually swim off within a couple of seconds, whereas a winter pike may take half a minute. My experiences, therefore, do not tally with those of anti-summer pike anglers; I can only assume their experience of summer piking is different from mine.

I have found that winter pike caught from deep waters that have the odd shallow bay or broad here and there, are much fitter than pike caught from shallow waters that do not have any deep-water areas. Pike caught from deep flowing rivers are, in my view, the fittest of them all, and rarely ever come to the net without putting up a fight. As I usually fish from a boat during the winter, with anchor ropes often out, I have to keep constant pressure on a fish to get it in quick, keeping it away from the anchor ropes, and my line clear of the keel. During the winter period, I would much rather catch five or six 7–10lb pike from a deep, fast-flowing river, than I would one 20lb pike from a shallow water. When at anchor, or oar trolling, I always tilt my outboard so it is clear of water, to eliminate the risk of my line getting caught around the shaft and prop.

LANDING

To start with, it is important to carry a landing net that can take the biggest of the predatory species – you never know when it will be your turn! Only seven hours before I caught my 33lb pike, I had said to my boat companion, Mark Wilson, 'I'll never catch a thirty-pounder,

Mark.' Within seven hours, I had! You must *always* be prepared, tackle-wise, for the fish of a lifetime to come along. I, personally, use a very deep 126cm (50in) landing net.

When landing a fish, especially a big fish, never put your net into the water until the fish is ready to be netted. A flying treble hook could easily get caught in the mesh of a landing net if held beneath the water's surface while playing a fish. I have lost at least one good pike because my boat partner put the landing net in the water too early, before the fish was ready to be netted. The fish brushed past the net, engaging a flying treble, then shook its head and levered the other treble free. It's not a very nice feeling seeing a good fish get away at the net, especially if it's caused by your, or your fishing partner's, stupidity!

I would say that around 80 per cent of the pike that I've hooked over the last couple of years have been hand-landed by me. I carefully check out the situation before slipping my fingers behind a pike's gill cover. If I'm not happy about a flying treble, I'll use a filleting glove, or the net as a last resort. I prefer to hand-land – even when a flying treble is showing – because, if netted, the flying treble will usually get caught up in the mesh of a landing net should the fish thrash or roll. Hand-landing can save both time and injury to a fish. If a fish does start to thrash about in the net before the flying treble is dealt with, wire cutters soon sort the problem out! Worry about the fish, not about a cheap length of trace wire or hook that can easily be replaced.

I recommend a filleting glove for hand-landing and unhooking. When you have more experience, the glove can be dispensed with, although, having received a bad cut in June 1993, I went back to wearing one!

Once a fish is in the net, I always remove the handle of my landing net and take hold of the spreader arms to lift the fish clear of the water. There is nothing worse than a long landing-net handle getting in the way.

Netting a Fish when Afloat

When the fish is ready for netting, I slip my landing net into the water beneath it, holding the bulk of the net in the same hand that's holding my landing-net handle (in my case, the left hand). When the fish is safely over the net, I release the netting from my grip, and raise the front of the handle, which in turn raises the spreader arms. I then fix the landing-net handle across the gunwhales of my boat. If possible, I unhook the fish in the confines of the net. After unhooking I leave the fish in the landing net (in the water) until I have everything ready: that is, my unhooking mat/weigh sling, forceps and scales, and my camera set up on the boat tripod. When all is ready, I remove the landing net handle from the spreader arms and roll the netting around the spreader arms. I then lift the fish (via the spreader arms) aboard for weighing. When fishing from a small boat, which I do most of the time, you really have to have your act together – for the fish's sake.

If you're not boat wise, I would advise you not to lean over the side of the boat to unhook a fish within the net. Also, make sure you wear a life-jacket at all times – even when sleeping. If you cannot swim, it's not a bad idea to wear a life-jacket for bank fishing as well – I nearly drowned once, when I slipped off the bank into freezing cold water.

UNHOOKING

While writing the first edition, I found that my unhooking methods could be considerably improved with the help of an accommodating tackle company! I phoned Terry Eustace to ask him if he could make me up a 1.2m (4ft) unhooking mat/weigh sling that could handle the smallest and largest of pike, as I was unimpressed with some of the 'Mickey Mouse' versions that I had seen. Terry saw the need for such a product and now markets a 1.2m (4ft) unhooking mat/weigh sling, called the 'Mega Ulti-Mat'. Never mind thirties, even a fifteen-pounder needs a mat of this size. At 1¾lb in weight, the mat/weigh sling is very easy to carry around using the shoulder strap fitted to the bag it comes with. Mobile anglers take note! With such items of tackle becoming readily available, there is no excuse for not carrying some sort of adequate unhooking mat. If money is a problem, a cheap alternative can be made from a camper's foam bed roll (1.8m/6ft long by 50cm/20in wide), or something similar, preferably with a smooth surface that will not 'de-slime' the fish. When not being used for its primary purpose, a well-padded mat can double up as a comfortable boat seat, or for overnighters, even as a pillow.

When lure fishing from the bank, if the situation allows, I will lay my weigh sling out and place my unhooking tools close by it. I set the camera up on the tripod and usually position my lure box in front of the mat (for a nice picture). As soon as I catch a fish, it goes straight on to the mat, is quickly unhooked, photographed and weighed, and then returned to the water. The complete process takes about one minute. If I have to work on a fish slightly longer for some reason, I will often return it without weighing or photographing – even if it's a big one. If you have a friend with you, things can be done even quicker, provided you both have your act together. If you don't, it can take a sight longer!

THE FISH'S WELL-BEING

Here are a few more guide-lines to bear in mind whenever you go fishing. Always try to plan everything out before you even hook a fish.

Careful return is most important.

One reason for using a 48-inch unhooking mat. This 19lb 8oz pike only just fitted.

Try to keep a fish away from your clothes when handling and photographing. De-sliming a fish on your clothes does it no good at all.

Choose a level non-stony area for unhooking. If you have to kneel to unhook a fish, no unhooking mat, however strong or thickly padded, will prevent jutting boulders from digging into your knees. They could also cause a fish serious headache problems!

Check your line and trace wire regularly for flaws. I like to retie the knot that secures my trace on a regular basis: that is, two or three times per session. Make sure also that your

hooks and hook hangers are in tip-top condition. Replace cheap and cheerful ones with better quality equipment.

Check before you leave home that you have everything important, including your landing net, unhooking mat and tools, filleting glove, and so on. Such items are of the utmost importance for the well-being of the fish.

Finally, return your fish with care. *Do not* let go of the fish until it makes an attempt to swim away. If you let go before it's ready to swim off, the fish may sink straight down to the bottom and die.

14

ESSENTIAL EQUIPMENT

RODS FOR LURE FISHING

Tackle chapters can be incredibly boring, but there is no doubt that using a balanced outfit, made up of good-quality equipment designed for the job, will make your lure fishing much more efficient and enjoyable. Lure fishing is nothing if not a specialized area.

A rod has to be both a lever for casting, which requires stiffness, and a spring for playing the fish, which requires flexibility. Any rod design is necessarily a compromise between these two opposing qualities. Modern materials mean that almost any required action can be created in a rod that is light, strong and virtually maintenance-free.

Many people start lure fishing with a regular carp or pike rod of around 11–12ft long. This length certainly gives good casting range and control over a fighting fish, but, while it's not a problem on open banks, a long rod can be a bit clumsy on more overgrown and restricted swims, and accurate close- to mid-range casting is not as easy as you might think. The traditional short spinning rod of 6–7ft suffers from the reverse problems: it is very accurate at shorter range and easy to manoeuvre in 'jungle' conditions, but you'll find yourself struggling with longer casts, and find it harder work playing the better fish. The best compromise of manoeuvrability, casting range and control, is a rod in the 8–10ft range, leaving longer rods for long range hurling of big lures, and shorter rods for boat work.

Most conventional pike rods have a test curve of 2lb or more. This is for throwing heavy baits and leads around, not for playing the fish. Since lure rods should ideally be matched to the weight of the general run of lures used, it is obvious that a rod capable of launching mackerel to the horizon won't be quite the thing for accurately flicking a $\frac{1}{2}$oz plug a mere twenty metres or so. A rod of around $1\frac{1}{2}$lb test curve will handle most lures under 2oz, and feel comfortable while doing so. If you regularly fish snaggy water full of huge fish, you may want to step up the power a bit, but don't get carried away. Remember, the late Dick Walker landed his 44lb record carp on a $1\frac{1}{2}$lb test curve rod.

Using a through-action rod means that you can take advantage of the 'soft rod–strong line' principle! That means you can step up the line strength beyond the range of the rod's test curve. The cushioning action of the rod, line stretch, and presetting the clutch to slip well before the rod or line snaps, prevent tackle breakage. The benefit of this is, that as long as you aren't ridiculously heavy-handed, you can use the whole of the rod's action, keeping to a lighter, more enjoyable outfit. After all, the average run of pike are less than 10lb. Why haul them in on a rod that feels like a dockyard crane, just because of its nominal line rating? Those ratings are pretty generalized (just multiply the test curve by five) and there is quite a bit of leeway you can take advantage of if you are sensible. For an ultimate illustration of the effect, just watch a fly fisherman: rod like a willow wand, line like an anchor rope!

It is obvious from all this that there is no such thing as an all-round lure rod, but it is possible to get closer to an all-rounder than it is in many branches of coarse fishing. A rod of about $9\frac{1}{2}$ft, with a test curve of around $1\frac{1}{4}$lb and a progressive through action, is a very ver-

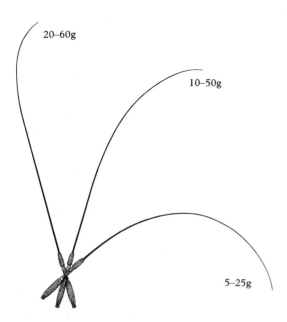

20–60g

10–50g

5–25g

These are the rod actions the author would expect for the casting weights quoted.

rods, designed for use with multiplier reels, are fun, but can put quite a strain on the wrist when playing a lively fish. If you want a lure rod for use exclusively with multipliers, look for a reel fitting with a projecting 'trigger'. This gives the hand a firmer, more secure grip on the rod.

Use a regular carp or pike rod until you are sure that you like lure fishing, or if you only expect to be an occasional plug-chucker.

Balancing Point

The choice of lure rod for fishing for small or large predators, is, in my view, a very important one. Careful thought should be undertaken before rushing out and spending your hard-earned money. Aim to buy a lure rod and reel set-up that will balance on the edge of your index finger, directly above the reel spool. This is particularly important when choosing a very lightweight, low casting-weight set-up.

Heavy duty 10–12ft lure rods can tend to be a bit front-heavy, which is only to be expected. If your favourite reel doesn't balance your new heavy-duty lure rod up as described, the only other way to achieve balance is to glue lead weight into the end of the rod's butt. Believe it or not, an additional counter-balance weight will appear to make your rod and reel set-up lighter!

Buying a Rod

Below is an up-to-date (2001) list of rods that I am currently using.

Retrieve Technique 1 'RT1'

The RT1 Jerkbaiter is a 6ft 6in trigger grip lure rod capable of casting lures from 28–84g (1–3oz) with ease. Although termed 'Jerkbaiter', it is absolutely spot-on for casting medium-weight crankbaits, spinners, spoons and the like. The left-hand wind Shimano Calcutta 251 and Abu UC5601C complement this rod nicely.

satile lure rod, handling the widest possible range of lures with reasonable comfort and control. It needs to be light enough, action- and weight-wise, to let you enjoy the smaller pike, perch, zander, chub or trout.

Nowadays, good-quality lure rods are sold with a lure casting-weight range quoted, rather than a test curve. At 1oz of casting weight per pound of test curve, and 28g to the ounce, a 1/lb rod would have an average lure rating of 35g and so on.

Fittings are a matter of personal taste, but aim for modern rings lined with aluminium oxide, since they will not groove quickly from the constant casting the way chromed and stainless ones sometimes do. Always have a screwlock reel fitting. If you have ever had a reel drop off with an angry fish on the other end of the line, you will not need to ask why! Handles can range from duplon split grips to the traditional full cork type. Again, choose what you feel most comfortable with.

Short, American-style pistol-grip casting lure

Rod and reel balance is very important to the serious lure angler.

Retrieve Technique 2 'RT2'

The RT2 Jerkbaiter is a beefed-up version of the RT1. It is the same in looks as the RT1 but can cast much heavier lures, ranging from 28g (1oz) to 112g (4oz). Like the RT1, it is absolutely spot-on for casting medium and heavy jerkbaits, crankbaits, spinners, spoons and the like. If you like using big lures loaded with ball bearings, as I do, this rod can really make them rattle. Again, the left-hand wind Shimano Calcutta 251 and Abu UC5601C complement this rod nicely.

Retrieve Technique 3 'RT3'

The RT3 'Medium Lure 'N' Bait' is a 9ft high-tensile, progressive through action lure/bait fishing rod, capable of casting lures from 28–56g (1–2oz). It is ideal for all types of fishing methods and techniques, for example light to medium bait fishing, plug fishing, spinning, top-water lure fishing, light sea fishing, and lots more! This is, in my opinion, a very good all-round rod. To complement the rod, the Shimano Stradic X 3000GTM and 4000GTM models would be ideal, loaded with 30lb braided line. For bait fishing, I recommend a Shimano Baitrunner or similar.

Retrieve Technique 4 'RT4'

The RT4 'Big Lure 'N' Bait' is a beefed-up version of the RT3. Without doubt, this is one of my all-time favourite lure and bait fishing rods. I use nothing else when it comes to bait fishing for big toothy critters on the Norfolk

Broads. I have boated many, many hundreds of pike, to just over 30lb, with this rod. It is rated at 28–112g (1–4oz). Personally, I cast a 4oz weight and whole herring with it quite comfortably. This rod, like the RT3, has a multitude of uses – bass fishing springs to mind! Reels to complement this rod are as follows. For lure fishing, I recommend the Shimano Stradic X 4000GTM, loaded with 30–50lb braided line. For bait fishing, I highly recommend Shimano Baitrunner reels, loaded with 50lb braid. Shimano Baitrunners are, in my opinion, in a class of their own.

Note: Make sure the reel clutch is set to slip at a sensible fish-pulling pressure when using strong breaking strain lines.

Retrieve Technique 5 'RT5'

The RT5 'All Rounder' is my all-time favourite lure fishing rod. Its high tensile strength and progressive through action make it the ideal rod for twitching, flicking and popping lures, that can stimulate pike and often trigger them to strike. At 7ft 6in long, it is light in weight and very, very strong. It has landed carp and pike to 30lb. If it had not been for this superb lure rod, my clients and I would not have stimulated, nor boated, a quarter of the pike that we have done over the years – a bold statement if ever there was one! To complement this rod, I highly recommend the Shimano Stradic X 3000GTM or 4000GTM, loaded with 30lb braided line. Personally, I use Newtech Power Cable braided line for all of my lure and bait fishing: 20lb for lightweight lure fishing, 30lb for medium lure fishing, and 50lb for heavy lure fishing and bait fishing.

Retrieve Technique 6 'RT6'

The RT6 'Ultralite' is a scaled-down version of the RT5, but still 7ft 6in in length. Designed solely for the ultralite lure angler, it can cast lures from 3.5–35g ($^1/_8$–$1^1/_4$oz). It is ideal for pike, zander, perch, chub, grayling and the like. The reel to complement this rod, in my opinion,

would be a Stradic X 1000GTM loaded with 15–20lb braided line.

Remember, never overfill the spool when loading line on to the reel. $^1/_8$in from the rim of the spool is absolutely spot-on.

REELS

Multiplier Reels

Here in the UK, for some mysterious reason, we prefer to use left-hand wind multiplier reels. I say for 'some mysterious reason', because American anglers prefer to use right-hand wind multiplier reels! Why that is, I don't know. Like us, the majority of Americans write with their right hand, but unlike us, they prefer to wind with their right hand too – strange!

I am not going to try to steer you towards buying a high- or low-profile multiplier reel here, but just offer you some advice. A multiplier reel should feel comfortable as you grip it, that is, when coupled to the rod. As people's hands vary in size, it pays to pop in and try out a few reels before buying. Ask if you can couple each reel that you look at to a/your rod, to see how it feels. With my experience of teaching and guiding clients over the last few years, I have come to appreciate that just because something suits me, it doesn't mean that it will suit everybody.

Multiplier reels have come a long way since writing the first edition of *The Art of Lure Fishing*. There are so many new models available in the UK now that it would be impossible for me to name them all, or talk about all their subtle little differences! All I will say is, look again at what I, personally, use and recommend, and go from there. *See* RT1 and RT2 under 'Buying a Rod' above.

Fixed-Spool Reels

With regard to fixed-spool reels, Shimano takes some beating. Shimano's new Stradic X series are spot-on for lure fishing. The thing that I particularly like about these reels is their back end clutches, which are far stronger than those of any previous models I have ever used. The Stradic X 1000GTM is ideal for ultralite lure fishing. The Stradic X 2500GTM, Stradic X 3000GTM and Stradic X 4000GTM are well suited to medium lure fishing. The Stradic X 4000GTM is also ideal for heavy lure fishing too. These are my preferred choice of fixed-spool reels – but they may not be yours. Nothing I say is written in stone!

What you should perhaps take into account is that I have probably landed more pike over the last twelve years than any other angler in the UK. The tackle I use has stood the test of time. I do not change tackle regularly. If something works well for me, I stick with it. I see no point in changing rods, reels or line when there is no need to. I am definitely not one of those 'in vogue' anglers who have to have all the latest gear – properly tested or not. It is here that I must bite my lip and stay silent about tackle that I know from experience has design faults – faults that I have pointed out to manufacturers, only for them to carry on selling the product. Believe me, it doesn't take me very long to find any fault that has managed to elude prior

testers. There is factory testing and there is hard casting, hard-fighting fish testing: the latter finds faults much faster than any robot's precision opening and closing of a bail arm to see how long a spring will last. I dare Mr Manufacturer to let me test out any of his new products before releasing them for sale! I will never be offered the job of being a tackle consultant, simply because I am too honest when it comes to reviewing products! If I think something that I've been sent to test is bad news, I won't use it, let alone review it. I always try to put the fish first.

LINE

Line possibly takes more stick in lure fishing than in any other fishing style. It is probably fair to say that line can get the equivalent of a year's regular wear in a matter of weeks when lure fishing, so it is obvious that you are going to have to pay particular attention to it. The only way to be safe is to check the state of your line constantly and replace it regularly. Most good lines are available on bulk spools and, not only is this the cheapest way for a lure

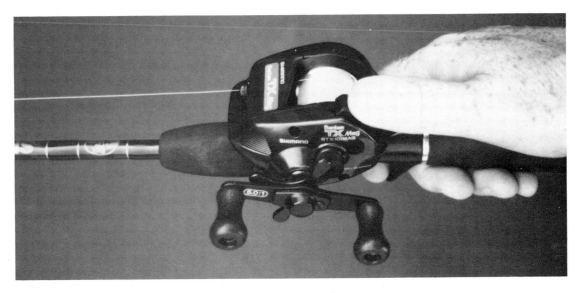

A pistol-grip casting rod, equipped with a low-profile multiplier reel.

fisherman to buy, it also encourages you to change it on a regular basis. Do not risk one more trip with 'iffy' line as that could be fatal to a fish.

Nylon lines needs to be supple to cast well (especially when using a fixed-spool reel), as well as tough and abrasion-resistant. Since those two qualities are mutually opposed, all good line is something of a compromise. You also need to consider knot strength, impact-resistance and stretch, all of which tend to vary from brand to brand. Also bear in mind that all nylon line is weaker when wet, and that the breaking strain quoted is usually dry. One thing I would advise you to do is forget these pre-stretched and ultra-thin lines, since line thickness is not that critical when lure fishing.

Some brands overrate their lines with regard to breaking strain, and some underrate them. Watch out for IGFA-rated and tournament lines; these are usually made to break at less than the quoted breaking strain. They are made for line class fishing – avoid them at all costs! At the other end of the spectrum, many of you may remember the old Sylcast 11lb line. Sylcast eventually rerated this at 14lbs, which is what it really was! Some American lines are still underrated this way, which is not totally truth-ful, but at least you know the quoted breaking strain is probably a minimum and not a maxium! The easiest way to be safe is to choose a known brand with a name to lose: most name brands have a high basic quality. What you can do is find which one has a balance of characteristics that suits you. Try a 'reel-fill' spool, which is about 200 yards of several different possibles, and see which you like most. Then buy a bulk spool.

At the time of writing, I personally am using Newtech Power Cable braided line in breaking strains 20lb, 30lb and 50lb, which I consider to be the best lines for my lure and bait fishing needs: 20lb for lightweight lure fishing, 30lb for medium lure fishing, and 50lb for heavy lure fishing and bait fishing. It is ideal line for when it comes to mimicking chicks leaving the nest!

Imagine this: you cast your imitation rat lure into the reeds and slowly start to twitch it back out. As the rat lure plops onto the water, a pike lying in wait at the edge of the reed bed hits it hard – and I mean hard! It totally engulfs the rat lure. 'YES! – I'm into a big one!' You get the idea. This technique (using 30lb braided line) would not be possible using stretchy mono line. The slightest nick in a reed stem, and it would be time to up anchor and rescue the lure, disturbing the swim on the way! Braided line is also superb for 'weed walking' lures over weed and lily beds.

Nowadays, I never go below 20lb braided line for serious lure fishing, and I only use that in relatively clear, snag-free water, when ultra-lite lure fishing. An area of water that I used to fish when I lived in Southend-on-Sea, Essex, required casts of up to 70yd to reach pike-holding features. Lighter line was used to get the distance with the required lures: I needed to use 8lb mono to get that distance! Nowadays, I can easily achieve that distance using 20lb and 30lb braided line – how times have changed! Believe me when I say that if I had to go back to using mono, I would give up fishing. For those that still use mono, though, please read on.

Store your line spools in a relatively even temperature and out of direct sunlight, prefer-ably in a box or bag, or wrapped in tin foil. Take the spool off your reel when you are not using it and wrap it in tin foil as well, especially if your reels are stored in sunlight! The ultra-violet rays in sunlight can literally destroy the strength of nylon line. For the same reason, when you buy line from a shop, insist on getting it in its original wrapping, or from a box. Buy your line from a shop with a good turnover, because then the line is more likely to be fresh stock. Do not buy exposed spools from shelves, counters or even – God forbid! – the window. You don't know how long it's been sitting there sunbathing, soaking up the ultraviolet.

Finally, use knots that retain a high percent-age of the original breaking strain, although

Various tackle items used by the author.

any knot will weaken the line to some degree. Good examples are the Grinner knot, the Palomar knot, the uni-knot and the tucked half blood knot, all over 95 per cent strength. Tie them carefully and moisten them before drawing them tight. Minimize your weak spots as much as possible.

TRACE WIRE

For pike fishing you need a wire trace. Use one even if you are after chub or perch, if there is a risk of pike being present, as a small pike can slice through nylon line like a hot knofe through butter. The only exception to the wire trace rule is when using flies. Modern stranded stainless wire is thinner than nylon of the same breaking strain, and it is possible to get very

fine 10lb breaking strain wire as insurance when after other species. For pike there is no real need to use wire of less than 15lb, and 20lb is even better. The main brand names like Marlin, Berkley and Drennan Seven Strand are all of high quality and can be easily twisted when trace making. I currently use 20lb and 28lb QED for medium and heavy lure work and 15lb Drennan Seven Strand for light lure work. Drennan wire, pound for pound, is thinner than QED wire.

I only use twisted traces, *never* crimped ones, as there is always a risk that wire strands will be damaged as you squeeze the crimp. Also, continual lure casting can weaken the wire where it enters the crimp. Weakening is caused by the wire grating against the edge of the crimp, or by what I call the whiplash effect! Even if only one of the seven strands of wire break, you lose a lot more than just one-seventh of the original breaking strain, more like three-sevenths. The biggest risk with wire is breaking: if a trace gets sharply kinked, scrap it! The life of a fish is worth a lot more than a few inches of wire. Nylon-coated traces do not tend to kink, but they are rather thick and clumsy.

In my mind, 45cm (18in) is the minimum safe length for a lure trace. A hooked pike will often roll on the trace and end up with it wrapped around itself. When that happens, your nylon line will be in danger of being severed by the pike's teeth. If the nylon line should encounter the pike's teeth, you could have a bite-off, which will result in a pike swimming around with a lure attached to it, which may possibly cause its death.

The odd lure or two can suffer action-wise when a long trace is used, for example, Heddon's Tiny Crazy Crawler. Sometimes it's possible to overcome this problem by twisting the wire directly to the eye of the lure, eliminating the weight of a snap-link and swivel. Any such lures can then be kept pre-rigged. To neutralize the weight of the trace, balsawood, or a small polystyrene ball, can be drilled and slid on to the wire when it's being made.

SWIVELS AND SNAP-LINKS

Always use the best quality swivels and snap links when making up wire traces. Fox round-eye swivels roll easily and are very reliable. Swivels make good attachments even when used with lures that don't actually spin, that is, for eliminating line twist when playing a hard-fighting, tail-walking, twisting and turning, thrashing and crashing pike! Don't use too small a swivel. I have bought some in the past that have given way while testing them for strength. Some swivels have the breaking strain quoted on the packet. I recommend 30lb or stronger. If you find revolving lures are causing line twist, try using ball-bearing swivels, either the traditional long Hardy type, or the more compact

American type. A 'Charlie-type' anti-kink vane will eliminate any line twist.

For snap-links I prefer the American duolock type. Not only do they have a rounded wire loop which doesn't interfere with the action of the lure, but they are designed so that the stronger the pull, the more tightly they lock shut. Traditional safety-pin snaps are very poor in this regard. I currently use size 7 and 10 Fox Safe-Lok links and Fox Safe-Lok link swivels. They are fine for most sizes of lure.

MISCELLANEOUS ITEMS

Leaving aside the actual lures, rods and reels, there are a number of other items that you will need. Some are absolutely essential, and anyone caught lure fishing without them should be chopped up and used as ground bait! Other items are optional and will vary according to the kind of fishing you are intending to do on the day.

I always carry an assortment of small items . . . I wouldn't leave home without spare hooks, traces, snap-links, swivels, split rings, sharpening stone, nail clippers/scissors, a selection of weights and a spool of 4lb line for weak links. A set of small screwdrivers, or a top-of-the-range Swiss army knife can come in very handy for undertaking running repairs on reels and plugs.

UNHOOKING EQUIPMENT

Forceps, in my opinion, are a must for unhooking treble hooks, doubles or singles. I always carry three pairs of forceps with me – one 20cm (8in) and two 30cm (12in) pairs. Forceps are one of those things you can lose absolutely anywhere if you're not careful. For ease of location, I keep mine on a quick-release clip, attached to one of my jeans belt loops.

A filleting glove, or a leather glove, is also essential if you have never hand-landed pike – and you intend to give it a try.

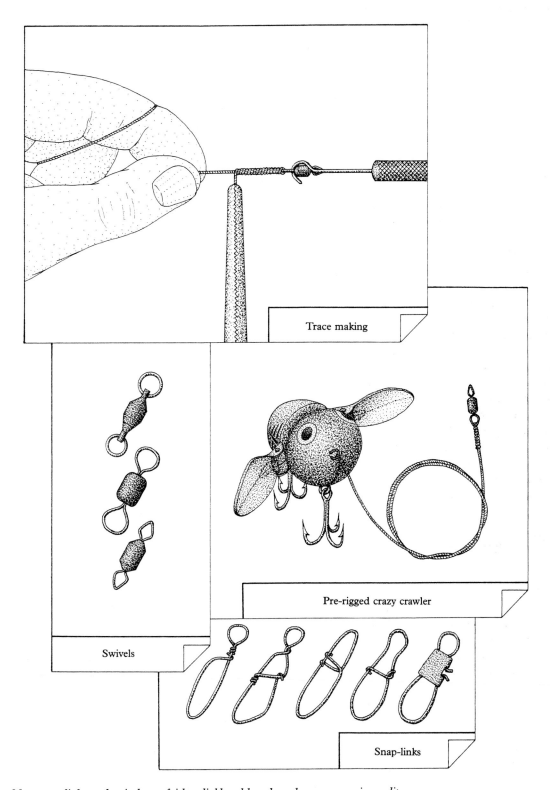

Trace making

Swivels

Pre-rigged crazy crawler

Snap-links

Most snap-links and swivels are fairly reliable, although makes can vary in quality.

Another vital unhooking item that I carry with me, is a rubber mouth pad, which is one of my own inventions. I call it a 'third hand', and use it at times when a third hand is required; for example, for keeping tension on the trace (if required) while unhooking. For bait fishing, I use a mouth pad that has a swivel and snap-link attacked, and clip the snap-link of the mouth pad on to the swivel of the wire trace tied to the main line. I grip the mouth pad in my teeth and lower the fish to apply tension to the trace. A mouth pad with snap-link can come in very handy when you have a hook set deep inside the fish's mouth, near the entrance to the throat, or even in the throat itself – heaven forbid.

I use various different designs of mouth pad. For lure fishing, I use one that has a long wire arm fitted, which has a hook at the end, like a pirate's missing hand! I use the hook version for supporting a free(d) treble while I unhook

another; the freed hook is thus prevented from falling back into the mouth.

You will also need some kind of unhooking mat to avoid damaging the fish.

Even if you prefer to hand-land your fish, still take a landing net with you: the day you hook a big fish from a jungle bank, you'll be glad you did. I would recommend a 30in (75cm) or larger frame, equipped with knotless netting. A landing net equipped with mesh netting of, say, 1.25–2cm (fi–flin), will help to minimize the risk of lure hooks snagging in it – and make it easier to release them from it. It can take ages to release treble hooks from micro-mesh netting – be warned.

For mobile lure fishing, I use a 30in-diameter, deep-pan landing net, manufactured by Quality Fishing Plugs. Its mesh is of the 2cm (flin) knotless type. When boat and static fishing, I use a 50in specimen landing net, manufactured by K. Taylor Precision

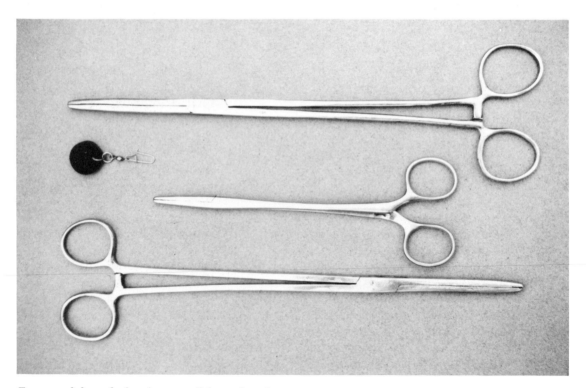

Forceps and the author's unique snap-link mouth pad.

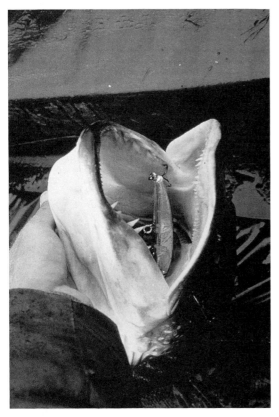

A 15cm (6in) set of forceps would be of no use on this fish! Always carry long forceps. The teeth on this 24lb 8oz pike could cause the ill-equipped angler quite a few problems.

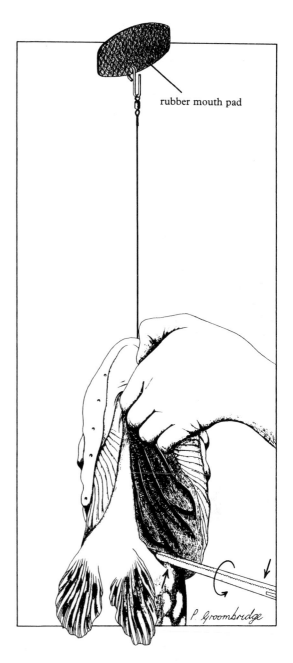

rubber mouth pad

P. Groombridge

The author's rubber mouth pad with a quick-fit wire system.

Engineering, which has 1.25cm (fiin) mesh, also knotless. Both landing nets are well and truly capable of engulfing a fifty-pounder – don't I wish!

This brings us to strong wire cutters. It's very unlikely that a lure will become so awkwardly lodged that the hook will need to be cut to release it, but it might. More like a netted fish will snag the lure's free hook barbs in the netting. In both cases, if you can't quickly and easily free the hook, don't mess about – cut it. A healthy pike can cope with a bit of residual hook susprisingly well, and you can free the remains of the hook from the net very easily.

Strong wire cutters also come in handy if you

The author's brother-in-law, 6ft 4in tall Sonny Redzimsky, displays Charlie's huge landing nets.

get a hook embedded in your flesh. Firstly, cut the split ring/hook hanger of the lure, releasing the lure from the hook. With the lure removed, you can work on the embedded hook far more easily. If the barb of the hook is buried out of sight, you should visit the hospital. If the hook point and barb of a treble hook has entered your flesh and reappeared elsewhere, you will need to cut the shank of the hook, leaving as much of it as you can for pushing and pulling purposes, in order to pull the shank through your flesh. If removing the remains of the hook proves too stressful, as it did for Steve Gamble some years back, go to a hospital.

A first aid kit, or box of fabric plasters, are a must if you hand-land fish, or even if you don't. While writing this book, I suffered my worst ever cut at the teeth of a pike. The cut really needed a couple of stitches, but since the nearest hospital was twenty-five miles away, I got to work with my first aid kit and soon had the blood flow under reasonable control. I was able to fish again within half an hour – I think how long I would have been up at the hospital.

OPTIONAL EXTRAS

High on my list of optional extras would have to be food and drink. When I go lure fishing without sustenance, I'm never away for too long!

If you want an accurate record of your catch, you may want a good set of scales, a properly designed weigh sling, a camera and accessories,

Steve Gamble very kindly demonstrates how to get an embedded hook out of his finger, using forceps. Unfortunately, Steve never succeeded – Norwich hospital did!

bulkier gear; Wychwood makes a very tough and roomy one. Alternatively, you could use a specimen-style rucksack. There are a lot of small compartmented plastic boxes on the market, which will take lures and other bits and pieces. By using them you can be very selective as to what you take, but avoid boxes made of hard brittle plastic or ones with poor hinges and catches, or you'll find everything rattling around in the bottom of the bag one day.

Plastic cantilever tackle boxes aren't too bad, but if dropped or knocked over everything gets tangled up together. I found the answer in American satchel-type tackle boxes. These are rather like briefcases made of polythene plastic, with an adjustable, compartmented interior. Some open at both sides, some on only one. I

and even a notebook and pen. A good keepnet, sack or pike tube can be handy for holding fish for a short time, while you get everything set up for photos and weighing. Carry tent pegs to hold your sack/tube in position; *don't* tie it to grass or reeds.

Polarized glasses and a peaked cap, or sun visor, are handy in a lot of conditions, not just bright sunshine. Miniature binoculars or a small telescope will enable you to scan the water in detail, while a tube of metal polish will enable you to keep a shine on spoons and metal blades. If you fish from a boat you could take a lure retriever for freeing snagged lures, and a boat magnet for retrieving metal objects dropped overboard. Americans fish with boat magnets around bridges retrieving guns and similar items thrown from them!

On a boat you can usually find space for extra gear, but if you are on foot, remember you are going to have to carry everything. This may be important to all those of you not built like Arnold Schwarzenegger! A good hold-all with a shoulder strap can swallow a lot of the

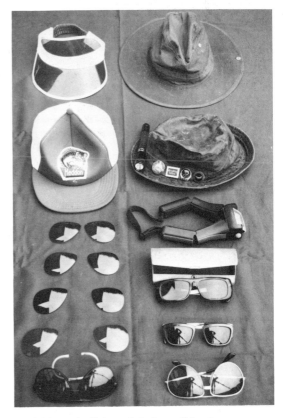

Useful items for light and dark conditions!

prefer the type that only open on one side, as you do not have to keep turning the box over to get to different lures. Most have translucent lids so you can see what's inside, and the compartments are all sealed from each other to avoid tangles. The two biggest ranges of lure boxes are made by Flambeau and by Plano. They are not cheap, but in my opinion, well worth the investment. Steve Gamble and I used to use the Plano Magnum 1257 Over and Under box, and find it absolutely superb.

Tackle Tip

Put together your gear and try carrying it around before going off to fish. That way you'll find out what carrying set-up suits you personally, and also what you can definitely live without!

Put everything together before you set off.

15

PREPARATION FOR THE DAY'S FISHING

I think the best way of explaining how to prepare for a day's fishing would be to tell you how I go about it. Others may do it differently, some might not bother at all. Somewhere, sometime, they will suffer!

There have been too many times over the years when I have arrived at a water many miles from home, only to find that I'd forgotten to load an important item of tackle. The worst instance I can remember was when I forgot to pack a spare reel. On arriving at a river many miles from home, I unloaded my lure fishing gear and set off along the bank. When I got to a known hot spot, I started to cast a lure about. Within five minutes of my starting to fish, my reel's bail-arm spring broke, and that was the end of that day's fishing. There have been many other times when I have forgotten something of importance. As I tend to fish on the spur of the moment, mistakes do happen unless I follow certain procedures carefully.

As you can appreciate, if you are going to be fishing miles from home the following day, it pays to have everything needed ready and waiting. What I do nowadays is keep lists of all the possible items of tackle that I may need. All I have to do is check down my lists before I leave home, or better still the night before, to see if everything is laid out ready and waiting. I use five lists for reference: boat items, tackle items, bait, miscellaneous items, and clothing items. Below I have included bait under tackle items.

THE LISTS

These lists are all based on what I personally use. You don't have to use the same items; use what suits you.

Boat Items

Boat   I have two boats. One is 2m (7ft) long which fits into the back of a van. The boat is very buoyant due to built-in buoyancy tanks which act as seats; I wouldn't recommend the use of a small boat that did not have buoyancy of some kind built in. My other boat is a 4m (14ft) aluminium craft. It has to be transported on a trailer.

Outboard engines   I use a 4hp petrol engine which fits on to either of my boats. Remember to take a can of petrol with a shot of oil in, and a large petrol funnel. I also use a Minn Kota 35W electric engine. Sometimes I mount the petrol and electric outboard on to my boat at the same time, since the electric is very useful for approaching an area quietly, or trolling, whereas the petrol is good for getting me from A to B quickly. In winter, time is of the essence!

Oars   A good set of oars is a must if you are going to oar-troll, or if the outboard fails.

Rowlocks   I always take a spare rowlock in case one should happened to snap or fall overboard, as has happened in the past. I tend to use plastic rowlocks which are prone to snapping in cold weather, but have the advantage of being kind to the oars and reducing noise! If you hire boats regularly, it pays to take your own rowlocks and oars just in case. Hire boat fixtures and fittings are never quite as you would expect. If you arrive at a water late, you can also expect your hire boat to have been picked clean by the vultures!

Anchors Where I fish, light and heavy mud anchors are in order, and I make my own using sand and cement. My two lightweight mud anchors weigh 12lb each, and my heavier ones 28lb each. On some waters, you may find a grappling anchor necessary. To make a 28lb mud anchor, grease the inside of a 5-litre plastic tub, then fill it with not too wet a mix of sand and cement (two parts sand to one part cement). When levelled off, push an exhaust clamp (or similar) down into the middle of the levelled mix; this acts as a rope attachment point. Make good around the eye to finish. Again, if you hire boats, it may pay to take your

own anchors. Finally, make sure your anchor rope is sound and long enough to reach the bottom!

Battery I use a 105AH deep-cycling battery. If you buy yourself an electric outboard you'll need a battery with a good AH rating. My battery not only has to run my electric outboard, it also has to power a fishfinder and a 250 candlepower spotlight. Deep-cycling batteries are made for regular recharging, which a car battery is not. Do not waste your money, buy right in the first place.

Fishfinder and transducer I use a Humminbird fishfinder/depth sounder. A fishfinder/depth sounder is a must for locating prey fish as well as mapping the bottom of a lake, river or reservoir. If you can find prey fish or features like drop-offs, you will usually be hot on the

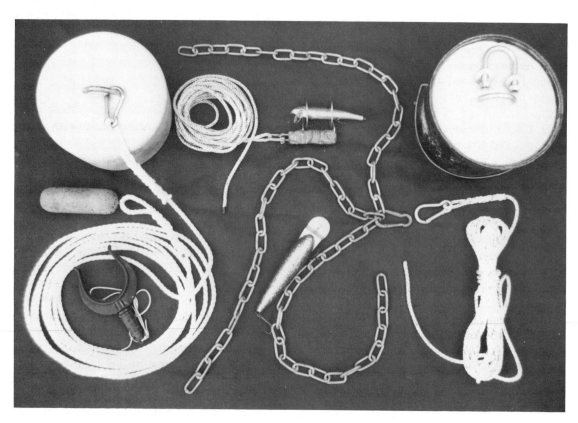

Mud anchors; anchor rope with cork floats fitted; hound dog lure retriever; chain lure retriever; strong rope; spare rowlock; exhaust clamps; 5 litre tub.

trail of pike, perch, and possibly zander.

Some hire boats are made of wood, which means a transducer with a suction cup will not suck properly, because of the uneven surface of painted wood. When I fish a water for the first time using a hire boat, I always take a clamp and a piece of wood just in case; the dimensions are 90cm long, by 5cm wide, by 2cm thick (3ft × 2in × ¾in). If the hire boat does have an uneven surface, I tape my transducer to the wood, and then clamp the wood to the aft of the boat.

Boat rod-rests I use various types of boat rod-rests (otherwise known as outriggers). My favourite type has to be the Taylor rod-rest, which was designed for use on trout fishery hire boats.

Some projecting boat gunwhales need to be blocked below the projection of the gunwhale to take a rod-rest securely. If you use rod-rests and hire boats regularly, you will know that it pays to have a few blocks of wood with you, of varying thicknesses.

Rope I use a good strong synthetic rope for anchoring. I also use the same rope for tying up to the bankside. It is attached to the anchor with a quick-release clip.

Sponge and water bailer Any boat will get a build-up of water. It collects in the bottom of the boat from anchors, fish (if you are lucky!), leaks and rain. A bailer is also handy in rough conditions for acting as a toilet, or protecting your modesty!

Downrigger Ball weight.

Carpet A carpet is handy for various reasons. It stops you and your tackle slipping about the boat, deadens noise, keeps your feet a bit warmer in winter and helps protect fish. I use a plastic mat (or unhooking mat/weigh sling) as well as the carpet. Additional small carpet mats are handy for resting anchors/batteries on.

Life-jacket Even good swimmers can drown. Always have some kind of life-jacket or flotation device along; I use a full flotation suit which is warm as well as safe. Never take children afloat without life-jackets.

Lure retriever A commercial or home-made lure retriever tends to be more effective when used from a boat, and it can save you a lot of time and money! A lure retriever is a must when trolling lures deep.

Boat magnet A powerful boat magnet can retrieve quite heavy metal objects lost overboard.

Drain plug Nowadays, I always check to make sure my boat's drain plug has not been tampered with, or that I've screwed it back in place after draining water. On at least three occasions, I have gone afloat with the drain plug missing from its hole. If your boat, or a boat you hire, is a single-skin vessel, a missing drain plug will soon become apparent: water will start washing around your feet. A double-skinned boat's cavity may fill up before you realize something's wrong. The first sign will be water breaking over the gunwhales! Be warned, and check the drain plug before launching any boat.

Tackle

Rods Various.

Reels Various.

Lures Assortment. Also a sharpening stone, and polish for spoons.

Licences For boat and rod.

Landing net I use a 50in (130cm) specimen landing-net frame, equipped with 1.25cm (½in) mesh netting, or a 30in (75cm) diameter pan-type frame, equipped with 2cm (¾in) netting. Both landing nets have deep netting and are capable of holding the largest of fish. I prefer to hand-land when possible. If you do not like the idea of hand-landing, I would suggest that you use 1.25–2cm (½–¾in) mesh netting on your frame. Lure hooks caught up in micro-mesh netting can cause all sorts of problems.

Weight sling I use the Terry Eustace 1.2m (4ft) unhooking mat/weigh sling, the Mega Ulti-Mat.

Sack When the need arises to retain the fish, I use a very large sack, which I prefer to a tube. However, in some circumstances, for example near a sloping concrete reservoir dam wall, or in gravel shallows, a tube may stop a pike damaging itself against the hard bottom. I would rather let a fish go straight back than take the risk of damaging it.

Tackle bag I use a big one, or a large weigh sling to carry things. Before setting off, I check in the bag/weigh sling to make sure all my important small items are present.

Forceps Three pairs. Two pairs of 30cm (12in) and one pair of 20cm (8in).

Hook disgorgers

Scales I carry Avon dial scales that will handle fish up to 30lb. I also carry a small dial scale that weighs fish up to 50lb – you never know!

Traces A selection of ready-whipped traces made of 5–20lb breaking strain wire.

Wire cutters I always carry a good set of wire cutters. If a trace needs cutting for some reason, I do not hesitate.

Hook cutters It is important to have a good pair of metal cutters with you. When a 'hook-in-finger' situation arises, you may need to cut the shank of a hook to get it out.

Lights I take a torch and headlamp when lure, or bait fishing from the bank or boat. For boat fishing, I also take a 250 candlepower spotlight, along with spare batteries and bulbs.

Weights I use ½oz, 1oz, 1½oz and 2oz leads for trolling and leger retrieving lures.

Oil and syringe

Silicon tube Various uses. Various sizes from 1mm to 3mm.

Floats For controlling the working depth of a lure or bait. I prefer to make my own.

Beads I use shock-absorber beads, stop-knot beads and quick-change beads.

Snap-links I use Fox Safe-Lok Snaps in sizes 7 and 10.

Spare hooks Spare hooks for lures.

Swivels I use American ball-bearing SAMPO swivels, Mustad 90lb and Berkley 65–100lb ones.

Line grease I sometimes use line grease when I'm using small top-water lures or flies and bugs.

Bait A few handfuls of groundbait, maggots, or worm, can come in useful, as they cause roach, perch and other prey fish to shoal. Shoaling prey fish sometimes bring in the predators!

Miscellaneous Items

Survival knife I use a Swiss army knife that has everything you might possibly need for running repairs: screwdrivers, a magnifying glass for those cold winter days, a pen, can-opener, pliers, and even a corkscrew for the champagne!

Compass

Polarized sunglasses Very handy on bright sunny days, especially when the water is calm and clear.

First aid kit

Camera Canon EOS 600 (28mm to 70mm zoom lens), and a Canon flash. Remember the film! I also use a Fuji Digital 2.3MP.

Rod-rest and camera adaptor I find a rod-rest far less bulky than a tripod. I prefer to use a rod-rest and camera adaptor when I'm doing a lot of walking.

Tripod Sometimes I prefer to carry a tripod. I use both a large and a miniature tripod, the latter being ideal for boat work.

Scope I also carry a 7cm (3in) spotting scope in my camera bag with 8 × 20 power, or a pair of binoculars.

Radio and watch It can get lonely out there.

Fox bedchair For overnight stints.

Sleeping bag German army, for overnight stints.

Large umbrella For overnight stints.

Bivvy For overnight stints.

Food Hot and cold. Tins of curried food go down well!

Drink Non-alcoholic. Remember coffee, milk, sugar and fresh water.

Cutlery

Coleman cooker

Petrol Small funnel for cooker.

Saucepan I cook and eat direct from the saucepan.

Lighter For cooker.

Careful preparation is required for success.

Change For phone.
Toilet paper

Clothing

Hat Thermal.
Hat Brimmed against the sun.
Jumper Warm.
Jacket Thermal.
Body warmer Thermal.
One-piece suit Flotation type.
Ground sheet For covering cloths, bedchair and so on.
Socks Thermal. I highly recommend Helly Hanson socks.
Boots Skee Tex.
Boots Waders. These are for bank fishing, or launching my boat – I never go afloat wearing them.
Mittens Thermal. Mittens will warm your hands up in a matter of seconds. I highly recommend Helly Hanson mittens.

That's about it, I think! I hang my lists somewhere close to hand ready for the following day. Usually I have one complete list indoors, one in the garage, and another in my motor. I usually load my small boat into my van along with any other large items the night before as it saves an ear-bashing from my wife on my return home! When completely loaded, I make one last check through my list then, then I'm off.

Every item listed is important, right down to the lighter. The reason I started my lists is down to various unfortunate omissions! For example, I have been anchored out in the middle of the Broads before, planning to spend the night; I have opened up a tin of food and popped it into my saucepan, only to find that I had forgotten my lighter. Another time I forgot to put oil in the petrol can. When I refilled the engine, in the middle of Heigham Sound, Norfolk, the engine died a death – it's a two-stroke! I won't even go into the problems that caused me.

You may find the need to compile your own personal lists. Mine cover every item of tackle you should need for any type of pike fishing from either the bank or boat; you will probably not need many of the things listed. If you do not want to compile your own list, look through mine before you set off. You should know straight away if anything of importance is missing from your necessities. My lists comprise both lure and bait fishing equipment.

16

WATER TYPES

RIVERS

I like to fish rivers more than any other type of water – especially the Norfolk rivers, which link up with the Broads. The nice thing about fishing rivers is that you never know what you may catch next. Above all, I hate fishing still waters where all the fish have pet names, such as Percy the Pugnose Pike!

The well-known Broadland pike anglers, past and present, are always on my mind as I fish from my boat. I'm sure that the likes of Jim and Edwin Vincent, Dennis Pye, Bill Giles, Reg Sandys, Derrick Amies, John Watson, Martyn Page and so on, will never be forgotten by the pilgrim pike anglers who venture to Norfolk's rivers and broads. Nostalgia for the Norfolk Broads environment – which is totally unique in this country – will make you return time after time after time, however bad the fishing is!

No living Broadland pike angler that I know of, has caught anywhere near as many big pike from the broads system as Derrick Amies, who has nine different pike over 30lb to his credit, two of which were over 40lb. Derrick has also had something like eighty 20lb-plus pike. Bill Giles landed his first Broadland 30lb plus pike twice in two days from the River Bure system. It took Bill many, many years to catch that first Broadland thirty-pounder though – and he's a vastly experienced Broadland pike fisherman. Dennis Pye, on the other hand, caught twelve thirties during the years he fished the Broads, his biggest being 34lb 2oz. Dennis also obviously knew a lot about the waters he fished. Derrick Amies, from the age of eleven, served what can only be described as a pike fishing apprenticeship under Dennis's watchful eye,

and it would appear, from Derrick's results, that Dennis passed on his trade secrets! When you consider the amount of time Dennis Pye and Derrick Amies put into catching their combined total of twenty-one 30lb-plus pike, thirty-pounders obviously never came that easy for them as they fished Norfolk's river systems. If you desperately want to catch a 30lb pike, in my view, the big water reservoirs have to be your best bet. Paul Stephenson caught four 30lb-plus pike in just two seasons from Lland-egfedd Reservoir in Wales – all taken on lures.

Derrick Amies's 42lb 2oz ex-record pike is always on my mind when I'm afloat on the Broads. 'Today could be the day, Charlie', are

Derrick Amies with his one-time record Norfolk pike.

the words that I hear echoing around inside my head as I fish. I'm confident that one day, when I'm least expecting it, I'll crack a big 'un . . . It'll be so big that Jim Vincent, son Edwin, Dennis Pye, and all the other Broadland greats that have passed on, will have hooked and lost that monster pike at some time during the many thousands of hours they spent fishing there!

The Thurne system, which can vary greatly from one area to another in depth, movement and water clarity, can be very cruel to both visiting and local pike anglers. As shallow slow-moving water gets very cold during the winter period and very weedy during the summer period, very different fishing methods are called for. During the summer period, highly vibrant, noisy top-water lures tend to produce the best results; during the winter period, trolled baits will usually outfish lures. When the water temperature drops during the winter, shallow rivers and broads can be very unproductive – usually because they're frozen over! If my morale needs a boost in order to keep me motivated, I'll divert a few of my fishing sessions to a deeper, faster-flowing river. Deep rivers, especially fastish-flowing, or tidal rivers, are far more reliable when it comes to catching winter pike in numbers. In the summer, however, shallow rivers can be far more productive than deep; but because of weed growth they are much harder to fish in general.

Fish will burn up far more energy in fast-moving water than they will in slow-moving. The more energy a fish uses, the more food it requires; fish that have to eat more, are obviously going to be that much easier to catch! Fastish-moving waters do not suffer from stratification (where layers of water have different temperatures) like still, calm waters do – they're continually mixed by water movement. A still, calm water may fish its socks off after a strong wind has caused the different temperature layers to mix.

When rivers are in flood, look for dykes, back waters and so on, where pike and other coarse fish can hold up out of the flow. Because fish visit dykes and back waters regularly through rainy periods, they're the first places I usually send a lure to investigate, even when the flow has returned to its normal speed!

When a river is flowing fast, it pays to cast up the flow: chub and trout especially, prefer lures that are worked with the flow. On many fast-flowing rivers it's almost impossible to work a lure up and against the flow in any case. Fast-flowing water can cause undercuts in the river bank and drop-offs in the river bed; such features are great holding spots for pike. Pike seem to prefer leger-retrieved propbaits, and hybrid chugger propbaits retrieved up the flow, tight along the bottom.

When drift trolling fastish tidal rivers (that is, when the boat moves with the tidal flow rather than being propelled or rowed forwards), I have far more takes going with the flow, than I do rowing or motoring against it. What I try to do (tides permitting), is to go with the flow on the in-tide, then go back over the same ground on the out-tide, or vice versa! You would be amazed at how much ground you can cover in one day just using tidal power. In my view, tidal power presents a lure or bait at the perfect speed. When moving along on the tide, I use weighted, ultra-lightweight snagless spoons, or hybrid propbaits, dragged tight along, or just off, bottom. A lure retriever is a must when trolling lures along the bottom.

Most rivers have fish-holding areas; find those areas and you'll be half-way there! Winter is the time when river fish shoal up in vast numbers; find those shoals and you should be guaranteed some great winter sport – provided you have the right size and type of lure in your lure box to entice them . . .

Refer back to all the lure chapters, trying all the types of lures as described. Look for a feature, or bottom structure, and work it using the appropriate lure. If it doesn't produce fish on the day, don't dismiss it; it may produce on your next visit, or a month later. Many of the features and structure formations that I've taken big hauls of pike from, are vacant for many months of the year!

Gareth Edwards	45lb 12oz	Mepps spinner
Pete Climo	42lb 5oz	Mepps spinner
Paul Stephenson	38lb	Mepps spinner
Paul Elborn	37lb 4oz	6in copper spoon
Dave Chilman	36lb 8oz	spinnerbait
Mick Rouse	36lb	spinnerbait
Paul Stephenson	35lb 11oz	spinnerbait
Paul Stephenson	31lb 8oz	spinnerbait
Paul Stephenson	30lb 10oz	spinnerbait
Pete Climo	30lb 10oz	spinnerbait
Andy Mundy	30lb 8oz	spinnerbait

Out of all the lure-caught Llandegfedd fish that were listed for me, only four pike fell to plugs.

Roy Lewis	46lb 13oz	Creek Chub Pikie – unconfirmed record!
Tony Clegg	33lb 12oz	6in plug?
Phil Pearson	33lb 12oz	handmade Creek Chub Pikie copy
Paul Sullivan	32lb	Shakespeare Big S

Gareth Edwards, the Welsh rugby star, was very careful as he touched down this beauty. Gareth's scales converted the fish's colossal size into pounds – a record-breaking 45lb 12oz.

WATER RESERVOIRS

Water reservoirs can be very productive at times. However, when they are totally unproductive, they can only be described as soul-destroying for all concerned.

Llandegfedd Reservoir in Wales, is the best example of a big pike and perch water. Over the years, the water (which is usually clearish) and the water's inhabitants (some enormous pike), have responded well to shiny, flashing lures. Below is a list of big fish caught on lures from the reservoir.

Gareth Edwards's 'record' pike has to be the ultimate goal for any lure angler. Who said that lures don't catch big fish?

For the lure fisherman, choosing the right reservoir is most important, since they can vary greatly in their water clarity. If you are prepared to spend your hard-earned money on petrol, a fishing permit, a boat and accessories, you really want something to show for it at the end of the day, such as a few photographs and memories of boated fish. Your chances of catching on lures will be greatly improved if a water's clarity is good. Using a highly visual (because of water clarity and lure finish) and vibrant (because of action) lure, is better than just relying on vibrant action alone to entice

Pete Climo with his 42lb 5oz pike. Pete's fish held the British record from 1988 to 1989.

predators. Remember what I have said about water clarity making a difference to my strike rate during daylight and darkness.

A murky type of reservoir, like Bough Beech was in 1991–2, causes lure and bait anglers all sorts of problems. The reason for the fishing being so poor during that period, was put down to the amount of water feeding into the reservoir. I would have put money on the fish responding to lures if the water had turned clear on any day of that period, irrespective of the amount of water feeding in. As it was, the fish got a good rest. Anglers like Simon Marshall, Rob Milford, John Milford and Phil Probert, who caught pike of 40lb 2oz, 30lb 8oz, 31lb 4oz and 32lb 1oz the previous year (1990–1 season) when the water was much clearer, were in the right place at the right time, doing the right thing. That's what fishing is all

about: being in the right place at the right time.

During the winter period, pike, after feeding at depth (in any type of water), will often move up into clear, shallow, brightly lit water of about 1.5–2m (5–7ft) in depth, in order to speed up their digestive system. While there, they can be induced to feed by offering them small lures and baits. During very overcast days, pike either do not bother to come up into the shallows, or they come up, but do not feed.

At Bough Beech Reservoir, in 1992, the water was very murky on the days that Steve Gamble and I fished it. I saw to my amazement that there were other species of fish in water so shallow that I could touch them with my foot as I walked the bank. Do other species of fish also come up into shallow, brightly lit water to accelerate the digestive system? Perhaps, while everyone was fishing deep at Bough Beech, the

Rob Milford with his 30lb 8oz pike.

pike were just under the surface laughing at the anglers – did anyone try fishing 45cm (18in) deep?

The Americans have done tests using transmitters, which were implanted in muskies so their every move could be monitored. It was noted that big muskies would move into shallow water when the sun shone, and stayed deep on overcast days. The reason put forward for this was that muskies visit the shallows to speed up their metabolism, and in turn their digestive system. While the tests were being carried out, muskies were often monitored moving as far as fourteen to twenty-four miles in a single day. I know of a couple of instances on the Norfolk Broads where a fish has been hooked in the morning and recaught up to two miles away later that day by the same angler. It would

appear that pike, like muskies, may also travel considerable distances in a day.

Here is my own idea as to why pike move into shallow water on bright sunny winter days. The main aim of pike is to eat and get big, because the bigger a pike is, the better chance it has of not ending up inside another pike's stomach! To get big, a pike needs to eat; in order to eat as much as possible, they need to digest their food quickly. Pike, knowing far more about their environment than we do, react instinctively to the slightest change in light, temperature and possibly barometric pressure; to go on a feeding binge or lurk in the depths or whatever. A pike doesn't need a brain to do this – it's an instinct that has been built in over many thousands of years.

Heat radiating from the sun will penetrate shallow clear water, just like it will the glass of a greenhouse. Any live creature in its path will be warmed by it. A fish's back, being very dark in colour, is the perfect receiver for high-frequency vibrations. Absorbing the sun's radiation through the back, plus any minor increase in water temperature, will help to speed up a fish's metabolism and digestive system. In order to catch fish before they move back into the deeper water, you must be there at the right time; I have found that midday to two o'clock is the best time period for takes, if the sun is strong and the water clear. During the winter, the sun is not at its strongest until just after midday.

Fishing shallow water under these conditions really works; I've had huge hauls in the past, the biggest being 150lb-plus of pike in two hours – six of which were over 15lb. I have had many 100lb catches of pike, under the same type of conditions, fishing other types of water.

The right choice of lure or bait is very important once you have located the shallow water pike holding areas. Small and medium-size lures/baits seem to work far better than large, possibly because the pike aren't overly hungry before their return to the depths. When using big lures, pike have shown interest in them – following them through, but veering off as they come in sight of my boat; perhaps I should have used the figure-of-eight method (*see* Chapter 4, 'Jerkbaits'). Small and medium-size lures, are usually taken well before pike come into my view.

See Chapter 17 for more information on trolling lures shallow and deep. Chapter 5 tells you about deep-diving searcher crankbaits, which are perfect for reservoirs. Refer to Chapter 6 for advice on working the bottom of a reservoir from the bank, using weighted snagless lures. Refer to Chapters 6, 7 and 8 for information on 'flashy' lures.

GRAVEL PITS

Gravel pits have been very good to me over the years, and many hundreds of gravel-pit pike have fallen to my top-water lures. Nowadays, I prefer to venture to gravel pits that I've never lure fished before, because I find them a challenge – and more often than not, very rewarding. While writing this book, I lure fished for the first time a north Norfolk gravel pit, and caught nine pike over 17lb during my first ten visits to the water. My first pike of the season was 17lb and my sixth pike was 19lb 8oz – same day, same session!

During the summer period, pike will usually be located in the shallows of a gravel pit; 1.5–2m (5–7ft) is the ideal depth for locating pike, provided the water is clear. If it is not clear, there will be less weed growth and so fewer pike. At that depth pike use the weedy areas for spawning.

When fishing these water depths, where weed may grow to the surface as the summer progresses, the right choice of lure is critical. If you do not have any top-water, or shallow-diving lures with you, I'm afraid you are going to be missing out on a lot of potential action. Find a water where ducks, rodents and amphibians abound, and top-water lures will score heavily.

It is well worth mapping a gravel pit in order

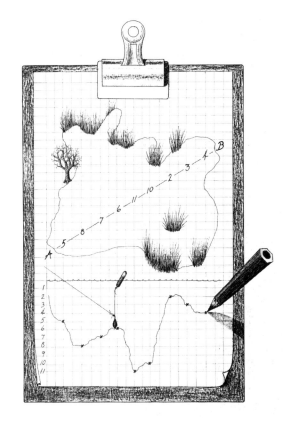

Mapping a water can improve your catch statistics.

to build a mental picture of what its bottom looks like. It is very easy to map a water using a weight, float, stop-knot bead and stop-knot. Draw graphs from A-B, C-D, E-F and so on. When complete, take the depths from each graph and pencil them into your outline map of the water.

During the winter, if top-water, medium or deep-diving lures do not get any response, work a weighted lure tight along the bottom. Some gravel pits are very deep which may mean your deepest diving lure will never reach bottom without help!

LOCHS

Lochs can vary greatly in depth. I would

Peter Hudspeth with a 26lb Lomond pike, taken on a 15cm (6in) Gudebrod Maverick lure.

venture out into the unknown. Learn its moods. Find out about boulder formations that lie just below the surface. If you happen upon one of these stony areas when rollers are lifting and dropping your boat, do not be surprised to see a rock suddenly appear through the bottom!

Lochs are for the very experienced boat angler. They are dangerous places and should be avoided until you are boat wise. With boating experience, and a map of the water giving depth readings and dangerous locations, you can go off in search of monster pike in depths of water that range from 30cm (1ft) to 100m (330ft) and deeper.

I have only made the pilgrimage to Scotland three times, fishing Loch Lomond on each occasion. I loved the sessions that I spent on the loch, even though the fishing was poor. Loch Lomond is the nearest thing I have found to fishing the Broads, in the sense I have of losing myself in all those acres of water. When you find yourself amongst the fish (I'm told), its like a dream come true. Peter Hudspeth and his brother Brian have had some very good catches on lures there, as has Gord Burton.

recommend the lure angler to start in shallow areas, because big lochs can be very dangerous places. Get to know the water well before you

There's not a Scottish wave big enough to stop Gord Burton from fishing! Foolhardy he may be, but he always plays safe by wearing a life-jacket.

Spinning for small perch can be a lot of fun, if you use a lightweight, balanced set-up.

I can't give any personal advice as to where, when and how to fish lures on the lochs due to my very limited experience. I know from others though, and from my own observations while fishing Loch Lomond, that pike congregate in the shallows during hot summer periods and can be caught in numbers by the ardent lure angler. I don't know what you should do to locate pike in the winter; buy Gord Burton's book when it comes out!

He is without doubt the most foolhardy angler to have ever fished the Scottish lochs, having taken chances on the lochs that no other person in his right mind would dream of taking. This is in no way meant as a put-down; Gord is an adventurer in every sense of the word, and lets nothing stand in his way. For those anglers who like to emulate their fishing heroes, I would advise you to think twice before emulating Gord Burton, as he is most definitely in a class of his own when it comes to trolling the mighty lochs of Scotland during obscene weather conditions.

NATURAL LAKES AND PONDS

Over the years, I have lure fished many lakes and ponds – some so small you would not give them a second look. Small lakes and ponds, for some reason, always seem to have a good head of perch present. When lure fishing a small lake or pond for the first time, I always start off by using small lures; if these get no response, I'll try larger ones.

When lure fishing lakes and ponds of an acre or more, I usually start off by using medium-sized lures; if they get no response, I'll try small lures, and if they get no response either, I'll try large. Some anglers prefer to start by using small lures, then work up, or vice versa. Whatever the order, at least you will have given the water your best shot. I'd cast in a teacup if I thought there was a chance of catching a small perch or pike on the lure; the size of fish doesn't come into it, it's the challenge of catching a fish from no more than a puddle that I find so fascinating. Try it for yourself and see.

17

TROLLING TECHNIQUES

Before I say one single word about trolling, I will warn you *never* to go afloat without a life-jacket, and *never* to go afloat wearing waders.

This chapter is for the lure or bait troller. Almost all of the trolling methods mentioned, apart from speed trolling, can be used by the bait troller.

Trolling is one of my favourite methods of fishing. I've never been one for following the crowd when it comes to fishing big waters! I rarely ever fish from a static position, much

preferring to be afloat, keeping on the move – tracking fish like a mountain man would track game. I feel that lounging about on a bedchair within the rounded walls of a bivvie, making hot drinks from sunrise to sundown, waiting hours and hours for a specimen fish to happen upon a well-baited hook, is such a waste of life.

Being an active person, I need to be doing something every minute of the day; casting, or trolling lures or baits all day long, seems to satisfy my hyperactive brain cells. If I go off

Various ways to troll using two rods.

A nice pike, taken while trolling a silver spoon.

fishing for a couple of days, the only times that I'll stay still for any length of time are when I'm eating or sleeping. At first light, I'll be up and on the move again.

HI-TECH TROLLING

Using a depth-sounder or fishfinder and an electric trolling motor, can only be described as heaven! It gives you the freedom to alter your course with one hand while using the other to adjust something else, or to hold a rod. The electric trolling motor is a very important item of equipment for the serious troller. Being able to monitor constantly the water depth, bottom contour, structure and fish beneath your moving boat, has taken trolling one step beyond. Some of the more expensive fishfind-

ers also give water temperature, trolling speed, and sound an alarm if fish appear on screen, or if a specific depth is reached. There are fishfinders that will show the bottom in a three dimensional view. There are even fishfinders that will scan sideways.

A depth sounder will allow a troller to float troll lures or baits at a constant depth around the outer edge of a deep reservoir, or will keep him on course, if, for example, working along an old river bed that runs from one end of a reservoir to the other, or across it. An LCD fishfinder will allow you to form a mental picture of what the bottom looks like. It will show you bottom structure and shoals of fish that have to be seen to be believed. Quite often, I have passed over thousands of fish holding in mid-water, while matchmen, leger fishing within casting distance of the suspended shoals, have not had a single bite! I can remember one match angler, who, at the end of his day's fishing, was convinced that the manager of the reservoir had removed all the coarse fish; if only he could have seen my fishfinder view screen.

Fishfinders are great for finding the food of the pike: the prey fish. A lot of anglers are under the delusion that a fishfinder will allow you to locate pike; this, I can assure you, is not the case. During the winter, pike will lie flat on the bottom and will not show up on a view screen as actual fish, but as bottom contour. Using a fishfinder to locate shoals of prey fish is a much better game plan!

FLOAT TROLLING DROP-OFFS

For float trolling, the lure troller will need a controller float, and the bait troller will need a large standard-type pike float: one that can support 1–2oz would be ideal. For visual and

buoyancy reasons, I much prefer to make my own long (18cm/7in), very buoyant (balsa-wood) pike floats, with a swivel attached at the bottom end. I also make my own controller floats.

When trolling steep drop-offs, it pays to troll thoroughly between two predefined points – say point A and point B. I would usually start my troll off by positioning my boat over 2m (7ft) of water. Using controller/pike floats and double stop-knots, I'll set one lure or bait to work at approximately 1.5m (5ft) deep, trolling it on the side of the boat nearest the bank that I'm working. The other lure or bait will be set to work at approximately 2.5m (9ft) deep and trolled on the deeper water side of the boat, furthest from the bank that I'm working. Those depth settings take into account that the drop-off is falling at about 1.2m (4ft) every 3m (10ft) from the bank; my rod tips are positioned 3m (10ft) apart. At this incline, the water at 21m (70ft) out from the shore line would be approximately 8.5m (28ft) deep.

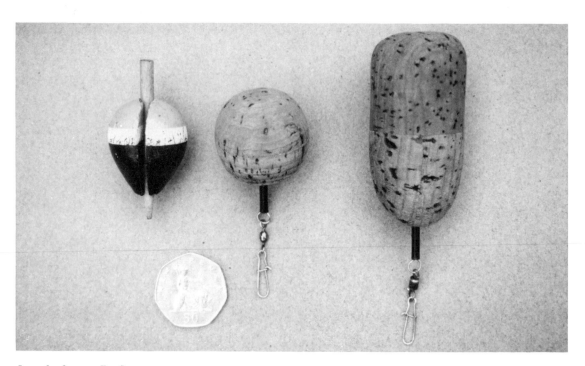

Lure depth controller floats.

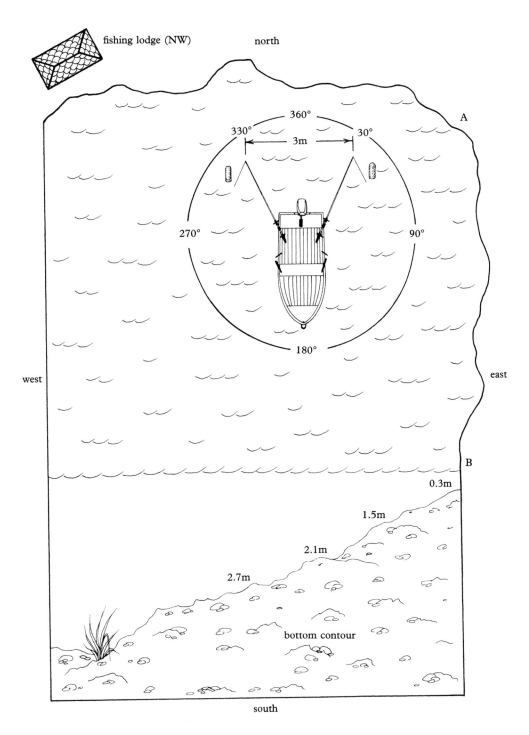

Float trolling drop-offs.

Obviously not all drop-offs fall at the same rate, but within a short time of using a depth sounder, you'll soon get to know at what rate the drop-offs drop off at various locations around a water. I work different depths when float trolling drop-offs, because of the angles I set my rod-holders at. Looking from forward to aft of my boat, my engine being at 360 degrees, I set the rod-holder on the starboard (right) gunwhale to about 330 degrees, and the rod holder on the port (left) gunwhale to about 30 degrees. When the rods are placed in the rod-holders, the rod tips are approximately 3m (10ft) apart. As I've said, over this distance, the drop-off will have dropped 1.2m (4ft), hence the 1.2m (4ft) difference in stop-knot settings. The advantage of trolling two depths at the same time, is that it saves time and covers the bottom more thoroughly.

Rod-holders are not only handy for positioning your lures or baits wide apart, but they also protect your rod butts. A good quality rod-holder will allow you to position your rods at just about any angle you require.

Example

Start your first troll from A to B with your boat positioned over 2m (7ft) of water. Set your stop-knots to the depths you require your lures or baits to work at, then place your rods in their rod-holders and start trolling. If nothing happens on your first run from A to B, reposition your boat over deeper water, and alter the running depths of your lures or baits (via the stop-knots) to suit the depth change. Then head back to point A. When you have worked the drop-off from the shallow to the deepest water, move on and work points B to C and then C to D, and so on.

When trolling with controller/pike floats, it pays to have enough weight on the line to stop the lure or bait lifting in the water because of forward movement. It also pays to have a lure retriever on board.

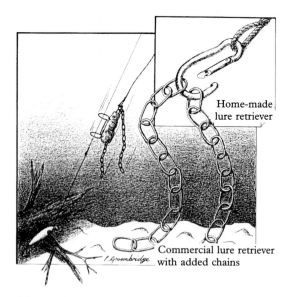

Home-made lure retriever

Commercial lure retriever with added chains

A lure retriever can save a lot of money and heart-ache!

DEPTH TROLLING

If I intend to float troll fairly deep, about 9m (30ft), and the water is quite murky, I'll position my leger weight to about 9m (30ft), or even let it drag bottom. I would rarely ever position it higher. During the years of fishing deep murky waters, I have found that big pike, and especially perch, love to hold or swim tight to the bottom. When I've trolled lures or baits well up off the bottom in deep murky waters, I've rarely ever had much luck. In ultra-clear waters, though, it can be very rewarding. When, or if, you get the chance to troll a deep clear water, it pays to try all the different depths from the bottom to the surface. If you're fishing two rods, set one high in the water and the other deep.

VARIABLE DEPTH TROLLING

To keep in constant contact with a quick-changing, variable-depth bottom, float trolling is a no-go area! A 2–3oz sliding weight on the main line, or tied to a 4lb breaking strain weak link, is ideal for dragging lures or baits tight along, or just off bottom. Leger trolling was the name I gave to this trolling method when I first started using it back in 1987.

Keeping weighted lures or baits tight to the bottom is not an easy task for the angler not equipped with a depth sounder and electric trolling motor. With this equipment, you can view every change as it happens, and alter your lure or bait depth accordingly by releasing the throttle for a few seconds.

I find that it's best to hold the rod that I'm working the bottom with, in my right hand at all times (I'm right-handed!). All I do to alter my lure or bait's running depth is take my left hand off the throttle for a few seconds and pull off, or retrieve, line. Every now and again, to be on the safe side, I open my bail arm, or press the spool-release button of my multiplier, and let my 2–3oz weight fall to the bottom, my lure or bait following close behind. I then position my rod tip ready for trolling, take up any slack line, and wind my reel handle one half-turn; retrieving 25cm (10in) of line. One full turn will retrieve 50cm (20in) and so on. It pays to know beforehand, exactly how much line is retrieved with half, one, or two full turns of your trolling reel's handle. Half to three turns of your reel's handle, after the weight has hit bottom, could mean the difference between catching, or not! Three turns of my multiplier reel's handle, would mean that my weight would be working 1.5m (5ft) off bottom, my lure or bait being 45cm (18in) from the weight. In my opinion, it's a must to keep a lure or bait working tight to the bottom in murky water conditions.

Bear in mind that electric trolling motors are not permitted (by NRA regulations) for trolling on many of our inland waters, including the Norfolk Broads.

TOP, SHALLOW, AND MEDIUM-DEPTH TROLLING WITH LURES

Top-Water Trolling

Trolling top-water lures can be very productive over shallowish warm water. It pays to use oars for this, as pike prefer lures retrieved and trolled very slowly. Steer the boat forward in a winding, snake-like fashion so that the top-water lure passes over fish that haven't been disturbed by the boat passing overhead!

Shallow and Medium-Depth Trolling

When I'm trolling shallow and medium depths of water (1.2–2.4m/4–8ft deep) in a lake, pit, or broad that has a constant depth throughout, I will use either minnow plugs, my own hand-made shallow-running plugs, or float-controlled crankbaits, spoons, tailspins, vibrating plugs, weighted propbaits, or hybrid chugger propbaits. One of my most effective lures for trolling the Broads is a large handmade, very lightweight, silver spoon (see Chapter 6, 'Wobbling Spoons'). Worked just beneath the surface of warm or cold, fairly clear, shallow water – up to 1.8m (6ft) deep – the wobbling spoon never fails me.

There is a very good reason why a flashy lure is so effective when float retrieved or trolled high in clear water, well above the weed-beds that the predators hold-up within: the higher a lure is worked above the weed-beds, the longer it will stay in a predator's field of vision. Also, because the lure is so near to the surface, it will reflect more light from it, making it an easy target to the eyes of any onlooking predators. Looking up at a flashy object from below when it is flashing against a strong background light, will make it hard for a predator to decide whether or not it is an erratically moving fish, or a fish-catcher!

Working lures tight to features such as reed-beds and fallen trees is also a very productive method. Precision trolling will be called for, especially in strong winds. Rod-holders, otherwise known as outriggers, set at 90 or 270 degrees, help to eliminate the risk of spooking the pike that lie resting in the reeds! With a rod-holder set to either of these angles – using an 11ft rod, your boat positioned at about 3m (10ft) out from the reed-bed – you can troll your lure or bait tight to it.

When working reed-beds in calm conditions, I prefer to use my electric trolling motor – discreetly! When trolling in windy conditions, I much prefer to use oars and arm power – they're much more reliable in strong winds.

When my local waters get murky, things are never easy. In such conditions, I try just about everything in my lure box until I get a take. I much prefer to lure fish clearish waters, and if I knew a water was very murky before I ventured to it, I honestly wouldn't bother!

SPEED TROLLING

Speed trolling, using an electric motor or petrol engine, is best suited to clear waters. Some slim-bodied deep-diving lures (such as deep-diving minnow plugs) do not need any form of weighting to get them down there, searching out predators. Other lures may need to be weighted down with heavy (2–12lb) cannon-ball-type lead weights, attached to a wire and suspended from an arm protruding out beyond the gunwhale. These arm, wire and cannon-ball trolling devices are called downriggers. On cheap models, a handle is turned to lower or retrieve the cannon-ball weight: the Roberts downrigger, for example, lets out, or retrieves, 30cm (1ft) of wire with each full turn of its handle. A crocodile (quick-release) clip attached to 15cm (6in) of wire, is fixed to the main length of wire just above the cannon-ball weight. This rubber-padded quick-release clip is clipped on to the reel line at any distance from the lure you wish. When the nylon line is in the clip, the bail arm is opened, or multiplier spool-release button pressed. The downrigger handle is then turned, lowering the lure to its required working depth. Then the bail arm is closed and tightened up until the rod has a nice bend in it. When a fish strikes, the rod tip will spring up.

The further the crocodile clip is attached from your lure, the more slack line you'll have to take up when a fish strikes. In order to set the hook after a take, the slack line must be taken up quickly, which can be done by accelerating the boat forward as soon as your rod indicates that a fish has struck. Before you start trolling, make sure your clutch is preset to slip just under the breaking strain of the line.

The amount of line from the lure to the quick-release clip, and the type of lure that you're trolling, have to be taken into account to determine the lure's actual working depth. A deep-diving crankbait would dive below the cannon-ball weight if 6m (20ft) of line was trailing behind the quick-release clip, whereas a propbait would stay horizontal to the cannon-ball.

Like electric trolling motors, petrol engines are also not permitted to be used for trolling on the majority of our inland waterways.

Fish Seeker

A fish seeker depth-controller vane is a much cheaper way of getting your lures to run deep. The fish seeker has ten settings that will allow you to work lures from 1–21m (3–70ft) deep. It is tied on to the main line; two clips are then clipped into position to achieve its required diving depth. A lure is attached (via a snap) to a wire trace, which in turn is attached to the fish seeker. The fish seeker is then lowered over the side. Leaving the bail arm open, start to move forward, letting out about 36m (120ft) of line; then close the bail arm. The lure should then dive to the fish seeker's predefined diving depth. I prefer to use the fish seeker for slowly trolling small lures in clear water.

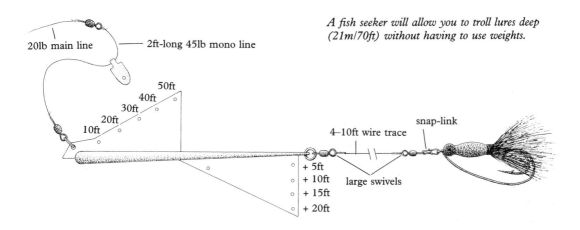

20lb main line

2ft-long 45lb mono line

50ft
40ft
30ft
20ft
10ft

A fish seeker will allow you to troll lures deep (21m/70ft) without having to use weights.

snap-link

4–10ft wire trace

+ 5ft
+ 10ft   large swivels
+ 15ft
+ 20ft

ANCHORS AWAY

When you have a take trolling in very windy conditions, it pays to put an anchor over the side straight away. My anchor-rope lengths are made up with my local waters in mind! I put a big loop at the end of my anchor ropes and attach a large cork to it. If I get a take, I strike into the fish and then lower the anchor over the side with my free hand, slipping the loop over the rowlock; this way I avoid any messing about tying knots!

The idea of the large cork, is in case a fish gets caught up in weed and I have to move my boat position quickly to free it. All I have to do is pull the loop off the rowlock and let go! I keep pressure on the fish to stop it getting any deeper into the weed, at the same time, my boat moves position, and is soon overhead. I then drop another anchor and set about freeing the fish. As soon as the fish is unhooked and returned, I up anchor and return to the floating cork which holds aloft the discarded anchor rope.

With regard to dropping anchor after you've had a take trolling over very deep water, this can present a problem for the beginner and old hand alike. Mud anchors, like those issued with trout reservoir boats, are very heavy indeed, and have to go down a fair way before hitting bottom. I recommend that you tie on the end of the anchor rope well in advance of takes,

keeping it coiled up neatly off the deck (floor) of the boat. When you get a take, drop the anchor over the side and just let it go. If there is a wind blowing, pushing the boat in one direction, it will take up any slack rope, keeping the anchor rope well away from the fish that you're playing.

Keeping the anchor rope up off the deck of the boat is important; otherwise you are in danger of getting a coil of rope caught around your ankle as you let go of the heavy anchor, which could pitch you overboard. Believe me, it could happen. I've heard many a story back in my Navy days, of seamen that have lost a foot, leg, or a hand, as a ship's anchor chains or mooring ropes were released.

When going afloat on a big water, it pays to have a compass with you. If fog should all of a sudden come in on a water, you would be amazed how easy it is to lose your bearings. Take a compass reading before you go afloat, from either the boat mooring area, or the fishing lodge. The latter will usually have a light switched on.

Always be prepared for the worst weather conditions when you go afloat. Water can change from being calm one minute to being turbulent the next. I can't stress this enough – you only live once, so wear a life-jacket at all times and don't take risks with other people's lives!

18

LURE MAKING

MY FIRST HANDMADE LURES

When I started lure fishing, I bought Barrie Rickards and Ken Whitehead's book *Spinning and Plug Fishing*. I found the book very interesting, especially the snippets on hand-made lures. After reading the book, I fancied the challenge of making and catching on a hand-made lure, so I looked around the house for things that I could possibly use. On finding some bottle corks, I thought I would have a go at copying one of the cheap, jointed, plastic plugs. Some of you old-timers will remember the ones: you would find them on most tackle shop walls. They had curtain rings for hook hangers and sold at about £1.50 each.

I wanted to make my lures as strong as possi-ble, so I threaded copper wire through each body section and formed eyes at the end to act as a hook hanger, a joint, and a trace attach-ment eye. For strength I soldered all the eyes closed. I fixed the diving blade on using Arald-ite and pins! Don't laugh – it worked. I made three jointed lures in one night, complete with a coat of 'Hammerite' paint. I thought they were great for my first attempt; when tried in the bath they worked really well. I never had a take though. I was so pleased with those first cork plugs, that I couldn't bring myself to use them: I used to lose quite a few lures when I first started lure fishing, mainly because the pit I regularly fished at had every snag you could possibly think of in it, or around it!

One day I took a grappling iron to the pit to try and recover a couple of expensive lures that I had lost to submerged snags, and I brought up from the depths a moped, a wheelbarrow and a forty-gallon drum, not to mention a push-chair. You'll be pleased to know that I also recovered my lures. The next time I visited that spot, the items mentioned had vanished; I wonder where to? Besides losing lures to snags below the surface, I also lost many above the water line, since I wasn't very accurate at cast-ing back in my early days. I think I must have caught every type of tree possible, along with overhead cables, bridges and so on. Now I look back, I'm glad that I never used those first handmade cork plugs, as I'm sure that I would have lost them to snags. As it is, I still have them to remind me of how much I've pro-gressed over the years!

After making the cork plugs, I thought that I would have a go at making something a little more difficult. I decided to make a 'Cahokie spoon'. I needed some sheet metal to get me started, so off I went to the fireplace shop and bought a 60cm × 60cm (2ft × 2ft) copper sheet (20swg). I left the shop with a hole in my pocket, I can tell you! Upon my return home, I set about designing a template on my com-puter. I had an arts software package which made it very easy for me to put a shape to screen and then to printer. All I had to do then was cut around the printed-out shape, glue it on to my copper sheet using a glue stick, and then cut around the paper template. I kept the first metal cut-out as a hard template, as I still do with any new lure that I design – be it wood or metal. I then set about shaping my metal cut-out into a Cahokie spoon. Within an hour the spoon was complete and polished.

I couldn't wait to use it, so off I went to the test pit to put it through its paces, and within an hour I had caught a small pike on it. I went

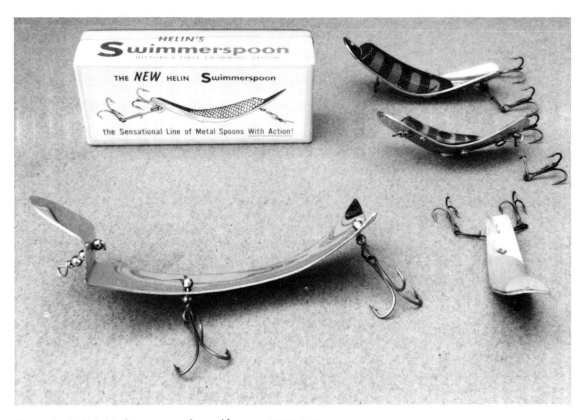

The author's Cahokie Spoon copy, along with some of Helin's Swimmerspoons.

on to land two more pike that day, the biggest being about 6lb. The size didn't matter, it was the catching that counted, and I was over the moon at catching on a handmade lure. Only two hours before I caught that first pike, the lure had been part of a copper sheet! You really have to experience the feeling yourself to understand just how I felt that day.

Someone else might have stopped there, content with what they had achieved . . . not me though: I had to push on, making more and more of my own lures – I was *obsessed*.

I was lure fishing fairly shallow pits back in 1986, but I could find very few plugs that did not dive deep, so I decided to have a go at designing my own shallow-diving plugs. That took me until the summer of 1987. I came up with some good designs, all of which were sub-surface shallowish runners. I hadn't made any

top-water plugs – I didn't even know what a top-water plug was at that time.

I went over to the pit in May 1987 to have a look round and make plans for 16 June (the end of the close season). On arriving at the water, I was shocked to see the place thick with weed, approximately 30cm (1ft) below the water's surface. That called for a rethink straight away, since I hadn't designed any lures that worked that shallow. I shot straight down to Jetty Anglers to see if Bob had any lures that worked that shallow – he hadn't, but he knew of a company that did. T & G Lures.

Bob placed an order straight away for a few different types of shallow-diving and top-water plugs. The lures arrived just in time for 16 June. I bought one or two of each type, including Heddon Crazy Crawler, Dying Flutter, Torpedo and Lucky 13. I wasn't holding out much hope for my lure fishing that summer, as I really didn't know what to expect from the new lures I'd purchased – especially the top-water plugs.

I went over to the pit at the start of the season, and the weed was even thicker; it was actually touching the surface in places. There were still the odd weed-free channels here and there, which called for very accurate casting. Fortunately, by then, my casting had improved, thanks to the garden! I tried a couple of different top-water lures along the weed-free channels but didn't get any response. I then put on a Heddon Dying Flutter top-water propbait. I cast it out... then retrieved it back slowly, guiding it through a weed-free channel with my rod tip held high... all of a sudden the water erupted, and bingo, I was into a fish. To cut a long story short, for the rest of that summer the water just kept on erupting. Every time I went out I just kept on getting 'full houses' – my reel clutch would 'clickity click' and I would often catch 'two fat ladies' in a session. My 'legs eleven' would really ache after a day out stalking the kings and queens of fresh water.

Some days, I would have take after take – nearly every take making me jump. At the end of a session my nerves would be in tatters (even very recently, I was so shocked when a pike hit my top-water Jitterbug, I actually choked). I had never experienced such violent takes before, and they really made the adrenalin surge through me. It doesn't seem to flow anywhere near as much when bait fishing, because you don't get that initial shock – unless, of course, you're one of that noisy lot that have fire engine sirens built into their backbiters. They're enough to make anybody's adrenalin surge!

On some occasions, I would see a bow-wave coming over the top of a weed-bed, starting at least 6–9m (20–30ft) away from my top-water lure, which would be totally out of view of the pike. I would say to anglers fishing alongside me, 'here she comes... here she arrgh!' I would still jump with all that warning. I have talked to other lure anglers and it seems to

have the same effect on them too, so it does not seem to be just a bad case of the nerves! As I have said to people before, I do not recommend top-water lure fishing to anybody who has a weak heart. I have seen pike smash into my lure and take it way into the air, perhaps as much as 90cm (3ft), if not more; it was like nothing that I had ever experienced before. Most of the time the bow-wave takes were near doubles. There are no two ways about it: lures do attract the fittest of pike. There is no better time than summer to lure fish: leaping and tail-walking pike are the norm during this period.

I started going to different waters in Essex and Suffolk to see if top-water lures would have the same effect on their pike populations; they did seem to, but I found some waters to be far more productive than others. The best waters for takes on top-water lures, were those that had plenty of waterfowl and rodents present; for example, Flatford Mill on the River Stour (a duck's paradise) was one place that always produced double-figure pike for me. I found that on waters that didn't have much in the way of waterfowl, rodents or amphibians, but had plenty of prey fish, surface takes would be rare – if there were any! There was definitely a good head of pike in those waters, though, since I caught some on sub-surface lures. In the waters that did hold a lot of waterfowl and rodents, I would catch as many as twelve to fifteen pike in a day – and perhaps miss as many again.

During the summer of 1987 I landed approximately 200 pike from one pit alone. From various other places I would estimate to have landed another 100 – all on one Dying Flutter, now retired and resting in a snag at the bottom of the River Stour! There's no sound chamber in a Dying Flutter, but its blades make a nice rattling noise, that can be heard from a fair distance. They also send off good flash patterns, especially on sunny days, making a good target for an attacking predator.

I went back to the computer to try to design some top-water lures for the coming summer of 1988. I paid serious thought to why I had

(1) *Searcher Crankbait;*
(2) *Wooden Wiggle Lure;*
(3) *Jointed Wiggle Lure;*
(4) *Charlie's Mouse;*
(5) *Roll 'N Rat;*
(6) *Charlie's Worker;*
(7) *Buzz Stick;*
(8) *Buzz Stick;*
(9) *Buzz Stick;*
(10) *Buzz 'N Pop;*
(11) *Yare Popper;*
(12) *Revolving Plug;*
(13) *balsa crankbait;*
(14) *balsa crankbait;*
(15) *top-water spoon;*
(16) *Derrick Amies' spoon;*
(17) *Snagless spoon;*
(18) *spring-activated spoon.*

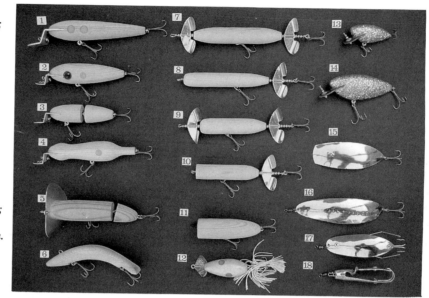

Some of the author's handmade lures.

caught so many pike on top-water lures during the previous summer. I was really starting to think about what I was doing, and, what was more important, I had started thinking more about what the fish were doing. It had taken hundreds of hours of lure fishing before I started to realize there was a pattern forming.

Around October 1987, I started doing some experiments with lures at night. I would go to the pit after dark and lure fish until 1 or 2 a.m. in the morning. I did not have too much luck with the top-water lures in October because the water temperature dropped too much at night. I tried sub-surface lures and a definite pattern started to emerge. I could fish for a couple of hours using lures without sound chambers and not have a touch, but as soon as I put a Big S on, or any lure with a good sound chamber, I would start having knocks. That was the beginning for me, and I really started thinking noise and vibration from that time on. Pike were definitely homing in on the vibrations emitted from the sound chamber. Fortunately, some time before I started lure fishing, I had been involved in side-band radio, and had learnt a

lot about vibrations and frequency from that hobby, which I put to good use.

Years ago, most of the pike anglers that I'd spoken to, who dabbled with lures to keep warm, were mostly in agreement that a sound chamber was just a gimmick. Nobody, it seemed, gave any serious thought to a predator specifically homing in on the noise vibrations emitted from it. I must point out here for new-comers to lure fishing, that over the years most pike anglers thought that pike were always frightened off by noise. That, as many of us now know, is *not* the case. The breaking of surface ice, for example, can instantly attract pike into the area.

WOODEN WIGGLE LURE

When I first started making lures, I used to whittle all my wooden lure bodies into shape. I soon got fed up with that method because it was hard on the wrist and took far too long. I invested instead in a hobby lathe which requires a drill to power it. For those who have a lathe

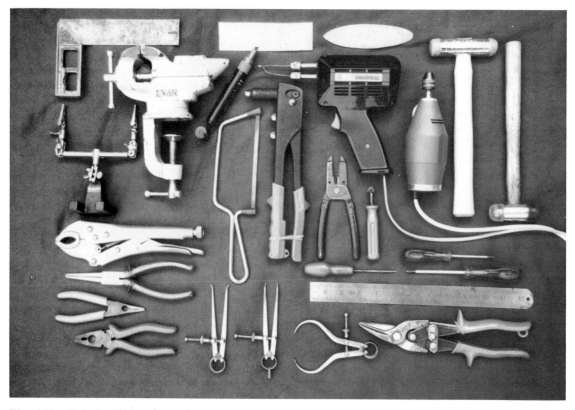

The tools used for lure making.

already, you should find plug bodies easy to turn.

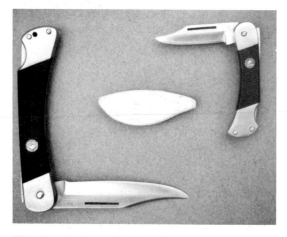

Whittling requires a sharp, good-quality knife.

Whittling Knife

For those that do not have a lathe, whittling will be your only option – it's not that hard once you get the hang of it. A good whittling knife is a must; it should be about 13cm (5in) long (handle 7.5cm/3in blade 5.5cm/2in) as this will fit into the palm snugly. Stanley-type knives are best avoided as their blades snap very easily.

Lure-Holder

Refer to the diagram on p. 150 as you carry out these instructions. A lure-holder is very handy when it comes to undertaking the saw cut for the diving blade (*see* No. 2). The hole that holds/supports the wooden body tapers in from top to bottom, through the block of wood.

Before you drill the 2cm (¾in) hole, using a pencil and a 2cm (¾in) circle, draw around the circle where you intend to drill the hole. Then, draw another larger circle around that circle of 2.5cm (1in) in diameter. When you have drilled the smaller hole, whittle to the outer circle, forming a taper through the block of wood. Taking a 2cm (¾in) strip of sandpaper, smooth off the taper. Similar diameter wooden lure bodies should fit tightly into the hole.

Block of Wood

This should be 11cm (4⅜in) in length, and 3cm (1¼in) square. The thickest part of the lure body will be 3cm (1¼in) from one end of the block of wood.

Mark the two ends of the block of wood with a pencil as seen in the diagram, No. 1. Then draw a dot approximately 8mm (¼in) round over the cross hairs in the centre of the wooden block. Draw a line around the block of wood 3cm (1¼in) in from one end, to represent the thickest part of the lure body. The line is only deleted by sandpapering when the whittling is complete.

Whittle to the outer edge of each dot from the 3cm (1¼in) line that marks what will be the thickest part of the plug body. When whittling is complete, you should have a shape like the one seen in the diagram (No. 1 – After). Now the wooden shape can be sandpapered until smooth. Fondle the body until all the whittled blemishes are completely smoothed out. After you have finished whittling and sanding the block of wood, the thickest part of the body should be about 2.5cm (1in) in diameter, with the nose of the body rounded off as in the diagram.

Saw Cut

Before you start sawing, use a pencil and draw a 'mouth' that you can use as a guide for the saw blade to follow. The saw cut needs to be no deeper than 1.7cm (⅝in). Make a vertical line at this depth from the nose on each side

of the wooden body before you saw; that way you will not over-saw!

Always have your wood grain side-on as seen in No. 5 of the diagram. This will make the lure a lot stronger when completed. If you have not made a lure holder or jig for holding your wooden body (as seen in No. 2 of the diagram), hold your lure body in your hand, and lock the hand as tightly as possible in between your legs; then carefully saw (remember what you've got to lose!). Keep checking both sides of the body to make sure your saw blade is following the mouth line.

The Diving Blade

The blade is to scale in No. 6 of the diagram. Trace it out with tracing paper, then turn the tracing paper over and place it on your aluminium sheet and scribble over it! When you take the tracing paper off you should be left with the outline of the diving blade. Cut out the blade then pencil on the two bend lines and dot. It's a good idea to keep the first blade made to use as a hard template; then in future, you can draw around the hard template with a needle or similar object.

Follow the bending plan in a vice or on the edge of a block of hard wood. Using a 2mm drill bit, drill a hole through the dot mark. This hole will take the wire-form trace attachment eye. Use a pointed punch before you drill the hole.

Wire Form

This is made using a piece of 18 gauge (1mm) stainless steel wire – the type used for making sea weights. Cut off a 10cm (4in) piece of wire, then take a pair of pointed-nose pliers and grip the wire in the middle. Now bend the wire around one half of the pliers using your thumb and index finger; then do two turns around the other half of the wire length and cut off the surplus – you have formed a wire eye! Now slide on a metal bead and pass the end of the wire through the diving blade from the front.

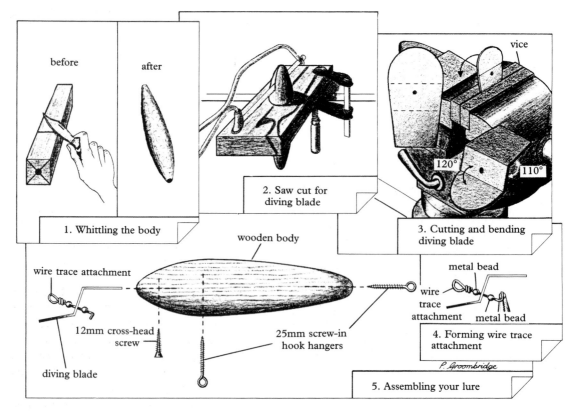

before **after**

1. Whittling the body

2. Saw cut for diving blade

vice

120° 110°

3. Cutting and bending diving blade

wire trace attachment

wooden body

metal bead

wire trace attachment   metal bead

12mm cross-head screw

25mm screw-in hook hangers

4. Forming wire trace attachment

diving blade

P. Groombridge

5. Assembling your lure

Making a wooden wiggle lure.

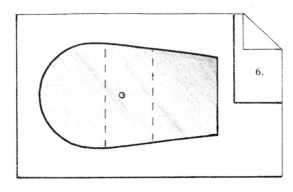

6.

Now add another metal bead and cut wire to the required length before bending the end round 90 degrees with your pointed-nose pliers – as seen in No. 4.

Assembling Your Plug

This is very straightforward. Apply some epoxy to the saw cut using a fine needle and then push in the diving blade. Make sure the diving blade is in a true position before the epoxy sets. After about fifteen minutes you can drill a hole under the chin of the plug to take the diving blade screw. Start by using a bradawl, then use a 2mm drill bit to drill the hole. Do *not* drill right through the body; stop drilling as soon as you feel the drill bit go through the metal blade. Counter sink the hole so the head of the screw sits snugly in it. I use a zinc-plated cross-headed screw. Now simply add the hook hangers, split rings and hooks to complete your plug.

If you want, you can then paint it, glitter it, or leave it natural. You can add plastic eyes, a sound chamber, tail or belly spin-blades, or both.

All the parts required for the making of this plug, except the aluminium sheet, can be purchased from Pro Am Products (*see* Useful Addresses).

Aluminium sheet can be purchased from any decent model shop that specializes in radio-controlled model cars and planes. The thickness should be 0.8mm ($\frac{1}{32}$in).

Gord Burton with a nice pike taken on a Wooden Wiggle lure.

MAKING A SPOON

The thing that puts most DIY lure makers off the idea of making a spoon, is the initial shaping. When you know how, it's easy, however. The instructions below refer to the diagram on p. 152.

1. Take a sheet of A4 paper, fold it in half and then draw half a spoon on the folded edge. Then cut along the drawn line. When complete, open the fold, and there is the spoon design, with both its sides in perfect proportion to each other. No more do you have to waste metal trying to get the spoon shape right; if you are not happy with your paper cut-out, bin it and do another.

2. To achieve the concave shaping of the spoon, I use a rubber hammer and a 1.2m (4ft) length of wood 5cm deep by 10cm wide (2 × 4in). I draw the spoon shape on to the centre of a block of wood. Using a chisel, I gouge out the traced spoon shape, and shape the hollow to how I want the curvature of the finished spoon to look. When complete, I sandpaper until smooth. I would advise you to gouge out to a depth of about 1.2–1.5cm ($\frac{1}{2}$–$\frac{5}{8}$in), shaping the sides and ends according to the style of spoon you require. This wooden beating-template can take some time to shape, but once completed, it can be used time after time – even for other things like concaving spinner blades. I tend to use one size of wooden beating-template for making three or four different sizes of spoon! If you want to make a smaller version of the original gouged-out spoon shape, you work at one end of the beating template first, then slide your spoon to the other end and shape that end of the spoon.

3. This shows how to make a hard spoon template from your paper one. After you have cut out the paper shape, glue the back of it and stick it on to your metal sheet. I, personally, prefer to use a glue stick. Once glued on to the metal sheet, mark around the paper template with a thick marker pen. Give the ink a couple of seconds to dry then remove the paper template.

4. Cut around the marked shape with a pair of good quality metal cutters, keeping to the inner edge of the ink line, not the outer.

5. Using a punch, drill and 1.5mm drill bit, make your holes.

6. Position the length of wood on your knees and using a rubber-headed hammer, start to beat and shape the metal cut-out into a spoon. A rubber-headed hammer will leave no blemishes in the metal if you're careful. If you have any little bends/dents along the outer edge of your spoon, stand your block of wood upright so that you can use the end as a small beating table; then, using the harder nylon head of the

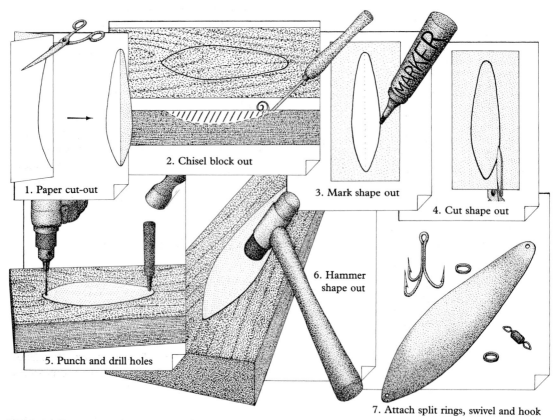

1. Paper cut-out

2. Chisel block out

3. Mark shape out

4. Cut shape out

5. Punch and drill holes

6. Hammer shape out

7. Attach split rings, swivel and hook

Making a Spoon.

hammer, gently straighten out the bends/dents.

7. When complete, look at the spoon side-on and do the final shaping with your fingers. When you are happy with everything, add the split rings, swivel and hook.

MAKING A CONTROLLER FLOAT

I use a single 38 × 38mm cork rounded off for retrieving and trolling lightweight lures, and a 76 × 38mm (shaped) cork for use with heavier lures.

To make one of each type, you will need three 38 × 38mm wine-making corks, or simi-

lar, one length of stiff boom tube, two swivels, some stainless steel wire, and some strong glue.

1. For the larger-sized controller float, all you do is glue two corks together. For rounding off, use coarse sandpaper; to finish, fine sandpaper. In the bottom of the floats, drill a hole 3cm (1¼in) deep. The drill bit diameter will depend on your boom tube diameter.

2. Cut two 15cm (6in) lengths of wire and make a couple of wire eye forms like those seen in part 2 of the diagram on p. 153. When complete, trim the shaft lengths to be 5cm (2in) long, and then add the swivels. *See* spinner-making section for instructions on bending wire, page 156.

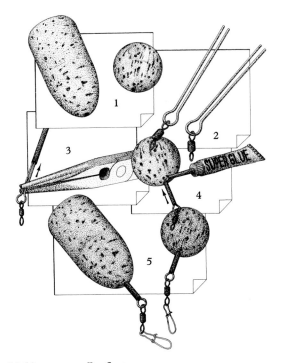

Making a controller float.

3. Cut off a 5cm (2in) length of boom tube. Make sure that the boom tube slides easily into the 3cm (1¼in) deep hole, leaving 2cm (¾in) sticking out. Make sure that the wire shafts fit the boom tube.

4. If everything is OK, glue the boom tube into the hole. When set, slide the wire shafts into the boom tube, but do not glue them in. They should be a firm but *not* tight push fit. You may need to put a slight bend in the wire, half-way along the shaft, to achieve this.

5. To finish, just add a couple of snap-links.

I do not glue in the wire shafts because, when I troll 45cm (18in) below the surface, I often clip my float directly to the wire-trace swivel. If a fish were to snap me up, in the first snag that my float gets caught in, the fish would pull the wire shaft out of the boom tube, releasing the float – a bit like pulling the pin from a hand grenade. For the same reasons, when float

trolling, it pays to have your stop-knots as loose as possible. If a break should occur above a tight stop-knot, due to frayed or nicked line, the float would probably get caught up in the first dense snag the fish ventured through. Unable to pull the line free of the float because of the stop-knot being so tight, the fish would possibly die.

I usually connect my controller float to a quick-change bead. I have a stop-knot bead and a (not too tightly tied) stop-knot each side of the quick-change bead. This method comes in very handy when you want to alter the working depth of a float-controlled lure quickly.

MAKING CHARLIE'S WORKER

This lure is unique! It has a nice side-to-side tail end action when retrieved slowly. When jerked hard, it will corkscrew. The plug can be made as described, using a one-piece wire system, or by using 2.5cm (1in) eye-type hook hangers. The following instructions refer to the drawing on p. 154.

1. Take your block of wood and draw the shape on to it with a pencil. Make sure the wood grain runs along the side of the wood block. When complete, cut around the shape using a band saw. If you don't have access to a band saw, as I dare say most of you won't, use whatever method's available, such as whittle, fret saw, surform, or similar. I always keep the first cut-out shape as a hard template, which I use for drawing the outline shape of additional replica plugs.

2. Now draw the fish shape. When complete, band saw, or cut, around the outline.

3. This is what the wire form would look like when the plug is complete, if you could see inside the plug body! I use 1.5mm copper wire for the form; the type used for electrical wiring is ideal.

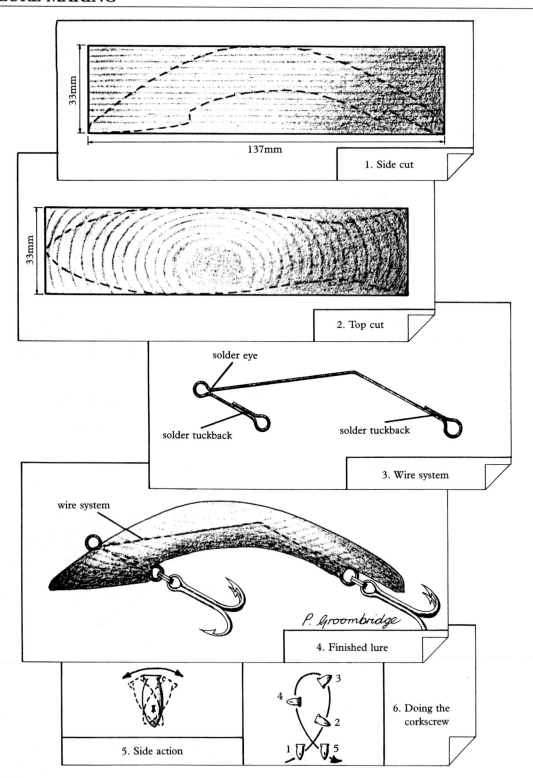

1. Side cut

33mm

137mm

2. Top cut

33mm

3. Wire system

solder eye

solder tuckback

solder tuckback

4. Finished lure

wire system

P. Groombridge

5. Side action

6. Doing the corkscrew

Making Charlie's Worker.

4. Whittling is now in order. Round off all right-angle corners along the sides of the plug body. After that get to work with the sandpaper. A good hand, eye and mind are needed to carry out the drilling. Drill in from the front and rear of the plug, using a long 1.5mm drill bit, making sure the drill holes meet in the middle of the plug body; this is *not* easy. When complete, drill up from the belly to meet the front trace attachment hole. Again, I like to drill into the plug body from both sides, my drill holes meeting up inside.

4A. Now, cut off a piece of 1.5mm copper wire, twice the length of the plug body. Make an offset bend 2.5mm from one end of the wire and thread the bent end through the plug body; take my word for it, this is not easy. You can thread the wire from the front or rear of the plug body; sometimes the wire will feed through from one end better than it will from the other! Once you've succeeded in threading the wire through the length of the plug body, the rest is easy. Form a loop and tuckback at the rear of the plug body, as seen in No. 3 on the far right, then solder the tuckback. When complete, pull the wire through the plug body, using a pair of pliers, until the tuckback has disappeared inside the body. I like to apply a drop of glue to the hole before the tuckback is pulled into it, for added strength.

4B. Double the front end of the wire back into the same hole and down to the belly hook hanger position. Take a nail or similar object and place it through the large loop which will become the wire-trace snap-link attachment loop, seen in the top left of Nos. 3 and 4. Take your pliers and pull the end of the wire until a wire loop is formed tight around it, then slip the nail out. Holding your soldering iron on the wire loop, feed solder to the neck of the wire loop, which should be level with, or just below the front drill hole, hidden inside the plug body!

4C. After you've formed and soldered the wire-trace snap-link attachment eye, there should be plenty of spare wire sticking out of the belly hook hanger hole. Take a ruler and cut it off 2cm (3/4in) from the plug body. Feed the end of the wire back into the same hole with a pair of pointed-nose pliers; at the same time, form a nice tidy wire loop. Again, holding your soldering iron on this loop, apply solder to the tuckback via the belly drill hole. Solder will automatically feed itself along the tuckback inside the plug body!

5. This shows the action of the plug, as if it were coming straight towards you.

6. This shows the plug doing the corkscrew.

This is probably one of the hardest plugs for the DIY enthusiast to make. If you manage this one, any other type of plug will seem easy!

SPINNERS AND HYBRID LURES

by

John Worzencraft

There are lots of good reasons why you should try customizing commercial spinners as well as making your own; the cost is low and the satisfaction you get will be enormous. You may find it difficult to buy exactly what you want in terms of spinner size, colour, style and weight, especially in the larger blade sizes, so DIY is the obvious answer; this means that you don't have to compromise.

Lightweight and Heavyweight Spinners

Using a pair of long-nosed pliers, a small drill bit and some wire-cutters, you can make a start on the fun road to building your own collection of custom-designed spinners. Wire shaft, beads and split rings will cost about £5 for a basic selection.

A size No. 4 or 5 Mepps Comet comes complete with a ribbed brass body, the whole spinner weighing 8g or 11g. To make its lightweight companion spinner, cut the wire shaft, remove the beads, blade and clevis, and brass body and hook. Put the brass body in your box of DIY spinner parts for use later, and take a new wire shaft; twist it round a 3mm diameter drill bit using pliers to make a loop in one end, and trim off any excess wire.

Next, add extra beads and/or a much lighter body in place of the one you have removed, making sure that the combined length of these extra beads and new body is just greater than the blade length. Then put the deflector and spacer beads, and clevis and blade, on to the wire shaft; if there's not one already, I always like to add a spacer bead between the clevis and the trace-link loop. Then twist a second loop in the end of the wire shaft. Finally, join the original hook to the bottom loop with a split ring and there you have your very own lightweight version of the Comet. The customized French-bladed spinner will be good for covering the upper levels of the water, varying its speed of retrieval, while another, heavier, original can be used in deeper or faster flowing water.

This simple method can be repeated for even heavier spinners like the Willow-bladed Mepps Aglia Long. With the Colorado-bladed Ondex spinner, the problem is just the opposite – the commercial spinner is quite light and you will need to make a heavier version for deeper, faster waters. Here the process is equally easy; cut the shaft and replace the blade and beads on a new shaft, add one of your spare metal spinner bodies left over from lightening other spinners and you'll have your own unique heavy Ondex.

Making a Bodied Spinner

Your spinner body will have to be at least 2.5cm (1in) long for this. Refer to diagram above.

1. Cut a length of wire; the length will be

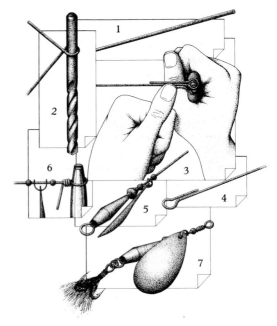

Making a spinner.

determined by the overall spinner length, plus eyes.

2. Using a 3mm diameter drill bit, or larger, twist one end of the wire around it as seen in No. 2 of the diagram.

3. Using a pointed-nose pair of pliers, form an eye and tuckback as seen in No. 3.

4. When complete, the wire form should have a 2.5cm (1in) tuckback.

5. Slip on a 2.5cm (1in) (or longer) spinner body, then a deflector, then a metal bead, then the clevis and spin blade. Finally, add one more metal bead above the clevis, which acts as a weed-guard for the clevis.

6. You have a couple of options open to you now. (a) The wire shaft can be finished off just above the clevis, as seen in No. 6. (b) The eye can be formed 2.7cm (1⅛in) past the clevis! If you do this, you can slide the body up and down the wire shaft to change hooks quickly. To stop the spinner body slipping up and down while casting, you put a little off-set bend at the end of the tuckback. (c) Instead of a tuck-

back feeding inside the spinner body, you can form an eye like that seen in No. 6 of the drawing. Use a split ring to connect the hook to the eye. This method has to be used when making lightweight spinners. Whichever method you chose . . . to finish off, using a pair of pointed-nose pliers, hold the wire shaft just above the clevis. Bend the surplus wire back round the nose of the pliers and then twist it two to three times around the wire shaft. Cut off any surplus wire and there you have it – a finished spinner.

Deflector Beads

If you are making your own spinners from scratch or if the shop-bought one you are modifying doesn't have a deflector bead between the clevis and the spinner body, it's always worth adding one. It will help the blade stay clear of the body, unless, of course, you want it to clatter against the body to make more vibrations! I prefer spinners with blades that revolve smoothly when the spinner is moving at the slowest possible speed, and have found that deflector beads are important for this.

Bodies and Blades

Traditionally spinner bodies are made from metal, usually brass, and come in various shapes, sizes and weights. Super lightweight ones can be made from salmon tube flies, plastic-lined copper tubing and mini-coils of brass or stainless steel wire. Tulip beads can also be added to the shaft before attaching the hook, adding a flash of red.

You may want to spin in deep, fast water using tiny blades with a high spin rate; this too is simplicity itself for the DIY spinner enthusiast. Replace the big blade of a heavyweight spinner with a much smaller one and you will have just what you need. The smallest sizes of French, Colorado, Indiana and Willow blades will work but special DIY Hi-Spin blades are available from several suppliers.

Neutral-Buoyancy Suspending Spinners

Even after making your customized lightweight spinners, you may still find that, under certain conditions or when you are after a particular species, a spinner which doesn't sink at all is what you need: a suspending one with neutral buoyancy.

Balsawood is the key to suspending spinners; your local model shop will stock some. It is very easily shaped with a Stanley knife and finished off with sandpaper or emery cloth and a coat of tough varnish. Make up a cylinder of balsa to match the length of your spinner blade and wire shaft, say 6cm (2⅜in) long and 2cm (¾in) thick, and round off the ends. Assemble all the beads, hook, split rings, blade and clevis on to the wire shaft that you want to use, and simply push one end of the wire shaft through the balsa body; then check whether the spinner floats or sinks. If it sinks, you will need to make a larger body! If it floats, it's just a matter of whittling away the balsa until the spinner sinks very slowly.

After testing it in water, let the balsa body dry overnight, and then seal it with epoxy or yacht varnish. Next you can assemble all the components as you would a normal spinner. The spinner you have made may sink gently on its own, but don't worry, linked to a lightweight trace, the slight lifting force on it while being reeled in will make it run level, neither sinking nor floating. Even if you stop retrieving for a second or two, it will hardly sink at all, hanging temptingly in the water.

Other Ideas

Having made some of your very own spinners, there's much more you can do if you want to experiment. You can paint some or all of the blade and body. Red is a very effective colour but it's always worth trying others like yellow, white and black. Plastic tail fins can be added to the hook hanger to make the spinner even more realistic and attractive; I have found that adding red wool soaked in an attractant oil to the treble hook also helps. If you want to increase your chances of catching nice big perch (and what more beautiful fish are there?), try adding a red plastic teaser-tail worm to the treble hook; it works wonders.

Hybrid Spinners

Hybrid spinners are combination lures made from a spinner blade and wire shaft plus any one, or more, of the other types of lure, plugs, spoons, and flies. They are very effective in conditions where it's difficult to decide whether to use a plug, fly, spoon or spinner. Spinnerbait hybrids are based on a combination of a spinner and a natural bait or artificial jig.

There are a few examples of manufactured hybrid spinners. Mepps make fly-spinners and plastic fish-spinner combinations; Kilty Lures also make spinner-plastic fish hybrids. An American lure called the Heddon Hellbender is a plug-spinner hybrid. For a much wider choice the only option is to make your own.

Permutations and Combinations

With all the options and variations available for spinner-plug, fly-spinner, spinner-spoon and spinner-bait hybrids, a whole new world of opportunity is opened up to the lure angler at little cost. The advantages of combining two types of lure are obvious. With modern materials and more freely available DIY lure-making components, the permutations and combinations are almost endless. Although DIY lure making is still really in its infancy in coarse fishing, it is much more common in the game fishing world, which has several good stockists of spinners, DIY components, plugs and other lures.

You can use standard spinners or design your own, and add them in front of, below or behind any suitable plug. There are some good add-on spinner blade systems available now, with a plastic clevis that actually allows you to change the blade without having to remove the wire shaft or clevis – nothing could be simpler.

Hybrid spinners have most of the good points of the original lure with the added advantage of vibrations and flash created by the blade; this makes them very good lures for almost any conditions of weather or water, and for every species of predator fish.

Whatever types of hybrid spinners you decide to make, you should remember the important factors that determine the plug's characteristics. The weight, buoyancy, centre of gravity and trace-attachment point of the plug combined with any integral or added diving lip will make the plug float or sink, dive and wiggle. The plug may also have internal weights which rely on the action of the plug to provide an enticing rattle.

Obviously, when converting a successful plug into a hybrid spinner, it's important to avoid affecting the action of the original plug too much. Of course, some slight change is inevitable but this can be kept to a minimum with a little care and forethought.

Spinner-plug hybrids can be made with the blade attached to the plug body in several alternative positions, in front, below and behind; with jointed plugs, a blade can also be inserted between the two sections.

Flies are good lures for many species of coarse and game, carnivorous and predator fish. They can be made even more effective by adding a highly polished spinning blade to make a fly-spinner hybrid. Jumbo flies and fly-spinners are needed for jumbo grandmother pike and salmon. The larger the hook, the easier it is to tie on the various coloured hackles and feathers, the more outrageous the better! Many anglers prefer to use single hooks for pike flies and fly-spinner hybrids; these and other fly-tying materials are available from game fishing shops and mail order outlets.

— USEFUL WEBSITES —

Charlie Bettell

Author of *The Art of Lure Fishing.*
charlie@esox.co.uk
charlie@norfolkguide.co.uk

Predator Fishing UK

The website for serious pike and predator anglers.
www.esox.co.uk
charlie@esox.co.uk

Guided pike and predator fishing trips on the Norfolk Broads

With professional guide Charlie Bettell.
www.esox.co.uk/pikefishing2000
charlie@norfolkguide.co.uk

PikeTech.co.uk

In association with TackleDirectory.com.
sales@tackledirectory.com

TackleDirectory.com

For all your pike and predator fishing needs.
www.tackledirectory.com
sales@tackledirectory.com

Specialist Innovations

Tackle developed to meet angler's exact needs.
www.spinn.co.uk
sales@spinn.co.uk

BaitBoat.co.uk

Pike and carp remote control bait boats.
www.baitboat.co.uk
sales@spinn.co.uk

In-Fisherman

A superb magazine for the predator angler.
www.in-fisherman.com

Coarse Fisherman

For all your coarse fishing needs.
www.coarsefisherman.co.uk

Norfolk Broads Direct

One of Norfolk's biggest tour operators: day boat hire, river tours and cottages.
www.broads.co.uk

INDEX